SCENIC DIVERSIONS

50 AMERICAN DRIVING TOURS

by

Dorothy "Dollie" Carruth

with

Susan Farewell

The H.M. Gousha Company
Comfort, Texas 78013

SCENIC DIVERSIONS™ is a trademark of The H.M. Gousha Company.

SCENIC DIVERSIONS
50 American Driving Tours

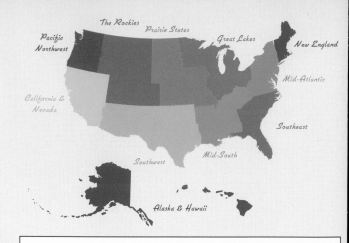

Ever feel as if your alarm clock is the starting bell of a horse race? One minute you're suspended in dreamland, the next, it's "And they're off!" You spend the day running around full speed.

It's easy to get caught up in the high-tech fast-forward pace of the nineties. You're faxing this, faxing that. You do your banking by computer. You shop by modem. When it comes to traveling— whether it's to a local tag sale or clear across the country—you always ask "What's the fastest way to get there?"

Though you can zoom across and throughout the U.S. on highways and interstates (or fly above it all), you can also meander along slowly and take time out to enjoy the journey as well as the destinations.

From the Andrew Wyeth landscapes of Maine to the sun-bleached shores of Florida's coast to the deep orange-hued canyons of Utah's national parks and the mighty rivers of the Oregon wilderness, the variety in this country is endless, the wildlife abundant, and the scenery astoundingly beautiful. On top of all that, there are all sorts of interesting stops to make along the way from New England country stores (complete with penny candy) to futuristic museums and sculpture gardens.

Here are 50 scenic driving tours designed to take you to and through some of this country's most memorable landscapes. Some are easy day trips, while others can take up to two weeks. All originate in a city; most of them begin and end in the same city. These reflect a mere fraction of what the U.S. has to offer. Use them only as a guide. The best way to explore this country is to be spontaneous and improvise as you go along. If a road looks intriguing, by all means, follow it. You'll eventually get where you're going.

These 12 easily identifiable icons are used throughout the book's sidebars to provide you with a quick reference to the content of the information provided within the highlighted area.

How to Read Your Tour Maps

●	National Park/Monument		Interstate Highway
	National/State Forest		Toll Road
▲	Places of Interest		Featured Route
⁄ ⁄	Mountain Pass		Other Roads
✕	Mountian Peak		Scenic Tour Route
✪	National Capital	▪▪▪▪▪	Tunnel
✪	State Capital	- - - - -	Ferry
○○○	City or Town		Indian Reservation
95	Interstate highway	23	U.S. Highway	284	State Highway

To help guide you, and to have some fun too, Dollie and her traveling companion, Darcy, appear from time to time throughout this book participating in some of their favorite activities. These two have had fun putting together 50 of this country's most scenic tours for you. They hope you enjoy traveling down the scenic byways of America, and they look forward to showing you some of their favorite spots along the way.

| Activities for Children | Dining | Events Schedule | Helpful Hints | Hiking | Lodging | Performing Arts | Quotes | Shopping | SideTrips | Sightseeing | Vineyards |

Table of Contents

Map Key

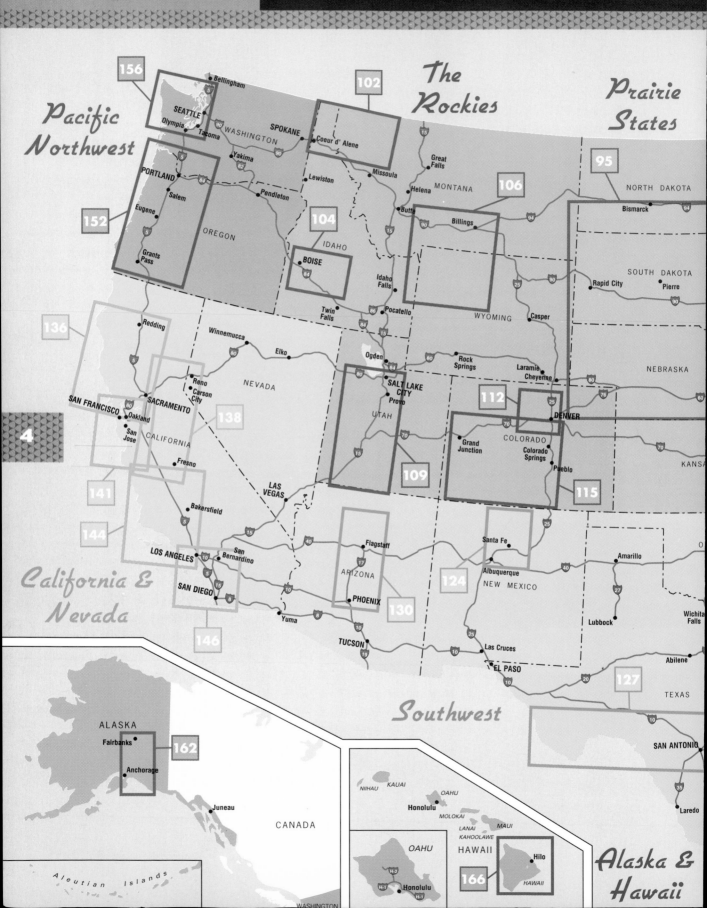

Pacific Northwest

156 — Bellingham, SEATTLE, Olympia, Tacoma, WASHINGTON

152 — PORTLAND, Salem, Eugene, OREGON, Grants Pass

The Rockies

102 — SPOKANE, Coeur d' Alene, Missoula, Lewiston

104 — BOISE, IDAHO, Idaho Falls, Twin Falls, Pocatello

106 — Great Falls, Helena, MONTANA, Butte, Billings, WYOMING, Casper

Prairie States

95 — NORTH DAKOTA, Bismarck, SOUTH DAKOTA, Rapid City, Pierre, NEBRASKA

California & Nevada

136 — Redding, Winnemucca, Elko, Reno, Carson City, NEVADA

138

141

144

146

SAN FRANCISCO, Oakland, San Jose, SACRAMENTO, CALIFORNIA, Fresno, Bakersfield, LOS ANGELES, San Bernardino, SAN DIEGO, LAS VEGAS

112 — Ogden, SALT LAKE CITY, Provo, UTAH, Rock Springs, Laramie, Cheyenne

109

115 — DENVER, Grand Junction, COLORADO, Colorado Springs, Pueblo, KANSAS

Southwest

130 — Flagstaff, ARIZONA, PHOENIX, Yuma, TUCSON

124 — Santa Fe, Albuquerque, NEW MEXICO, Las Cruces, EL PASO

127 — Amarillo, Lubbock, Wichita Falls, Abilene, TEXAS, SAN ANTONIO, Laredo

Alaska & Hawaii

162 — ALASKA, Fairbanks, Anchorage, Juneau, CANADA, Aleutian Islands, WASHINGTON

166 — NIIHAU, KAUAI, OAHU, Honolulu, MOLOKAI, LANAI, MAUI, KAHOOLAWE, HAWAII, Hilo

4

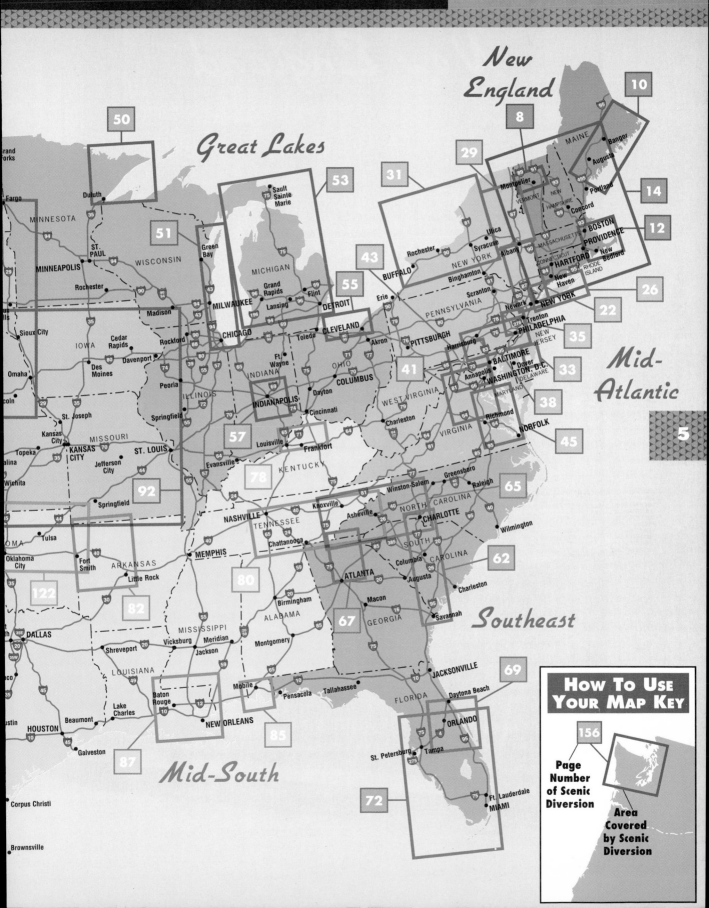

New England

Great Lakes

50

8

10

29

53

31

14

43

55

51

12

26

22

35

41

33

38

45

Mid-Atlantic

5

57

78

92

65

80

82

62

122

67

Southeast

69

87

85

Mid-South

72

HOW TO USE YOUR MAP KEY

156

Page Number of Scenic Diversion

Area Covered by Scenic Diversion

New England

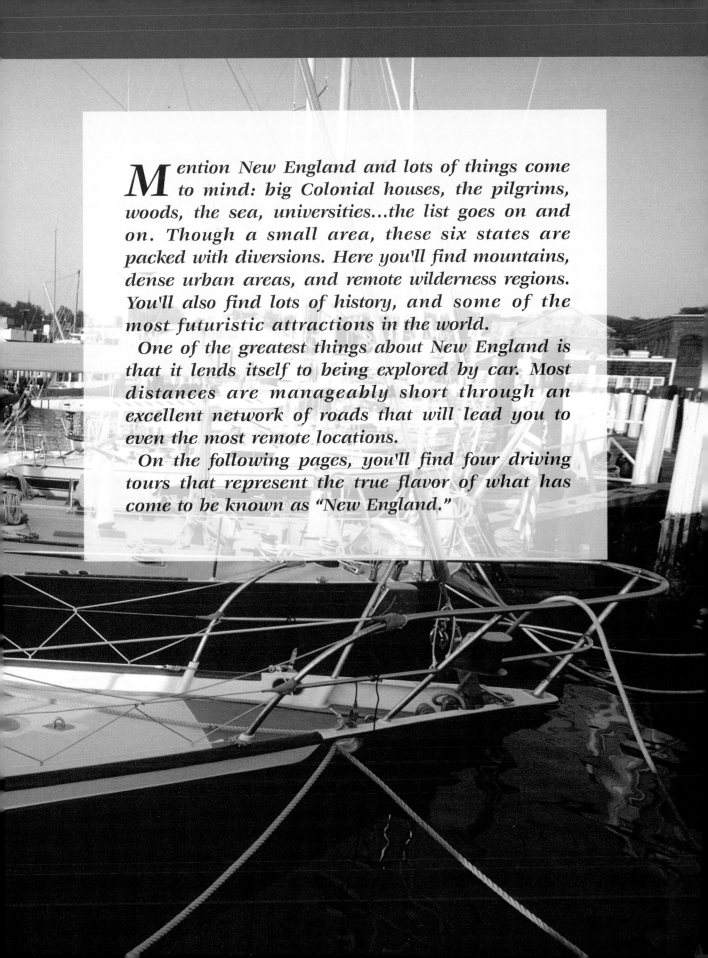

Mention New England and lots of things come to mind: big Colonial houses, the pilgrims, woods, the sea, universities...the list goes on and on. Though a small area, these six states are packed with diversions. Here you'll find mountains, dense urban areas, and remote wilderness regions. You'll also find lots of history, and some of the most futuristic attractions in the world.

One of the greatest things about New England is that it lends itself to being explored by car. Most distances are manageably short through an excellent network of roads that will lead you to even the most remote locations.

On the following pages, you'll find four driving tours that represent the true flavor of what has come to be known as "New England."

Vermont's Northeast Kingdom

Ben and Jerry's ice cream factory
Waterbury, Vermont

Distance: 203 Miles Round Trip, Burlington
Time: Allow one or two days
Highlights: Mountain scenery, picture-perfect villages, boutiques and antiques shops, Ben and Jerry's ice cream factory, distinguished inns, leaf viewing in fall, snow sports in winter.

Nearly every inch of Vermont is New England just as you pictured it—covered bridges, immaculate dairy farms, steepled villages, and sagging old farmhouses where big-pawed golden retrievers sleep on front porches. Add to that the fact that every season has its own appeals, and choosing exactly when to go and just where to go can be a happy dilemma.

Fortunately, you can't go wrong in Vermont. In the fall, the Crayola colors are fantastic (especially early to mid-October). At that time of year, the weather is often phenomenally beautiful, with flawless blue skies and plenty of sunshine. During winter, the hills are alive with skiers and snowshoers. When the snows thaw, the landscape awakens into an extravaganza of blossoms and green foliage. There's green everywhere, getting greener and greener each day as the state warms into summer.

Northern Vermont is perhaps the state's most sensationally scenic area (though many may argue that). There are miles and miles of cattle-dotted farmlands, silent lakes cupped in the hills as if precious jewels, and streams that really do sparkle. Add to that the backdrop of looming mountains, and

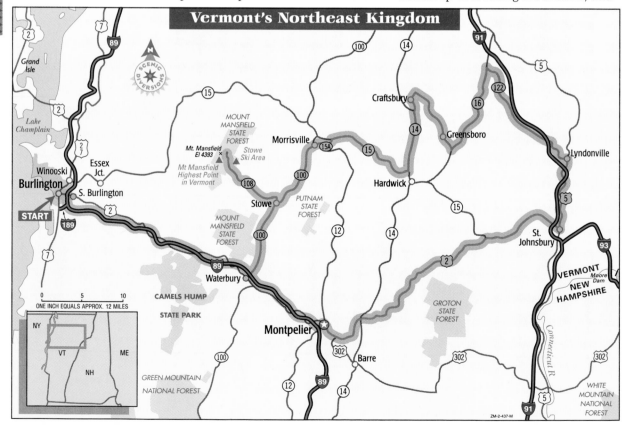

Vermont's Northeast Kingdom

you're looking at not just the state's, but some of our country's most beautiful scenery.

This drive starts in **Burlington**, Vermont's largest city, situated on the shores of *Lake Champlain*. Before setting out on your journey, take time to walk around downtown, which is a small enough area to negotiate on foot. It's centerpieced by the *Church Street Marketplace*, a four-block stretch of Church Street closed to traffic, with sidewalk cafes, benches, and all sorts of street performers.

From Burlington, it's about a 45 minute drive east to **Stowe** but first a refreshment stop. In **Waterbury**, you'll go right by *Ben & Jerry's ice cream factory*, which is worth stopping to see. There are tours, exhibits, a gift shop, and an all-around air of a carnival. Across the street is the *Cold Hollow Cider Mill*, where you can watch cider being pressed and see films on how cider and maple sugar are made. Now on to Stowe (take I-89 to Exit 10, Route 100 north).

In winter, Stowe is a mecca for skiers with its daredevil trails, its exuberant after-ski life, and its lodges that look like ones found in Austria. It's dominated by *Mount Mansfield*, Vermont's highest mountain (4,393 feet). But when the lifts are closed, Stowe is just as appealing. In town, there are all sorts of wonderful little emporia, selling everything from Christmas ornaments to handmade sweaters that look too pretty to wear. There are also several antiques shops to poke around in.

Stowe's natural beauty is by far its strongest appeal. Though you can drive around and see plenty (in fact, you can drive to the top of Mansfield) consider taking time out to explore by foot. Much of the landscape is part of Vermont's *Mount Mansfield State Forest*. There are many hiking trails, camping areas, and picnic spots. Another way to enjoy the area's scenery (in warm weather months as well as winter) is to ride the gondola to the top of Mount Mansfield. For the ultimate view, climb into a glider at *Stowe Aviation*. For 20 minutes—or

THE ULTIMATE INN

"Please turn on the lift, we'll be skiing today." Can you imagine staying at an inn that has its own ski mountain? For your honeymoon, anniversary, or any other extraordinarily special occasion, consider splurging on a stay at *Twin Farms*, an inn in **Barnard**, Vermont. Far from being an ordinary inn, Twin Farms—which is named for two farmhouses here that were owned by Sinclair Lewis and Dorothy Thompson—is a one-of-a-kind experience. Guests can stay in one of four lavishly furnished suites in the main house or one of the so-called cottages scattered around the wooded grounds. The cottages are decorated in different themes ranging from a log cabin in the middle of the woods (probably the most luxurious log cabin in the world) to a two-story art-filled house that can't be described as anything less than magnificent. The prices (which start at a lofty $750 a night for two) include three out-of-this-world meals (plus an elaborate afternoon tea), unlimited use of all facilities including skiing on the inn's private mountain in winter and—in warmer weather—tennis, mountain biking, canoeing, and fly fishing (all equipment is provided). Year-round activities include billiards, darts, an extensive video collection, open bars... and more. For more information or reservations, call (800) TWIN FARMS (894-6327) or (802) 234-9999.

more, depending on which flight you opt for—you'll soar over the peaks and valleys like a weightless bird.

From Stowe, head north on Route 100 and then turn right onto Route 15A in **Morrisville**. The landscape here is densely scenic. You'll find yourselves passing huge red barns with silver silos, old farmhouses settled into the contour of the land, and fields full of cows and spotted ponies with tangled manes. You'll see fishermen wading in rivers and thousands of white birch trees that look like fish bones against dark pine forests.

In **Hardwick**, take Route 14 north to **Craftsbury** (you'll see signs), a Grandma Moses kind of village with crisp clean white buildings, a billiard-green square, and flawless white fences all around. Consider stopping in at *Craftsbury Center* (follow the signs on the dirt roads), a camp for both kids and adults devoted to the graceful sport of sculling. In winter, it turns into a cross-country ski center.

From Craftsbury, follow the road to **Greensboro** (southeast of Craftsbury), which is home to *Willey's General Store*, an attraction in itself. Here, you'll find everything from parts for

INN-SIDE VERMONT

 Small, distinguished inns can be found throughout Vermont—tucked away in forests, set on farmlands, prominently situated in villages—you name it. A complete list of inns (and many bed and breakfasts) is published by the Vermont Chamber of Commerce. For a copy,

Write or call
> P.O. Box 37,
> Montpelier, VT 05601
> (802) 223-3443.

Vermont also has a reservation service for bed and breakfasts.

Write or call
> Vermont Bed & Breakfast,
> Box 1, East Fairfield,
> VT 05448;
> (802) 827-3827.

Covered Bridge, Vermont

balsa wood planes to farm equipment. Then carry on to **Lyndonville** where there are five covered bridges (one dating back to 1795) within the town limits. Follow Route 16 north and then make a sharp right onto Route 122.

From Lyndonville, head south on U.S. 5 to **St. Johnsbury**, which has some beautiful Victorian buildings along with an art gallery and a museum where you can learn all about the production of maple syrup.

From there, follow U.S. Route 2 to I-89 and return to Burlington.

The Coast of Maine

Distance: 524 Miles, between Portland and Eastport
Time: Minimum two days
Highlights: Atlantic Ocean scenery, seafood, inns, galleries, antiques shops, museums, sailing, boating, hiking, sports.

Freeport, Maine

For over one hundred years, Maine's coast has been a popular summer vacation area. It's made up of a series of deeply cut coves and narrow peninsulas, and has countless offshore islands. Along the way, there are dozens of little fishing villages bursting with character. On this particular tour, we take you north from **Portland** (Maine's largest city) up the coast to **Eastport**, near the Canadian border.

Tops on our list of sightseeing attractions in Portland is the *Portland Museum of Art*, which is housed in a striking post-modern building that was designed by Henry N. Cobb of I.M. Pei. It contains extensive collections of Maine-based artists such as Andrew Wyeth, Edward Hopper, and Winslow Homer. Other Portland attractions include the *Wadsworth Longfellow House* where the poet spent his childhood and the *Old Port Exchange*, a very attractive part of town where the streets are lined with restaurants, taverns, and shops that occupy former warehouses and other nineteenth-century buildings.

About 20 miles north of Portland, on U.S. 1, is **Freeport**, home of *L.L. Bean* and several name-brand factory outlets (*Polo-Ralph Lauren, Calvin Klein, Laura Ashley*...and more).

Continue up the coast on U.S. 1 and then take Route 27 to **Boothbay Harbor**. This town started life as a tiny lobstering and fishing community and grew into a tourist mecca of sorts. It's a great place to go with young children.

The sweet little village of **Waldoboro** is one of the next towns you'll come to as you continue up U.S. 1. It has several old homes and a Lutheran Church that dates back to 1771. Further out on that peninsula (following Route 220) is **Friendship**, a picturesque lobstering port. You have to go around the inlet, and then out to the tip of *St. George Peninsula* to get to **Port Clyde**, which is where the mailboat for *Monhegan Island* runs year-round. You can head out to the Island from here. On your way back to U.S. 1, take time out to visit the picture-perfect waterfront towns of **Tenants Harbor** and **Spruce Head**.

Around this point of the coast—at *Penobscot Bay*—you start to see the Maine Coast everyone has always raved about. There are startlingly beautiful islands rising abruptly out of the choppy waters. Sparkling sailboats gracefully skim about. Most beautiful though are the tall-masted windjamers that are famous in this area. You can spend a week on one eating hearty home-cooked meals and flitting about from one drop-dead gorgeous island to another. The main departure points are located in the **Rockland**, **Rockport**, or **Camden** areas.

As you continue up the coast, you'll come to **Searsport**, an old shipping port with stately old sea captains homes and a multitude of antiques shops. **Bucksport** is next. That's home to the *Fort Knox State Park*, a very impressively constructed fort that was manned during the Civil and Spanish American Wars. From there, you can take Route 15 right into **Bangor**, Maine's second-largest city. Take time to stroll around the *West Market Square Historic District* (a mid-nineteenth-century block of shops) and the *Broadway Area* where you'll see one lumber baron's mansion after another lined up as if contestants in a beauty contest.

Castine is the next stop up the coast. The town itself is the attraction, a collection of 18th- and 19th-century Georgian and Federalist houses standing in impeccable condition. Most of these were originally erected in the mid-nineteenth century when Castine was a prosperous ship-building town. Many of them have since been restored by people "from away" (in other words, big city folks with money to invest).

From Castine, it's a short scenic drive over to the village of **Blue Hill**, which is home to 75 buildings that are listed in the National Historic Register. Take time out

Deer Isle Bridge, Maine

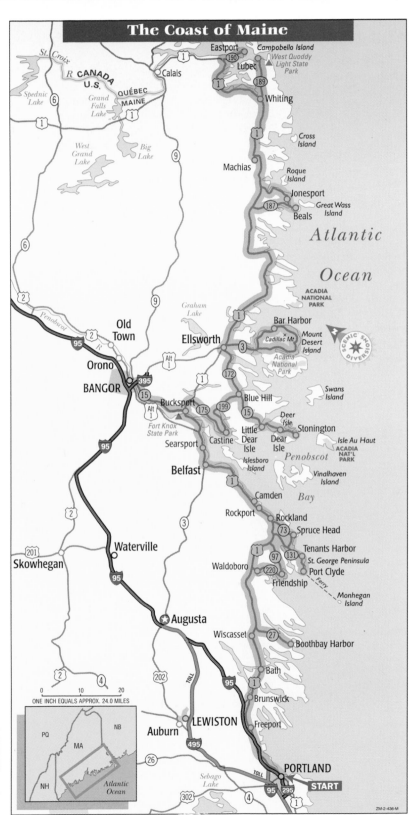

The Coast of Maine

ONE INCH EQUALS APPROX. 24.0 MILES

ZM-2-436-M

ISLAND EXCURSION

Consider taking time out to visit Monhegan Island, just off the southern coast of Maine. A mere smidgen on the map (less than two miles long and one mile wide), it has been known as a popular artists and writers retreat for years. The scenery is arrestingly beautiful: steep cliffs, powerful surf, rich green pine forests, and golden meadows. There's also a lighthouse that dates back to 1824. To reach it, you can take a boat from either **Port Clyde** or **Boothbay Harbor**.

12

to walk around and poke in the pottery and crafts shops, for which Blue Hill is well known for.

If you head southwest of Blue Hill, you'll eventually cut through a corner of *Little Deer Isle* and then climb an arching suspension bridge that takes you over to *Deer Isle*, a wonderful little island almost too beautiful to promote. Don't miss the sweet little town of **Stonington** at the southern tip of the island before going on to **Ellsworth**.

Ever since the mid-nineteenth century, *Mt. Desert Island*, east of Ellsworth, has been one of Maine's most popular destinations. Once you cross the bridge connecting it to the mainland, it's easy to see why. The island is home to *Cadillac Mountain*, which—at 1,530 feet—seems to scrape the sky. Looming all around are 16 other mountains that drop right down into the sea. Fortunately, most of the island (35,000 acres) is under the protection of *Acadia National Park*, which is threaded with miles of hiking, driving, and biking trails. The *Park Loop Road* takes in the major sights of the park.

The island's main town is **Bar Harbor**, which, back in the late 1800s was a thriving resort community for very wealthy and powerful American families. Today, it's quite a busy tourist hub with lots of shops, motels, and restaurants.

Back on the mainland, continue to follow U.S. 1, veering off whenever a road looks appealing. There are several worthwhile detours to keep your eyes open for including **Jonesport** and *Beals Island*, at the end of Route 187.

Next stop is **Lubec**, from which you can get to *Campobello Island*, *FDR's summer house*. Lubec is also home to the *West Quoddy Light State Park* which is the easternmost point of land in the continental United States.

Eastport is the next and last stop on this tour. At one time, it was a bustling town with 18 sardine canneries. But in the early 1940s, it went bankrupt, the canneries closed and much of the

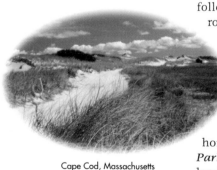

Cape Cod, Massachusetts

population left, leaving houses standing empty. Today, grand old Federal and Victorian houses stand as testimony to its better days.

From here, you can head inland and further north to explore the Maine woods or head back down the coast, stopping at places you may have missed on the way.

Boston and the Cape

Distance: 269 Miles Round trip, Boston
Time: Minimum three days
Highlights: Urban attractions, history, coastal scenery, seafood, beaches, boating, boutiques, galleries, inns, whale watching, nature walks, bike trails.

The curving coast between **Boston** and **Provincetown** offers visitors a combination-platter of sights to see. Within a period of two or three days, you can dip into the big-city attractions, visit *Plymouth Rock*, and tour the beach communities of **Cape Cod**.

Boston and next-door **Cambridge** offer a multitude of sights to see.

From Boston, it's an easy drive to **Plymouth** which is 39 miles southeast. Follow the Southeast Expressway and Route 3 south.

Plymouth is most famous because of Plymouth Rock, which marks the spot where the Pilgrims landed in 1620. The rock itself won't take more than a couple of minutes to look at, but there are several other attractions in the area devoted to early American history including a collection of historic houses, a full-size replica of the *Mayflower*, and a recreation of an entire *Pilgrim village* complete with costumed role-players.

To reach the Cape, continue south on Route 3 to the *Sagamore Bridge*, which will take you over the Cape Cod Canal. Though rarely referred to as such, Cape Cod is technically an island, separated from mainland Massachusetts by the canal. The Cape—which all writers and just about everybody else who has been there or lives there will tell you—looks like a flexed arm on the map. It's just seventy miles from the mainland to Provincetown, but its filled with little galaxies to explore.

Route 6A will take you right into **Sandwich**, which calls itself the "oldest town on the Cape." Take time out to stop and have a look around its antiques stores and gracious old houses. Sandwich is also home to one of the Cape's top attractions: the *Heritage Plantation* which has 76 acres of gardens, museums showcasing antique cars, colonial tools, and a working 1912 carousel.

From Sandwich, it's a short drive (on historic Route 6A) to **Yarmouth Port**, which is home to several old sea captains' houses. In fact, a stretch of Main

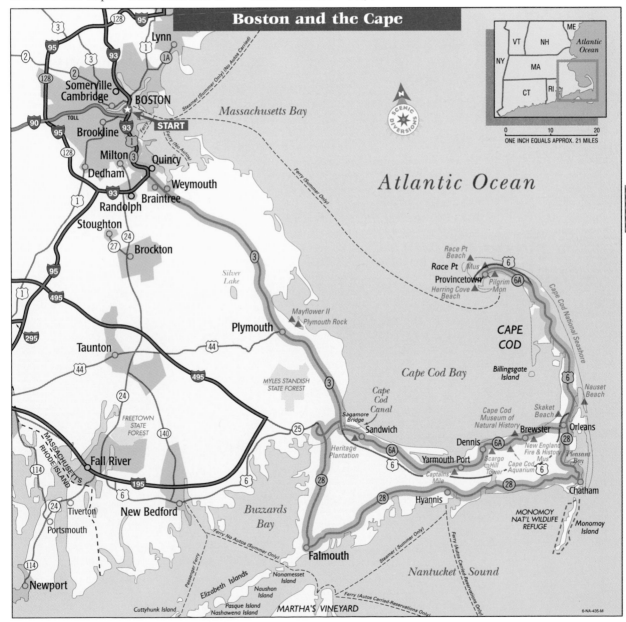

Boston and the Cape

Street (which is part of Route 6A) is known as the "Captains' Mile" because it's lined with them.

Carry on to **Dennis**, the next town. If it's a clear—or even partially clear—day, make your way up to the *Scargo Hill Tower* (from Route 6A, turn right onto Old Bass River Road and follow the signs). From the top, you can see the Cape stretching out below all the way to **Provincetown**.

Brewster is the next stop. Here you'll find three noteworthy attractions: The *Cape Cod Aquarium*, the *New England Fire and History Museum*, and the *Cape Cod Museum of Natural History*.

A little further up Route 6A is **Orleans**, where you'll find some wonderful beaches to take your pick of. On the ocean side, you'll find *Nauset Beach*, a gorgeous beach with major waves that stretches on for ten miles. Over on the bay side, *Skaket Beach* is also beautiful, but calmer—a good choice for families with young children. Before leaving Orleans, be sure to take a look at the *Bird Watcher's General Store*, which is devoted to our feathered friends.

Continue up the Cape to Provincetown or *P-Town*, which is a very lively community with lots of artists and writers. Though P-town is not that big, it's crammed with shops, galleries, restaurants, bakeries, night spots—you name it. Rather than wrestle with the P-Town traffic, consider parking your car in the first spot you find on Commercial Street and then walk in. You might also consider renting bikes (right in town) to peddle around and see some of the nearby attractions. Off Bradford Street (which runs parallel to Commercial Street), you'll find the town's biggest tourist attraction: the *Pilgrim Monument and Provincetown Museum*. From there, it's a short, mostly flat or downhill peddle over to *Herring Cove* where you can get on the *Province Lands Bike Paths*, a webwork of paved trails that take you over the dunes, through pine groves, and alongside the sea.

If you want to get in a couple of hours at the beach, drive over to *Race Point* which is part of the *Cape Cod National Seashore*. Sprawling over nearly 44,000 acres, this National Seashore was established by President Kennedy in 1961 to protect the area from commercialization.

Then work your way back down the Cape (take U.S. Route 6 to Route 28) pausing at **Chatham** which is a beautiful little village with gray shingled sea captain's houses, shops, restaurants, inns, and beaches, or any other little towns that strike your fancy. To return to Boston, get back on Route 3 once you cross the Cape Cod Canal.

Highlights of New England

Distance: 1307 Miles Round Trip, Boston
Time: At least 10 days

For this trip, we take you from **Boston** to Massachusetts' North Shore, along the coast of New Hampshire and up to the southern coast of Maine, then to the Western Mountains and Lakes region of Maine, through the mountains of New Hampshire and Vermont, and down through the Berkshires in Massachusetts, the Litchfield Hills of Connecticut, to the Connecticut coast, up to Newport, Rhode Island, and back to Boston.

The fastest way to reach the North Shore of Massachusetts from Boston is actually the least direct: Take I-93 north to I-95 north (Route 128 east). Get off at the exit marked for Route 114 and Salem. You could also head up on U.S. 1 from Boston, but traffic can be intolerably slow.

Whale watching off the New England coast

WHALE-WATCH EXCURSIONS

BOSTON

The A.C. Cruise Company
(617) 426-8419

Bay State Cruise Company
(617) 723-7800

Boston Harbor Cruises
(617) 227-4320 or
(617) 227-4321

The New England Aquarium
(617) 973-5277

CAPE COD

Provincetown
Dolphin Fleet Whale Watch
(508) 349-1900

Provincetown & Portuguese Princess
(508) 487-2651

Provincetown Whale Watch
(508) 487-1582

Barnstable Harbor
Hyannis Whale Watch
(508) 362-6088

The *North Shore*—which is roughly the area between Salem and Newburyport near the New Hampshire border—has long been a favorite escape for Bostonians. Back in the 18th and 19th centuries, magnificent ships were built in the coastal towns and would set sail for ports in Africa and Asia, bringing great wealth to the area. Today, many of the buildings—including majestic sea captains' homes—still stand surveying strikingly beautiful stretches of the Atlantic.

Make your first stop **Salem**, which is famous for the witch trials that took place back in 1692. Though it has never been proven that there were witches in this sea-fronting town, there are many attractions devoted to that scandalous time including *The Salem Witch Museum* (which has an audiovisual re-creation of the witchcraft trials), the *Witch House* (where one of the witch trial judges lived), and *Crow Haven Corner*, a tiny shop owned by Laurie Cabot, Salem's most illustrious witch.

From Salem, it's an easy drive over to **Marblehead**, a wonderful little village, well known among yacht and sailboat owners who come from around the world to race during the summer months. Consider taking tours of *Abbot Hall*, *Jeremiah Lee Mansion*, and *King Hooper Mansion*, three landmark buildings.

Then drive the loop around **Marblehead Neck**. This quiet residential community is made up of several grand ocean and harbor-front homes surrounded by handsome lawns and gardens.

Carry on up the coast, following Route 1A to **Beverly**, and then Route 127 to **Manchester**, which is poised on the shores of *Cape Ann*. Take time out to visit *Singing Beach*, a sensationally beautiful patch of beach.

Continue north to **Gloucester**, a major fishing port. Once in town, you'll see signs directing motorists along the city's "Scenic Tour," which takes you by the *Harbor Cove*, the *Inner Harbor*, the *Fish Pier*, and to the city's celebrated statue of a *Gloucester fisherman*.

SPECIAL EVENTS

APRIL. **Boston Marathon**. Takes place on the third Monday every April. Runners run from Hopkinton to the Prudential Center.

JUNE. **Harbor Festival, Bismore Park** on Ocean Street in Hyannis. An annual Blessing of the Fleet, clam-shucking and pie-eating contests, and all sorts of activities take place.

JULY. **Fourth of July Parade,** on Main Street and Old Colony Way in Orleans. This is a 2 1/2-mile theme parade held every year.

JULY. **Harborfest,** Boston. A seaside celebration with fireworks, chowder contests, boat races, historical reenactments, and a performance by the Boston Pops Orchestra.

JULY. **Esplanade Concerts,** Boston. Musical programs by the Boston Pops in the Hatch Shell on the Esplanade.

AUGUST. **Cape Cod Antiques Exposition,** at The Charles F. Moore Sports Center, O'Connor Way (exit 12 off Route 6).

This exposition attracts antiques dealers from all over New England.

AUGUST. **Festival of the Arts,** Chase Park on Cross Street, Chatham. A juried outdoor event attracting artists from all over.

AUGUST. **Festival Days,** Dennis. An annual festival with an antique-car parade, church suppers, crafts fairs, road races,... and more.

SEPTEMBER. **Annual Bourne Scallop Festival,** Buzzards Bay Park, Buzzards Bay. The largest scallop festival on the East Coast.

SEPTEMBER. **Cranberry Festival,** Harwich. Races, clambakes, barbecues, a parade—this is an enormous small town festival.

OCTOBER. **Charles River Regatta,** Boston. One of the rowing world's biggest races is held the third Sunday in October every year.

DECEMBER. **First Night Celebration,** Boston. Boston Common on New Year's Eve.

Next stop: **Rockport**, which started off as a quiet fishing village, was discovered by artists, and has since sprouted into a resort. During the summer, the *Bearskin Neck*—a narrow peninsula jutting into the water off *Dock Square*—is practically sagging with tourists. Here you'll find one souvenir shop after another interspersed with art galleries and restaurants.

Newburyport is the last stop to make before leaving the state of Massachusetts. It is a museum-like 19th-century town filled with ship

Jacob's Pillow, Massachusetts

owner's and captains' houses overlooking a yacht-filled harbor. There are a several museums in town (the *Coffin House*, *Cushing House*, and *Custom House*) worth browsing through if you have the time.

U.S. Route 1 continues through the state of New Hampshire, which has a impressive 18 miles of coast, and into the state of Maine. If time permits, consider stopping at one of the New Hampshire beaches; *Hampton Beach State Park* is one of the most popular.

The southern coast of Maine is quite developed and hence, not the picturesque Maine you might have had in mind. Nevertheless, it is home to some worthwhile attractions and towns including **Ogunquit**, a well-known art colony; **Wells**, which is home to the *Wells Auto Museum* with over 70 antique cars; and the "Kennebunks" which are

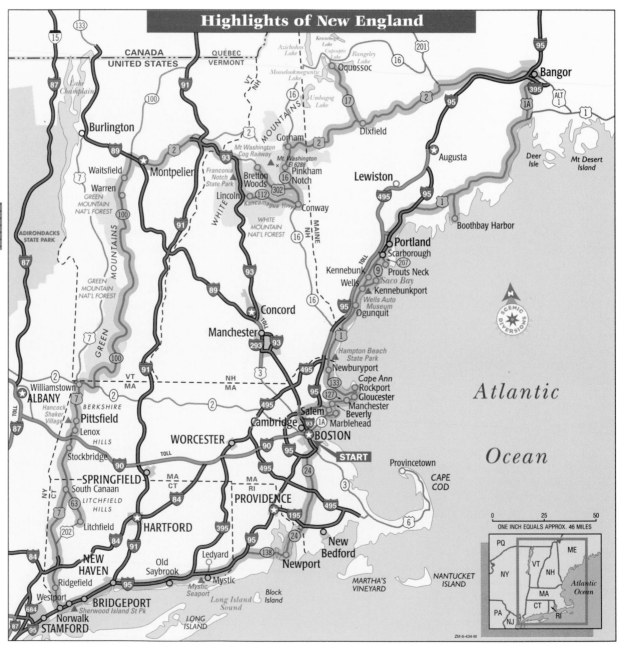

made up of the commercial center of **Kennebunk** and the port town, **Kennebunkport**. Both towns were early shipbuilding and fishing settlements.

As you continue north from the Kennebunks, you can either pick up U.S.1 (at Kennebunk) or opt for the more scenic Route 9 from Kennebunkport. The latter takes you past several sun-soaked beaches. After you have reached the town of **Scarborough**, turn right onto Route 207 which leads to *Prouts Neck*. This oddly-shaped peninsula juts into *Saco Bay* about eight miles south of **Portland**. Much of its coastal scenery—steep cliffs, swirling surf, and dwarfish rock-clinging trees—can be seen on the canvases of the American painter Winslow Homer who lived and worked there.

Continue up the coast on U.S. 1, making stops at Portland, **Boothbay Harbor**, and a handful of other towns before heading inland to the western part of the state. Take U.S. 1A to **Bangor**, and then pick up U.S. 2 West, which takes you across the state to the western mountains and lakes region. Turn right onto Route 17 (shortly after **Dixfield**) to get to the *Rangeley Lakes*. This area is almost solid wilderness punctuated with an occasional town (by town, we often mean a post office, a church, and a general store). The lakes, some of which have multi-syllabic names such as *Mooselookmeguntic*, *Kennebago*, *Aziscohos*, *Cupsuptic*, and *Umbagog*, are busy with boaters and fisherman in summer months. Come winter, the nearby ski areas of *Sugarloaf* and *Saddleback* come alive with skiiers.

Return to U.S. 2, and continue west over the border into New Hampshire. Here, you'll find yourself right in the heart of the *White Mountains*, home to *Mount Washington* (at 6,288 feet, it's one of the windiest places on earth). Depending on time, you can take the *Mount Washington Auto Route* (from Pinkham Notch) or climb aboard the *Mount Washington Cog Railway* at **Bretton Woods**. Otherwise, continue following Route 16 south to Conway, and turn right onto Route 112. The 33-mile distance between **Conway** and **Lincoln** is known as the *Kancamagus Highway*, and is one of the most spectacularly scenic drives you'll ever make.

Hop on I-93 North to reach *Franconia Notch*, a dramatic mountain gap surrounded by 6,500 acres of state park. A stretch of eight miles on I-93 is called the *Franconia Notch Parkway*.

Continue on I-93 North crossing the border into Vermont. Take U.S. 2 to **Montpelier**, the capital of the state and the smallest state capital in the country. A bit north of Montpelier, pick up Route 100 which you'll follow south through the state. You'll find several interesting towns along the way including **Waitsfield** and **Warren** (off Route 100 east of Lincoln Gap Road). Route 100 also takes you right along the edge of the *Green Mountains*, and through intensely scenic Vermont. Do detour on any road that looks appealing remembering to respect private property. Most of Vermont's best scenery can be found on dirt roads that don't show up on most maps and don't necessarily lead anywhere.

Once you cross into Massachusetts, head west to **Williamstown**, in the *Berkshires*. The Berkshire Hills—which occupy the western quarter of the state—are known for both their rural

Covered Bridge—Franconia Notch State Park, New Hampshire

17

Norman Rockwell Museum, Massachusetts

18

beauty (sprawling farms, tidy little villages, dozen of lakes and ponds, thousands of acres of forest) and their cultural assets (they're home to the *Tanglewood Music Festival* and *Jacob's Pillow Dance Festival*). U.S. 7 takes you right through the heart of them passing through a series of wonderful little towns including **Lenox** and **Stockbridge**.

Williamstown's most notable attractions include the *Sterling and Francine Clark Art Institute*, an outstanding collection of French Impressionists, Renoirs, and Old Masters, and the *Williams College* campus which has a fine collection of paintings itself as well as one of the nation's best collections of rare books.

From Williamstown, head south on U.S. 7. At **Pittsfield**, detour a bit to the west on Route 20. About five miles over, you'll find *Hancock Shaker Village*, a living history museum devoted to the Shakers.

Resume heading south on U.S. 7, making a stop at the *Berkshire Museum* in Pittsfield. Also in Pittsfield is *Arrowhead* the house where Herman Melville wrote Moby Dick.

Next stop: Lenox, home of *Tanglewood,* where legendary music can be heard under the stars throughout the summer months. It's the summer home for the Boston Symphony Orchestra. If you're not planning to attend a performance, do take time to stroll around the grounds (there are 210 acres including formal gardens) which are open daily.

Continuing south, near the junction of routes 7 and 7A, you'll find *The Mount*, which was the summer residence of novelist Edith Wharton. The house—a Classical revival—is sensationally situated on 49 acres.

Carry on to Stockbridge, which many people know from Norman Rockwell's famous illustrations that first appeared on the covers of "*The Saturday Evening Post*" and "*McCall's*". You can see some of the original covers as well as the world's largest collection of the illustrator's works in the *Norman*

Rockwell Museum. The *Red Lion Inn* on Main Street has been a major Stockbridge landmark for more than 200 years. Consider stopping in for a drink in the courtyard or on one of the rockers on the front porch. Then wander around the shops on Main Street.

U.S. 7 takes you right into Connecticut, where you can spend a little time exploring the *Litchfield Hills*. There are over three dozen towns scattered throughout the Litchfield Hills, most of them with fewer than 5,000 inhabitants. Especially pretty is the town of **Litchfield** itself (follow Route 63 from South Canaan), which is about as New England as a town can be complete with a village green, a bone white church, and huge 18th-century houses lined up along wide maple tree-lined streets.

You can follow U.S 7 right over to **Norwalk** on the coast of Connecticut (pausing to see **Ridgefield**, a lovely old village).

An outstanding attraction in Norwalk is the *Maritime Center* in "SoNo" (**South Norwalk**). Among its highlights: an aquarium with sharks and seals, an IMAX theater, a boat-building demonstration, and several interactive displays.

Just up the coast (hop on I-95 and get off at Exit 18), you'll find **Westport**, which is home to *Sherwood Island State Park*, a pleasant beach on *Long Island Sound*. The town is also rife with restaurants and shops.

Seiji Ozawa Hall—Tanglewood, Massachusetts

Get back on I-95 and head north, making your next stop at **Old Saybrook**. Once a shipbuilding and fishing town, it's now a popular spot for summer vacationers.

Carry on to **Mystic**, where you'll find the famed *Mystic Seaport*, a huge open-air museum where America's shipbuilding and whaling prosperity is magnificently captured. The star attraction is the 113-foot *Charles W. Morgan*, a whaling ship that was built in 1841. Another huge attraction in this area is the *Foxwoods High Stakes Bingo & Casino*, in **Ledyard**.

Continuing up the coast on I-95, you'll soon come to Rhode Island. To reach **Newport**, take Exit 3A, Route 138 east. Follow 138 east over the *Jamestown* and *Newport bridges*, directly into Newport. A city steeped in history, Newport needs little introduction. Plan to spend a good chunk of time on foot, exploring *Colonial Newport*. Then do the mansion tour by car. Route 24 north takes you back to the Boston area.

BOSTON

SEEING THE SIGHTS

You'll find history with just about every step you take in Boston and you'll take many. Indeed, walking is the best way to see the city's sights. The most complete—and affordable—way to explore the city's historical sights is to follow *The Freedom Trail*, a three-mile-long, self-guided walking tour. It takes you to many of Boston's most celebrated landmarks and is clearly marked by a red line (or double row of red bricks), starting at the *Boston Common Visitor Information Center* (near the Park Street subway station) and winding its way through the downtown district to *Faneuil Hall*, through the North End and into **Charleston**, where you'll find the USS *Constitution*. Some of the sites include *The Old State House, Paul Revere's House*, and the *Bunker Hill Monument*.

Boston's newer attractions (meaning anything after the Revolutionary War) include many museums. Its most famous showcase of art is the *Museum of Fine Arts* which has works by Rembrandt, El Greco, and Van Gogh. The nearby *Isabella Stewart Gardner Museum* is a 15th-century art-filled Venetian palace with an impressive collection of paintings and sculpture (including works by Rembrandt, Botticelli, Titian, and Raphael) collected by one woman. Boston is also home to a Computer Museum which has a giant walk-through computer and dozens of work stations for visitors to explore cyberspace.

One of the best views of the city can be had by taking the elevator straight to the 60th floor of the *John Hancock Building*.

There's lots more. If you have time, spend it wandering around the different neighborhoods including *Beacon Hill, Downtown, The Back Bay*, located just over the *Charles River*, in Cambridge.

Trolley Tours. If you're not up for sightseeing on foot, consider climbing into a trolley for a Boston tour. Boston Trolley Tours (617) 427-8687 is one of several companies that offer trolley tours. They have a large fleet of handcrafted trolleys that run year round. There are well over a dozen boarding stops scattered around the city. The narrated tour lasts about 100 minutes (though you can get on and off as you go along).

Walking Tours. In addition to the Freedom Trail, there are a variety of walking tours in Boston. The *Black Heritage Trail* (617) 742-5415 is a 90-minute walk taking you to the city's 19th-century African-American community landmarks. You can opt for a guided tour or pick up a map and brochure and follow it on your own. Boston by Foot (617) 367-2345 or 617-367-3766 for recorded information) has a variety of guided walks, from May through October. The Victorian Society in America (617) 267-6338 takes you to the city's Victorian sights. The *Women's Heritage Trail* (617) 731-5597 focuses on the lives of 20 women who made significant contributions to the city.

Mid-Atlantic

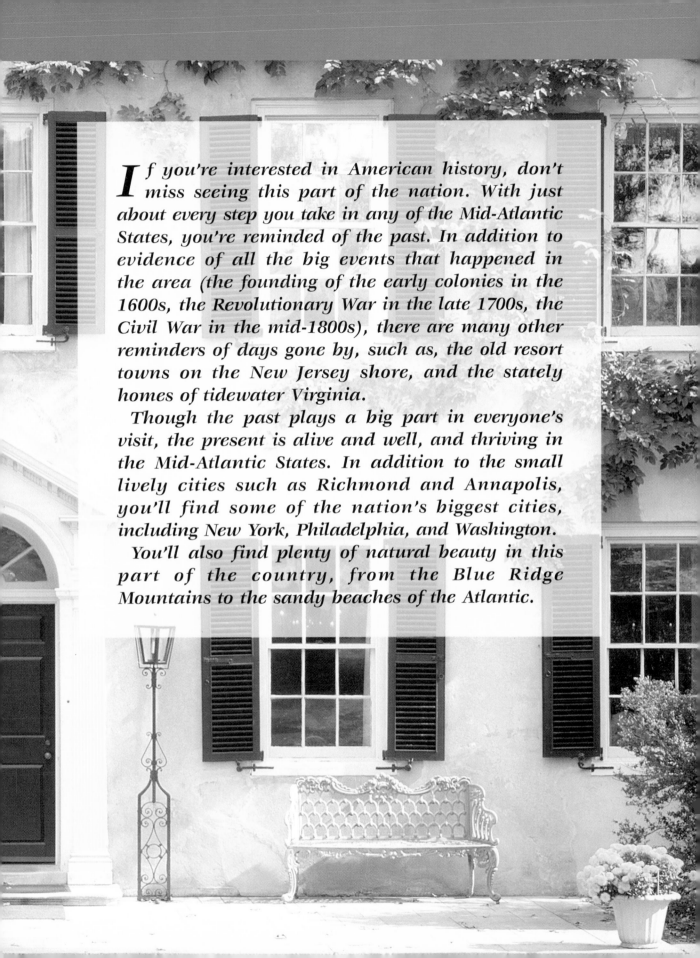

*I*f you're interested in American history, don't miss seeing this part of the nation. With just about every step you take in any of the Mid-Atlantic States, you're reminded of the past. In addition to evidence of all the big events that happened in the area (the founding of the early colonies in the 1600s, the Revolutionary War in the late 1700s, the Civil War in the mid-1800s), there are many other reminders of days gone by, such as, the old resort towns on the New Jersey shore, and the stately homes of tidewater Virginia.

Though the past plays a big part in everyone's visit, the present is alive and well, and thriving in the Mid-Atlantic States. In addition to the small lively cities such as Richmond and Annapolis, you'll find some of the nation's biggest cities, including New York, Philadelphia, and Washington.

You'll also find plenty of natural beauty in this part of the country, from the Blue Ridge Mountains to the sandy beaches of the Atlantic.

FDR's home, Springwood—Hyde Park, New York

The Hudson River Valley

• •

Distance: 281 Miles Round Trip, New York City
Time: Allow at least two or three days
Highlights: Riverside towns, historic houses, museums, U.S. Military Academy, mountains and woodlands, farms, wineries, antiques and crafts shops, hiking, horseback riding, sports resorts, skiing (downhill and cross-country).

The mighty *Hudson River* is one of America's most famous waterways, named after Henry Hudson who explored it in 1609.

Running 315 miles from the *Adirondacks* to the sea, it rushes by waterfront towns, stately mansions, vineyards, forests and mountains, and several historic sites commemorating Revolutionary War battles.

For this diversion, we suggest driving up the east bank, crossing over the *Rip Van Winkle Bridge* near the town of **Hudson**, seeing a bit of *Catskill Park*, and then returning down the western shore.

Start by heading north out of **New York City** (follow signs for

the *Saw Mill River Parkway*). Then jog over to U.S. 9 in **Hastings**, an exit off the Saw Mill. U.S. 9 roughly follows the Hudson shoreline, taking you through a string of historic towns and attractions.

Make your first stop **Tarrytown**, a riverside town that was settled by the Dutch in the mid-1600s and later made famous by the writings of Washington Irving, particularly "The Legend of Sleepy Hollow." There are several noteworthy attractions in the area including *Lyndhurst*, a Gothic Revival estate that was the former home of financier Jay Gould and *Irving's Hudson River Estate* called *Sunnyside*. In nearby **North Tarrytown**, you'll find *Philipsburg Manor*, a beautifully restored 17th-century manor house with a mill and mill pond. Also in North Tarrytown is the *Rockefeller Estate in Pocantico Hills*, a 40-room Colonial Revival mansion on 87 acres.

Continue up U.S. 9 to *Van Cortlandt Manor* in **Croton on Hudson**, which is a restored baronial manor offering insight into the life of a wealthy family in the early 1800s. From there, carry on to **Garrison**, home to *Boscobel*, an early 18th-century country home open for touring. Just to the north is the village of **Cold Spring** which is filled with historic 19th-century buildings. There are several antiques and crafts shops and the *Foundry School Museum* which displays Hudson River School paintings.

Once you've looked around Cold Spring, set out north on Route 9D picking up U.S. 9 above I-84. **Poughkeepsie** is the next major town. It's home to *Vassar*, one of the country's top colleges, which you can visit.

Continue north on U.S. 9 for six miles to reach **Hyde Park**, where you'll find *Franklin D. Roosevelt's home*. The estate (which is one mile south of town on U.S. 9) is known as *Springwood*. It was the president's birthplace and lifelong residence.

One of the Hudson's most famous attractions stands just north of Hyde Park. The *Vanderbilt Mansion* is a 54-room Beaux Arts mansion that was designed by McKim, Mead, and White

WHAT'S HAPPENING WHEN

May. **Rhinebeck Antiques Fair.** Held at the Dutchess County Fairgrounds. (914) 758-6186.

June. **Crafts at Rhinebeck.** A juried show of over 350 exhibitors. Held at the Dutchess County Fairgrounds. (914) 876-4001.

August. **Ulster County Fair.** An annual event at the Fairgrounds, 2 miles southwest of New Paltz on Libertyville Road.

September. **Hudson Valley Food Festival.** Uptown Kingston, Wall Street area. Includes music, tastings, and demonstrations.

September. **Harvest Moon Festival.** Seasonal foods, music, exhibits. Hudson River Maritime Museum, Rondout Landing, Kingston.

September. **Annual Radio Control Jamboree.** An air show and other aerial events at the Old Rhinebeck Aerodrome. (914) 229-2371.

October. **Crafts at Rhinebeck Fall Festival.** Over 200 exhibitors plus harvest-related activities at the Dutchess County Fairgrounds. (914) 876-4001.

October. **Rhinebeck Antiques Fair.** Dealers from all over New England show furniture, folk art, paintings, etc., at the Dutchess County Fairgrounds. (914) 758-6186.

for Frederick Vanderbilt. You can tour the house and grounds which gaze out at the shimmering Hudson River. Afterwards, continue north to **Rhinebeck** and have a look around the *Old Rhinebeck Aerodrome*, a museum devoted to vintage aeroplanes.

Shortly after Rhinebeck, turn off to the left on Route 9G and you'll come to two more of the area's most notable attractions: the *Clermont State Historic Site* in **Germantown** and *Olana*, just south of Hudson. Clermont was the home of Robert R. Livingston (and seven generations of his family), one of five men elected to draft the Declaration of Independence. He also was Chancellor of New York and administered the oath of office to George Washington. Olana was the

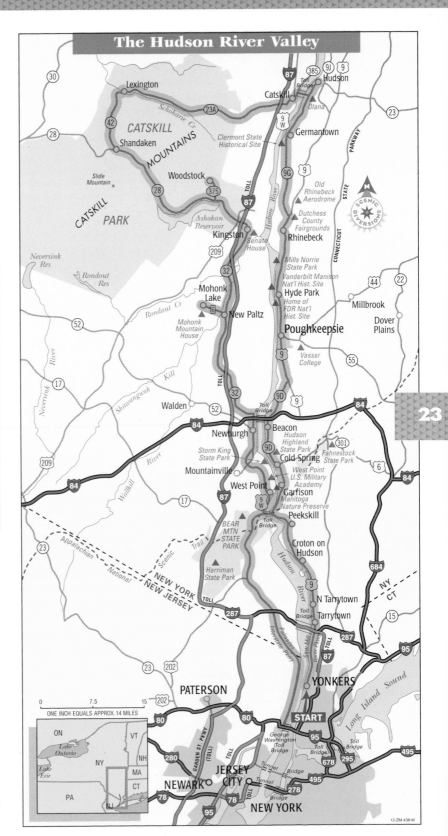

The Hudson River Valley

ONE INCH EQUALS APPROX. 14 MILES

12-ZM-436-M

24

home of the 19th-century landscape artist, Frederic Edwin Church. He built Olana (a five-story Persian-style villa atop a bluff overlooking the Hudson) in the 1870s.

Keep going north from there to the former whaling town of Hudson. Here you'll find several antiques shops as well as a handsome collection of restored Federal, Greek Revival, and Victorian houses that were built in the 18th century. Detailed walking tour maps are available in most of the shops.

From Hudson, backtrack a bit to cross the Hudson on the Rip Van Winkle Bridge. Route 23 takes you to **Catskill**, a gateway to the *Catskill Mountains*. To have a look at some of the magical scenery, follow Route 23A west to **Lexington**. Then turn south on Route 42, following that to **Shandaken**. From there, take Route 28 east and turn left onto Route 375 to see **Woodstock**, where the famed rock concerts took place in 1969 and 1994. There are several shops and galleries to browse through.

Kingston, which was New York State's first capital (back in 1777) is the next major stop. It's an old river port that was founded in 1652 as a Dutch trading settlement. Many of its early buildings stand today and are open to the public including the *Old Dutch Church* and the *Senate House*. There's also the *Hudson River Maritime Museum* and the *Trolley Museum* which showcases old trolley cars.

From Kingston, head south on Route 32 to **New Paltz**. Another history rich town, it was founded back in 1678 by half a dozen Huguenots who were

granted land by the Colonial governor of New York. Take a walk down *Huguenot Street* in town. The oldest street in America, it's lined with stone houses and a church that were built between 1692-1799. New Paltz is also home to the *Mohonk Mountain House*, a big old-fashioned country hotel on *Mohonk Lake* ("Mohonk" is an Indian word that means "lake in the sky"). Take time out to wander about its wooded trails. For a far-reaching view, climb the cliff-top observation tower.

From New Paltz, drive south to **Newburgh** to see *Washington's Headquarters* (during the last days of the Revolutionary War). From there, continue south on Route 32 about seven miles or so until you see a sign for the *Storm King Art Center* in **Mountainville**. It's the country's leading outdoor sculpture park and museum, sprawling over 400 acres of lawns, terraces, fields, and woods.

Dramatically situated on a bluff overlooking the Hudson River, *West Point*, home to the United States Military Academy, is next. It was founded in 1802 and over the years has turned out many prominent leaders including Robert E. Lee, Ulysses S. Grant, and George S. Patton. There's a museum devoted to military history.

From West Point, take U.S. 9W south and get off at the **Haverstraw** exit to reach *Bear Mountain State Park*, a 5,067-acre park that extends westward from the Hudson. Here you'll find the excellent *Trailside Museum* which consists of several small museums including a reptile museum, a nature study museum, a geology museum, and a history museum. There are also hiking trails, picnic areas, a mountain-top observatory, and a lovely drive up the mountain—called *Perkins Memorial Drive*.

It's an easy drive back to **Manhattan** from here—just 45 miles. Take the *Palisades Interstate Parkway* south to the *George Washington Bridge*.

ACTIVE DIVERSIONS

When visiting this part of the world, be sure to pack a good pair of hiking

HEY DUDES

If you thought you had to go west to have a dude ranch experience, you'll be pleased to discover the Rocking Horse Ranch Resort in Highland, New York (near New Paltz on the west side of the Hudson River). A great choice for families, this dude ranch is complete with horseback riding, all-you-can-eat chuck-wagon cuisine, and a whole "alphabet of activities." For information, call (914) 691-2927.

boots or walking shoes, binoculars, and clothes you can get out and explore in. Here are just some of the activities you'll find.

• *Biking.* Mountain bikes can be rented at Catskill Mountain Bicycle Shop on North Front Street in New Paltz (914) 255-3859; at Overlook Mountain Bikes, 107 Tinker Street, Woodstock (914) 679-2122; and Woodstock Bicycle Shop, 9 Rock City Road, Woodstock (914) 679-8388.

• *Bird-watching.* Slide Mountain in the Catskills is an especially good place for bird-watching. Among its many inhabitants are wild turkeys, ruffed grouse, pileated woodpeckers, yellow-bellied sapsuckers, and several different warblers and thrushes.

• *Golf.* Mohonk Mountain House, New Paltz (914) 255-1000 and Green Acres in Kingston (914) 331-7807.

• *Hiking.* Hiking opportunities abound in the Hudson Valley region. Here are just some you might want to find. *Hudson Highland State Park*, just north of Cold Spring has lots of trails to wander along, as does the *Manitoga Nature Preserve*, south of Garrison. In nearby Carmel the Appalachian Trail

Kykuit Mansion—Tarrytown, New York

cuts through *Fahnestock State Park*.

• *Hudson River Boat Tours.* In Kingston, there are several boat companies offering river trips including Hudson River Cruises, which has music and dinner cruises (914) 255-6515 and the Great Hudson Sailing Center (914) 338-7313 for sailing trips.

• *Skiing.* For downhill skiing and cross-country, there's Belleayre Mountain Ski Center, Highmount (914) 254-5600; for cross-country only, Lake Mohonk in New Paltz (914) 255-1000.

MEAL TIP

If you're in the area of FDR's home and it's time for dinner, you couldn't ask for a better place to eat. The Culinary Institute of America is in Hyde Park , 433 Albany Post Road (914) 471-6608. There are four student-staffed restaurants on the 150-acre campus: St. Andrew's Cafe offers contemporary dishes, The Caterina de Medici Dining Room features regional Italian cuisine, The Escoffier Restaurant serves French, and The American Bounty Restaurant specializes in American food. Reservations are a must.

Lower Manhattan, New York

New York's Long Island

Distance: 366 Miles Round Trip, New York City
Time: Allow at least two or three days
Highlights: Ocean beaches and views, farms, fresh seafood, chic boutiques, art galleries, estates, wineries, museums, wildlife, spa, tennis, beaches, boating, biking.

"The Island" (which is how most natives and visitors refer to Long Island) has long been a favorite summer escape for **New York City** residents. It stretches 120 miles from the tip of **Manhattan** to the edge of **Montauk**, and actually encompasses the metropolitan boroughs of **Brooklyn** and **Queens** (where both *John F. Kennedy International* and *LaGuardia* airports are located).

When most people talk about Long Island, they are referring to Nassau and Suffolk Counties. Within these two counties, there's everything from car-packed suburbs to beaches where there are no footprints in sight. There are dusty farms as well as conversation-piece celebrity estates. There are bustling malls and exclusive boutiques, diners as well as four-star restaurants, and roadside motels and top-drawer resorts.

This diversion takes you out of Manhattan and around the Island, hugging the coastline most of the way. Take time out to relax on the beach, stop at farm stands, and poke around the galleries and shops in The Hamptons—which include Westhampton, Hampton Bays, Southampton, Bridgehampton, and East Hampton—on the south shore of the island.

Start by taking the *Midtown Tunnel* from Manhattan to the Long Island Expressway (I-495). Head east to Exit 48 (about 32 miles) and then follow Round Swamp Road to *Old Bethpage Village*, a re-created farm village of the pre-Civil War era complete with costumed villagers demonstrating bread baking, butter churning, sheep shearing, and other everyday chores of days long gone.

From Old Bethpage, take Route 110 south for six miles and turn west on Sunrise Highway (Route 27) for four miles, then south for six miles on Wantagh State Parkway (Route 105) to reach *Jones Beach State Park*. In addition to being one of New York's best beaches (white white sand, significant waves, seemingly endless in length), Jones Beach has a wonderful theater company that performs nightly in the summer months. Follow Ocean Drive east and then head north to join Route 27, which you can take right through the five towns known as "The Hamptons." All five of the Hampton towns have long been a haven for writers, artists, and other celebrities in addition to summer visitors. The main attraction of all five is the beach, which—backed by rolling dunes—stretches out for miles, offering plenty of opportunity for sunning.

In **Southampton**, make your first

NOTEWORTHY LONG ISLAND RESTAURANTS

- For a huge, all-American breakfast: The Honest Diner, on the Montauk Highway ((516) 267-3535) is a massively popular spot in Amagansett.
- For a deliriously good seafood lunch: The Lobster Roll, also on the Montauk Highway in Amagansett ((516) 267-3740) is a no-frills, roadside eatery with lobster sandwiches and salads worth every minute you stand in line.
- For a splurge dinner: Located just three miles west of East Hampton, Sapore Di Mare, Winscott Stone Road, Wainscott ((516) 537-2764), offers unfailingly good Tuscan food and attracts a who's who clientele.

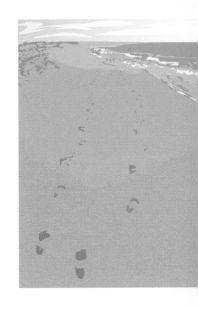

stop the *Old Halsey House*, which is the oldest English frame house in New York state. Also worth seeing is the *Southampton Historical Museum*. The main building, which was formerly a whaling captain's home (1843), is filled with period furnishings. There's also a one-room schoolhouse and a carriage house plus a 19th-century village street with over a dozen restored shops. Southampton's most famous shopping area is *Job's Lane,* where you'll find pricey boutiques competing for your credit card signature. Also on Job's Lane is the *Parrish Art Museum,* which has a good collection of 19th and 20th-century American paintings along with other changing exhibits.

After a look around the Parrish and a bit of shop-hopping, take time out to gape at the mega-mansions the town is legendary for. As with most affluent oceanfront areas, the biggest and the best homes are on the roads that run parallel to the ocean or intersect them. You can feast your eyes by driving down Meadow, Gin, Halsey Neck, Copper's Neck, and First Neck Lanes. If you want to get in some beach time, you'll find a wonderful public beach right on Meadow Lane.

Once you've "done" Southampton, continue east on Route 27, stopping at shops in the villages of **Water Mill** and **Bridgehampton**. Water Mill is named for its gristmill which is now a museum.

East Hampton has an impressive collection of old houses that have been declared historic landmarks. Best way to enjoy them is to stop by the Chamber of Commerce (4 Main Street) and pick up a free walking tour map. Most famous of them is the 1680 "Home Sweet Home" House, which was the childhood home of John Howard Payne, the composer of the song of the same title.

On East Hampton's Main Street, you'll find the *Guild Hall Museum* which is an art museum as well as the town's cultural center. Close-by is *Clinton Academy* which was the first prep school in New York state. It's now a museum exhibiting a collection of eastern Long Island artifacts. At the end of town stands *Hook Mill*, a wind-powered grinding mill, next to a burial ground with tombstones dating back to 1650. There are tours of the mill through the summer months. Before leaving East Hampton, take a drive down Lily Pond Lane to see more magnificent homes.

Amagansett has more shops to explore plus the *Town Marine Museum*

WHALE-WATCHING OFF MONTAUK

From May through September, the Okeanos Ocean Research Foundation in Montauk , Viking Dock ((516) 728-4522) offers whale-watching cruises aboard the *Finback II*. The waters off this coast are feeding grounds for humpback, minke, and fin whales, plus dolphins, seals, and sea turtles.

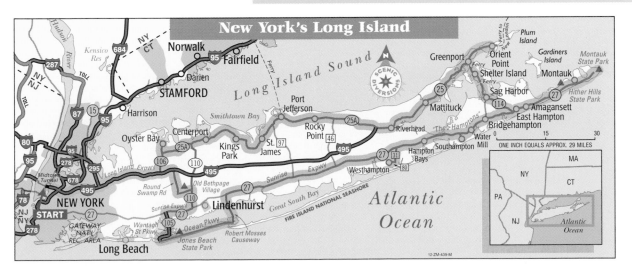

New York's Long Island

with shipwreck and undersea exhibits. There are also several town beaches on which to spread your blanket.

If you happen to be in the Amagansett area around breakfast time, head for the *Honest Diner*, 74 Montauk Highway; (516) 267-3535. A local hot spot, it's famed for its big, all-American breakfasts.

From Amagansett, carry on east to Montauk, which is truly land's end. Though just 120 miles from Manhattan, it honestly feels a million miles away. You'll start to feel the difference just after Amagansett, when the shops trickle out.

The one big sightseeing attraction is the *Montauk Point Lighthouse* in *Montauk State Park* (six miles east of town on Route 27) which has stood poised atop an ocean bluff for about two hundred years. It was built in 1795 by order of George Washington. Montauk is also home to the *Montauk Yacht Club Resort Marina* (a deluxe hotel with tennis, watersports, and spa treatments) that was frequented by the Vanderbilts, Astors, and Whitneys back in the 1920s and 1930s and Gurney's Inn Resort & Spa, a full-service spa poised up on a peach of an ocean beach.

Consider having lunch or dinner at *Gosman's Dock*, West Lake Drive, Montauk; (516) 668-2549. All summer long, this waterfront restaurant is packed. People come for the ultrafresh seafood (you can watch them unload catches right on the dock) and generous servings.

There's a take-out counter and some picnic tables in addition to the restaurant dining rooms inside.

From Montauk, return to East Hampton on Route 27, and turn right on Route 114. Head north for seven miles and you'll reach **Sag Harbor**, an old whaling town filled with 19th-century architecture and history. In fact, tiny Sag Harbor used to rival New York as an international port. Don't miss the *Custom House* which operated as a custom house and post office during the late 18th and early 19th centuries and the *Sag Harbor Whaling and Historical Museum* which tells the story of the island's whaling past.

From Sag Harbor, take the ferry over to **Shelter Island**, which is tucked between the North and South Forks. About a third of the island is nature preserve and the rest is beautifully unspoiled thanks to residents who are committed to keeping it that way.

Leaving Shelter Island, take the ferry to **Greenport** on the North Fork. From there, follow Route 25 west to Route 25A, which takes you to some of the island's *"Gold Coast"* towns such as **Centerport** and **Oyster Bay**, where name-name families (Vanderbilts, Woolworths, and Roosevelts—just to mention a few) had mansions at the turn of the century (several are open for touring). From Oyster Bay, follow Route 106 south for about six miles then take the Long Island Expressway back to Manhattan.

Montauk Point Lighthouse—Montauk, New York

The Adirondacks

Distance: 458 Miles Round Trip, Albany
Time: Allow at least two or three days
Highlights: Backwoods wilderness, lakes, hiking, canoeing, thoroughbred horse racing, family amusements, old fort, performing arts.

Winter Olympic Museum—Lake Placid, New York

When people talk about America's great wilderness areas, they're often talking about those in the western states. What usually comes as a big surprise, however, is that *Adirondack Park*, located in north-central New York state, is one of the country's largest—covering some six million acres.

You could easily spend weeks here, dividing your time between the different fresh-air activities (including hiking through birch and balsam forests and paddling canoes on lakes) and poking around the man-made attractions in **Saratoga Springs** and **Lake George**.

For this trip, we combine a brief visit to Saratoga Springs with a drive through the Adirondacks, including *Lake George*, *Blue Mountain Lake*, *Long Lake* and *Tupper Lake*, *Lake Placid*, and *Saranac Lake*.

From **Albany**, head north on I-87 to Saratoga Springs (Exit 14).

A resort town, Saratoga Springs has a beautiful collection of Victorian and Greek Revival buildings. In the addition to its proximity to the Adirondacks, Saratoga Springs has three major draws: thoroughbred horse racing, a stellar performing arts scene, and mineral baths for which the town is named. If you'd like to try the latter, you'll find some vintage bathhouses right in *Saratoga State Park*. Here, you can "take the waters" or—more specifically—soak in naturally carbonated water and follow with a half-hour rest on heated sheets on a cot nearby.

The bulk of the town's sights and shops can be seen on foot. Many of the shops on Broadway are in buildings that have been impeccably restored to their original Victorian appearance. On North Broadway, Circular Street, and Union Avenue, there are many mansions which were built in the 1800s. Be sure to wander into historic *Congress Park* which is home to two worthwhile museums that focus on the city's history and growth: The *Museum of the Historical Society* and the *Walworth Memorial Museum*.

If you're interested in the history and highlights of horse racing, be sure to check out the *National Museum of Racing* and *Thoroughbred Hall of Fame* and of course, the *Saratoga Race Course* on Union Avenue which is the oldest operating thoroughbred racetrack in the country (it was founded in 1863).

29

A SPECIAL FIND

Built in the 1930s by William Rockefeller, The Point is an exquisite 11-guestroom Adirondack lodge. There are hardwood floors, stone fireplaces, and lovely lake views. Guests can go canoeing, sailing, swimming, and hiking in summer (there's also tennis and golf nearby) and ice skating and cross-country or downhill skiing in winter. For information, write: The Point, HCR 1, Box 65, Saranac Lake, NY 12983 or call (800) 255-3530 or (518) 891-5678.

A GRANDE DAME RESORT

Located on a private island in Lake George is the grand old Sagamore Resort, which has been welcoming visitors for over a century. It's a beautiful Victorian hotel listed in the National Register of Historic Places. For information, call (800) 358-3585 or (518) 644-9400.

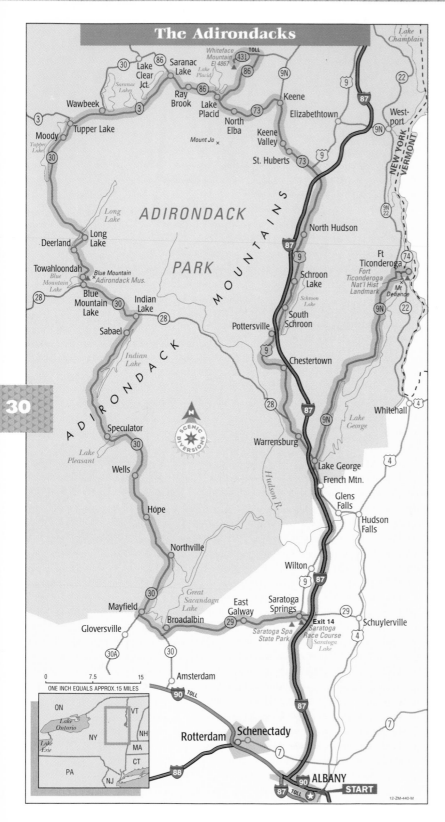

For information on events, call (718) 641-4700. If you have time, try to visit the *National Museum of Dance*. It's the only museum in the country devoted exclusively to professional American dance.

From Saratoga Springs, head west on Route 29 to Route 30 north. Route 30 is a magnificently scenic road, taking you right through Adirondack Park with its magical mountains and many lakes. Near **Speculator**, look for the vista of *Lake Pleasant* and a bit farther north, the shimmering waters of *Indian Lake* (on the right). The tiny hamlet of **Blue Mountain Lake** is home to an outstanding museum devoted to the Adirondacks. Standing high above the shores of Blue Mountain Lake, the *Adirondack Museum* is a complex of 22 buildings on 30 acres. One of the most popular exhibits is a display of the successive generations of Adirondack boats.

If you're up for some hiking, you can climb *Blue Mountain*. The head of the trail leading to the summit (3,800 feet) is about 1 1/2 miles north of town. It's a three-mile hike through lovely Adirondack scenery.

From Blue Mountain Lake, continue north (taking Route 30) to Long Lake for yet another sensational view and then carry on to Tupper Lake where you'll turn right onto Route 3. You'll soon come to **Saranac Lake**, which is well known for its winter carnival.

Mount Jo, looking south above Heart Lake, New York

From there, turn right onto Route 86, which will take you to **Lake Placid**, site of both the 1932 and 1980 Winter Olympics. The area just beyond Lake Placid is home to a range of mountains known as the *High Peaks*. You can drive up *Whiteface Mountain* which, at 4,867 feet, is the state's fifth highest peak. From the parking lot at the top, you can walk to the summit (or take an elevator) for a view of the Northeast you'd be hard-pressed to find anywhere else.

From there, it's a short, wonderfully scenic drive west on Route 73 to U.S. 9 (also a very scenic road) which you'll take south to the Lake George area. Though the town of Lake George itself is very commercialized (shops, entertainment arcades, family attractions), the surrounding lake and landscape is beautiful. You can drive the length of the lake on Route 9N to visit *Fort Ticonderoga*, the fortification and museum. Afterwards, follow the scenic drive up to the top of *Mount Defiance*.

Retrace your steps back to Route 87, which you'll then pick up and head south back to Albany.

WINTER TIP

In addition to being a wonderful warm-weather destination, the Adirondacks are truly lovely in the winter. If you ski, you'll find over a dozen alpine ski centers including Lake Placid. You can also cross-country ski and snowshoe through fragrant pine forests.

ON STAGE

The Saratoga Performing Arts Center, Saratoga Spa State Park, Saratoga Springs ((518) 587-3330) hosts a wonderful summer melange of cultural events including the New York City Opera in June, the New York City Ballet in July, and in August, The Philadelphia Orchestra. It also stages concerts by a variety of rock, pop, folk, and jazz artists.

New York's Northern Shore

Distance: 355 Miles, Niagara Falls to Massena
Time: Allow at least two or three days
Highlights: Niagara Falls, historic forts, beautiful countryside, lake and river scenery, farmlands, sportfishing, water sports.

Niagara Falls is high on lots of people's "Places To Go" list, which is not surprising. The monstrous falls, which are retreating about one foot a year, are split between the *American Falls* (which plunge 184 feet and are about 1,110 feet wide) and the *Horseshoe* (or Canadian) *Falls* (176 feet and about 2,500 feet wide). A visit to this part of the world however, should not only include the world-famous falls, but a drive along New York's North Coast, as it is frequently called, as well.

The *Seaway Trail*, which is the longest national recreational trail designated for mixed usage in the U.S., is a two-lane asphalt road clearly marked with green-and-white signs every few miles. It follows the shoreline, taking you through and to some of the area's most noteworthy attractions (both man-made and natural) including Niagara Falls, historic forts, rich farmland and beautiful countryside, and the *Thousand Islands*. If you're interested in following the complete Seaway Trail, it actually covers a distance of 454 miles, follow Lake Ontario from **Ripley** in the west to **Rooseveltown** in the east.

Here, we take you from **Buffalo** to Niagara Falls and then follow the trail from **Youngstown** to just beyond **Massena**.

From Buffalo, head north on I-190 to Niagara Falls. No matter how many photographs you've seen, nothing can quite prepare you for this natural extravaganza. For a close-up look at the falls, climb aboard the *Maid of the Mist*, a boat that takes passengers right

The Seaway Trail along Lake Ontario, New York

31

through the spray (everyone is issued a slicker to keep from getting wet). Another way to see the gushing torrent is to take the *Cave of the Winds* tour through the spray at the bottom of the American Falls. Other attractions include the *Aquarium of Niagara Falls*, the *Native American Center for the Living Arts*, and the *Niagara Power Project Visitor Center*.

Once you've finished feasting your eyes on the beauty of Niagara Falls, head north on the Robert Moses Parkway to Youngstown, where you'll find *Old Fort Niagara*. The restored fort played an important role in the French and Indian War and in the War of 1812. From there, drive east on Route 18, following the

green-and-white Seaway Trail signs alongside *Lake Ontario*. When you reach the **Rochester** area, consider detouring on Route 390 and I-490 to see the city's *International Museum of Photography* (located in the former home of George Eastman), the *Strong Museum* (devoted to everyday life in America since 1820), and the *Susan B. Anthony Memorial* (she lived in this house at 17 Madison Street for 40 years). Rochester is New York's third largest city and was founded back in 1817.

The Seaway Trail continues along Route 104 and alternates through apple and cherry orchard country. In **Oswego**, look for signs directing you to *Fort Ontario*. The original fort was built in 1755 by the British. It was taken by the

The American Falls—Niagara Falls, New York

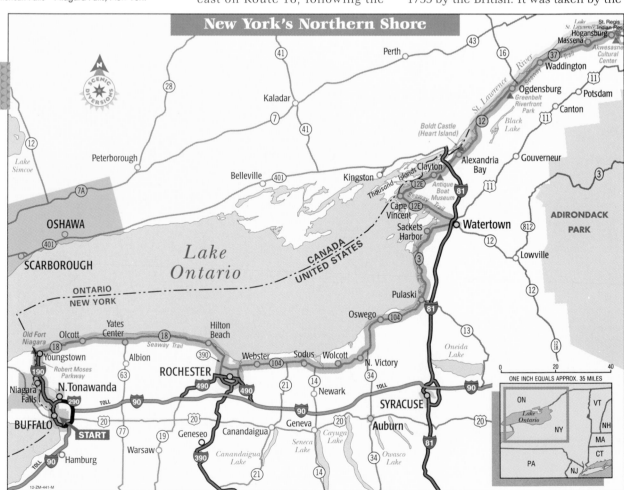

French and later used as a U.S. Army installation (1840-1946).

Carry on along the shoreline (The Seaway Trail continues on Route 3). Make your next stop at **Sackets Harbor**, a lakeside resort. The history of two major battles of the War of 1812 occurred here and are documented in the *Sackets Harbor Battlefield State Historic Site*.

The Seaway Trail continues along Route 12E, taking you by the Thousand Islands on the United States-Canadian border. There are actually closer to 2,000 islands here at the head of the St. Lawrence River, but who's counting? These beautiful rocky islands have many parks, summer homes that were built by American millionaires in the early 1900s, and private clubs. Some of the islands are linked by the *Thousand Islands Bridge* and Highway which runs between the New York and Ontario, Canada mainlands.

Along the way, there are a couple of worthwhile stops to make including the *Antique Boat Museum* in **Clayton** and **Ogdensburg** where you can take a *War of 1812 Battlefield Walking Tour* (in Greenbelt Riverfront Park). Don't miss taking the excursion from Alexandria Bay to *Boldt Castle* on *Heart Island*. One of the most famous of the Thousand Islands, this heart-shaped island and its castle were intended to be a wedding gift for millionaire George C. Boldt's wife. In 1900, the hotel magnate (he owned the *Waldorf-Astoria* in **Manhattan**) decided to build a genuine *Rhineland castle* with more than 120

rooms as a token of his love for his wife, Louise. The island's shoreline was dredged and formed into the shape of a heart and the construction well underway when suddenly, in 1904, Louise died. Boldt left the island with the castle unfinished, his dream destroyed.

In Massena, visitors can learn all about the St. Lawrence River's importance as an international waterway by visiting *Eisenhower Lock*. A bit further east, in **Hogansburg**, the *Akwesasne Cultural Center* on the *St. Regis Mohawk Reservation* offers insights into the life and history of the Iroquois Indians.

The Jersey Cape

Distance: 49 Miles,
Atlantic City to Cape May
Time: Allow at least one or two days
Highlights: Family fun, shore scenery, beaches, seafood, casinos, fishing, golfing, boardwalk amusements, Victorian buildings, biking, bird-watching, deep-sea fishing.

Back in the late 1800s, the sweep of Atlantic seashore that runs roughly from just below **Atlantic City** to **Cape May Point** was the place to vacation. So much so, that after a while, it became too popular and ultimately drove many vacationers away to other destinations. In attempts to bring back visitors, many towns introduced other activities such as amusement parks and convention facilities. The net result, unfortunately, is that many of the lovely shore towns now stand behind boardwalks that are

33

Atlantic City, New Jersey

Cape May Historic District—Cape May, New Jersey

lined with amusement arcades, bowling alleys and pool halls, fast-food restaurants—you get the picture. Nevertheless, this 50-mile portion of seashore still has its sandy beaches, and with all the activity, there's always a tipsy air of carnival.

For this particular route, we suggest starting in Atlantic City, then following *Ocean Drive* (a series of bridges connecting a series of narrow islands that run parallel to the mainland) down the coast to **Cape May**, making a couple of stops along the way.

Even if you're not gamblers, consider taking time to see Atlantic City, which was made famous by the board game, *Monopoly*, and continues to get national attention every fall when the Miss America Pageant takes place in town. In addition to its casinos, you'll find a 60-foot-wide boardwalk extending along five miles of beaches lined with shops, amusement centers, and food stands. You'll also find *The Shops on Ocean One*, a three-deck shopping complex built to resemble an ocean liner.

From Atlantic City, head south on Ocean Drive, making your next stop at **Ocean City**, which calls itself "America's Greatest Family Resort." Indeed, there is plenty to do for families on its two-mile-long boardwalk and eight miles of beaches. Ocean City prides itself on its wacky and inventive summertime festivals and contents. Every August, for example, there's a Hermit Crab Race and a Miss Crustacean Contest.

If you prefer natural over man-made diversions, continue down the coast to **Stone Harbor**, where you'll find *Leaming's Run*, one of the finest gardens on the east coast and *The Wetlands Institute*, an environmental center focusing on coastal ecology. At the latter, there's an observation tower, a marsh trail, and an aquarium.

Next on the itinerary are the *Wildwoods*, a quartet of shore towns. **West Wildwood** is a residential area, while the other three—**North Wildwood**, **Wildwood**, and **Wildwood Crest**—are lined with ocean-front hotels and motels. Wildwood's beachfront is where you'll find the biggest concentration of amusements including six amusement piers with carnival-like rides.

Less than ten miles away is Cape May (continue down the coast on Ocean Drive), which has been a popular beach resort since Revolutionary days and, ...in fact, is the oldest seashore resort in the country. Home to over 600 Victorian buildings (many of which have been faithfully restored), it's one of four U.S. seaports that has very successfully preserved its Victorian heritage

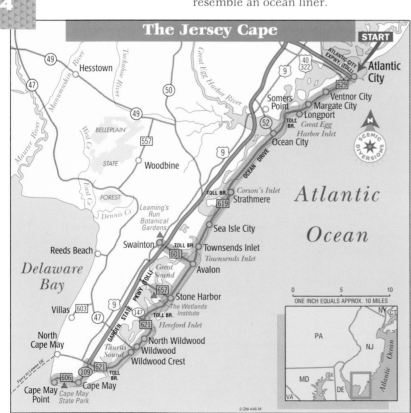

The Jersey Cape

ONE INCH EQUALS APPROX. 10 MILES

BIRD-WATCHING IN CAPE MAY

Every fall, thousands of migratory birds (including everything from small songbirds to falcons and eagles) stop here on their way south. The best viewing areas are: Cape May State Park, the Cape May Migratory Bird Refuge, and Higbee's Beach.

(Mendocino, California; Galveston, Texas; and Port Townsend, Washington are the others). In fact, the entire town has been proclaimed a National Historic Landmark, and for the most part, can be seen on foot.

The heart of town is the *Washington Street Victorian Mall*, which is a three-block-long stretch closed to automobiles and lined with shops and restaurants. The real focus in Cape May, however, is the promenade which runs along the Atlantic and offers a whole host of diversions.

To see the town's historic sites, consider joining a guided *Historic District Walking Tour*. These tours—which last about an hour and a half—are full of historical insights. Of course, you can also take yourself on a self-guided tour. The *Welcome Center* at 405 Lafayette Street can point you in the right direction and provide you with brochures. Several of the most beautiful Victorian buildings are now inns lined up majestically between the Welcome Center and the beach. These include *The Abbey*, a Gothic-Revival house at Columbia Avenue and Gurney Street, *Captain Mey's Inn* at 202 Ocean Street, *The Mainstay* at 635 Columbia Avenue, and the *Angel of the Sea* at 5 Trenton Avenue.

Once you've seen the town, take a drive out to *Cape May State Park* (follow Sunset Boulevard) for a beautiful walk through one of Cape May's best birding areas. There are three miles of trails and a boardwalk taking you over ponds and through wooded areas and marshlands. Then climb the 218 steps to the top of the *Cape May Lighthouse*. Stick around for the sunset, which is astonishingly beautiful from *Cape May Point*.

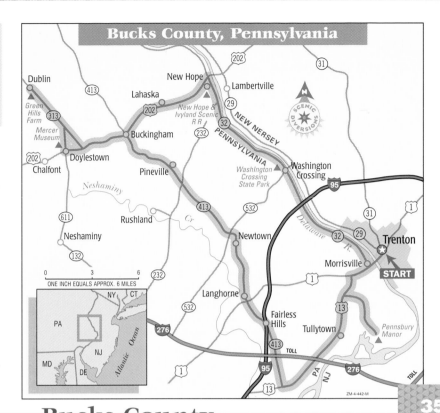

Bucks County, Pennsylvania

Distance: 98 Miles Round Trip, Trenton
Time: One day minimum
Highlights: Revolutionary landmarks, antiques, inns, natural beauty, farm country, galleries, fine dining.

Tucked away in the southeast corner of Pennsylvania is this lovely county which is bounded by Philadelphia and Montgomery County on the southwest and separated from New Jersey by the Delaware River to the east. The area was first known to the Lenni-Lenape Indians and later settled by Dutch explorers, followed by Swedes, English Quakers, and Germans.

Today's visitors find some history, dozens of antiques shops, and a wonderful collection of historic inns. The centerpiece of the county is **New Hope**, which has over 200 properties older than a century and listed in the

35

VINEYARDS TO VISIT

There are several wineries in the Bucks County area including the Buckingham Valley Vineyards in Buckingham, Peace Valley Winery in Chalfont, Rushland Ridge Vineyards & Winery in Rushland, and Sand Castle Winery in Erwinna.

Bowman's Hill Tower
Washington Crossing State Park, Pennsylvania

National Register of Historic Places.

This tour begins and ends in **Trenton**, New Jersey, which is just across the Delaware River. From Trenton, take U.S. 1 over the river to **Morrisville**. Turn right on Route 32, the River Road. One of Bucks County's many beautiful drives, it takes you right along the water's edge passing magnificent homes to New Hope, where most of the county's attractions are centered.

Along the way, you'll see signs for *Washington Crossing State Park* (right after Route 532). The park is divided into two sections. The lower part, which is seven miles south of New Hope is where George Washington and 2,400 soldiers in his Continental Army crossed the Delaware on Christmas night in 1776 to make a surprise attack against the Crown's Hessian mercenaries in Trenton. There are picnic grounds, historic structures (including the old Patriot general store and post office), and the *Washington Crossing Memorial Building*. The northern section of the park is dominated by *Bowman's Hill*, which is crowned by a tower commemorating a Revolutionary War lookout point. It's also a *Wildflower Preserve* (devoted entirely to Pennsylvania plants), the only wildflower preserve in North America to be accredited by the *American Association of Museums*.

New Hope is a short distance away. Keep in mind that the town attracts a lot of day trippers from Philadelphia, New York, and New Jersey—especially during the warm-weather months. So expect traffic and crowds. Your best bet for parking is to drive west of Route 32 and then walk back and see the town on foot.

Start along Main Street which has the *Delaware Canal* on one side, and the river on the other, popping into any shops or galleries that appeal to you. The canal was opened in 1831 to carry whiskey and raw materials between different local towns as well

Mule-drawn Barge—New Hope, Pennsylvania

as Philadelphia, **Pittsburgh**, and *Lake Erie*. Alongside the canal is a towpath which is used for walking, cycling, and jogging.

One of the highlights of any visit to New Hope is a ride on a *mule barge*. As you slide along the Delaware Canal on a flower-festooned barge, mules pulling alongside, a tour guide fills you in on New Hope's history. You can also take a ride on the *New Hope & Ivyland Rail Road* (station on West Bridge Street), a restored stream train, or take a horse and buggy ride over to *Phillip's Mill*, a gristmill complex built in 1765 by Aaron Phillips. For years, it was a political forum and social center for local farm families.

A most worthwhile museum is the *Parry Mansion* at 45 South Main Street. Built by Benjamin Parry in 1784, it now is a museum of decorative arts. Each of its rooms are furnished to reflect a different period from Colonial to American Federal.

If you're in town for the evening, consider taking in a show at the leg-

SCARY STUFF

If you want to be spooked, consider joining in on a ghost tour in New Hope. Tours meet weekly at the Cannon on Main Street every Saturday night at 8 p.m., from June through November. During October and early November, tours run every Friday and Saturday night at 8 p.m.

endary *Bucks County Playhouse*, 70 South Main Street; (215) 862-2041. Set on the banks of the Delaware, it used to be a mill but was converted into a theater in 1939.

From New Hope, drive west on U.S. 202 to the town of **Lahaska**. On what was the old coach road that connected **Philadelphia** with New York, this town used to be home to several chicken farms. In 1962, the farms were transformed into *Peddler's Village* which began as a collection of shops in reconstructed chicken coops but grew—very tastefully—as shops, and restaurants were added. Today, there are over 70 shops (purveying antiques, art, crafts, and other collectibles), several restaurants, and a carousel museum.

Your next stop is **Doylestown** which is home to two castles made of concrete and the *Moravian Pottery & Tile Works*. All three—which are designated as *"Mercer Mile"*—were built between 1908 and 1916 by Henry Chapman Mercer, a local eccentric. *Fonthill*—which is a fanciful building with turrets, secret rooms, and unexpected stairways—Mercer built as a residence for himself. A short walk through the park will bring you to the Moravian Pottery & Tile Works where you can watch tiles being made the same way they were made about 90 years ago. The other castle, which is the *Mercer Museum*, is on Pine and East Ashland Streets less than a mile away. Mercer used the latter to house an enormous collection of tools and farm implements that were used by tradesmen in the nineteenth century.

Adjacent to the museum is the *James A. Michener Arts Museum* which was named in honor of the Doylestown native. In addition to gallery space (which includes a permanent exhibition celebrating Michener's career as a writer, public servant, art collector, and philanthropist), it has a museum shop and a tea room. Other permanent exhibits include *"Nakashima Reading Room"* which is filled with furnishings by Bucks County's internationally-known woodworker George Nakashima and *"Visual Heritage of Bucks County,"* which traces the art of the region from Colonial times to the present. There are also traveling exhibits.

A few miles north of Doylestown (at 520 Dublin Road, off Route 313, one mile southwest of **Dublin**), you'll find *Green Hills Farm*, which was Pearl S. Buck's estate. Visitors can tour the 1835 stone house where the author lived when she returned to America (after growing up in China with missionary parents) from the age of 32 on. When the Nobel and Pulitzer Prize-winning author died in 1973, she was buried on the premises.

37

ICE CREAMS WITH A FOREIGN ACCENT

In New Hope, make a point of stopping at Gerenser's Exotic Ice Cream (22 South Main Street). The international flavors include Israel's milk and honey, Ukranian rose petal, and American pumpkin.

Reenactment of Washington crossing the Delaware, Pennsylvania

IN THE MARKET

You'll find farmers' markets at various locations around Pennsylvania Dutch Country throughout the year. On Tuesdays, the Roots Country Market takes place on Graystone Road near the intersection of Route 72 near Manheim. In Lancaster, the farmers' market takes place at Central Market (Queen and King Streets) on Tuesdays, and Fridays, and Saturday mornings. The Green Dragon Farmers' Market and Auction starts at 10 a.m. and goes to 10 p.m. every Friday on Green Spot Road, north of Ephrata, off Route 272.

MARK YOUR CALENDAR

On Christmas Day every year, the successful maneuver by George Washington and the Continental Army, which led to a decisive victory for the Colonies, is reenacted at Washington Crossing Historical Park, seven miles south of New Hope.

Head east again on U.S. 202, turning right onto Route 413. Follow that to **Newtown** which is made up of 18th- and early-19th-century houses that were laid out in a plan approved by William Penn. More than 225 properties are listed in the National Register of Historic Places.

From there, continue south on Route 413, then turn left onto U.S. 13 which will take you to **Tullytown**. Look for signs for *Pennsbury Manor* (400 Pennsbury Memorial Road), which was William Penn's summer mansion built on a bend in the Delaware. Penn's Georgian brick house stands on a multi-acre plot of land (originally, it was an 8,400-acre plantation, now it's scaled down quite a bit) overlooking the river where he would travel by barge to and from Philadelphia. It and its many out- buildings (bake and brew house, blacksmith's and joiner's shops) have been totally reconstructed by the Pennsylvania Historical Commission. Costumed guides take visitors through the compound on one-and-a-half-hour tours.

From there, it's a short drive back to U.S. 1 (at the end of Memorial Road, turn right and follow New Ford Mill Road to Route 1). Turn right on Route 1, cross over the river and you'll be back in Trenton.

Amish buggy—Lancaster County, Pennsylvania

Pennsylvania Dutch Country

Distance: 281 Miles Round Trip, Philadelphia
Time: Allow at least three days
Highlights: Farms and farmers' markets, Plain People communities, auctions, handicrafts, du Pont family mansions and gardens, traces of early Swedish settlers, Revolutionary War sites.

This diversion takes you to the *Brandywine Valley* in southeast Pennsylvania and northern Delaware and through the heart of *Pennsylvania Dutch Country* (Lancaster County) which is home to a large popu- lation of "Plain People" (Amish, Brethren, and Mennonite). It also takes you to the state's capital (**Harrisburg**), *Chocolate Town USA* (home of Hershey Chocolates), and **Valley Forge**, where George Washington's Continental Army endured the bitter winter of 1777-78.

From downtown **Philadelphia**, cross the Schuylkill River and get on the northbound Schuylkill Expressway. At exit 33, go west on U.S. 1 to **Chadds Ford**. Here you'll find several worth- while sites including the *Brandywine Battlefield State Park* (where Washington and Lafayette met) and the *Brandywine River Museum*, which has an impressive collection of American paintings (including some by Andrew Wyeth and other Wyeth family members).

The Brandywine Valley is where the du Ponts made their money (from gun powder and chemicals). It also was the home of three generations of Wyeth artists.

Just down the road from Chadds Ford (Route 1), you'll find *Longwood Gardens*, a 350-acre formal garden. Longwood was the estate of Pierre S. du Pont, chairman of the board of both du Pont Chemicals and General Motors.

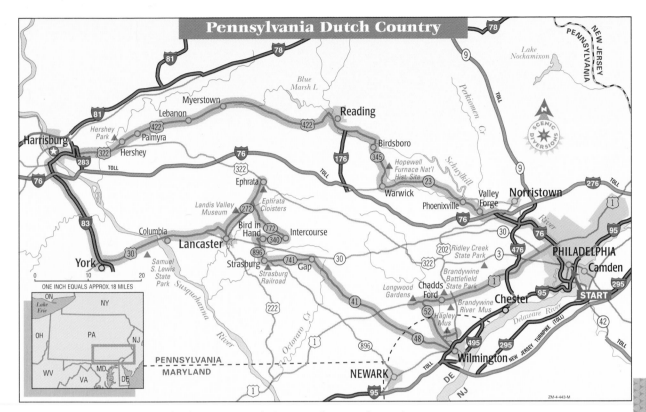

Pennsylvania Dutch Country

ONE INCH EQUALS APPROX. 18 MILES

Follow Route 52 to **Wilmington**, Delaware. Along the way, you'll see spacious farms and beautiful stone houses. Stops to make include the *Hagley Museum* (on Route 141, a half-mile north of Route 52) on the original du Pont Mills site along the Brandywine River; *Winterthur*, the famous du Pont Mansion where thousands of antique and decorative arts used in America between 1650 and 1850 are on display; and *Nemours Mansion and Gardens*, a modified-Louis XVI French chateau filled with antiques, artwork, and personal items collected by Alfred du Pont.

In Wilmington, take time to see traces of the first Scandinavian settlers. Check out the *Old Swedes Church*, *Hendrickson House*, and the *Fort Christina Monument* (where the Swedes landed in 1638). Also see the *Old Town Hall*, the *Grand Opera House*, the 18th-century houses at *Willingtown Square*, and the *Delaware Art Museum*.

From Wilmington, drive northwest on Route 48 to Route 41. Take that about 34 miles to Route 741, where you'll turn left towards **Strasburg** in Lancaster County. You're now in the heart of Pennsylvania Dutch Country and can expect to see Plain People at work using horse-drawn buggies as a mode of transportation and horse and mule teams to work farms. Most of them carry on their lives as they did in the 17th century, shunning anything modern such as automobiles, electricity, and chemical fertilizers.

Strasburg is home to the *Railroad Museum of Pennsylvania* and the *Strasburg Rail Road Co*. The latter offers 45-minute round-trip rides between Strasburg and nearby **Paradise** on wooden coaches pulled by steam locomotives.

From Strasburg, head north on Route 896 towards **Lancaster**, but before going into town, detour east on Route 340. Here you'll find a string of little towns with conversation-piece names (**Bird in Hand** and **Intercourse** just to name a few) and shops and other

The Pennsylvania Dutch—Lancaster, Pennsylvania

attractions (some are tourist traps, but some are worthwhile).

In Intercourse, head north on Route 772 and follow it to Route 272, which will take you up to **Ephrata**, home of the *Ephrata Cloisters*. Here you'll find a collection of half-timber and stone buildings with steep Germanic roofs that were originally erected in 1732 in a religious experiment by Conrad Beissel, a German Seventh-Day Baptist. Living as a recluse, he started a community of recluses and by 1750, there were 300. Many of them died from typhus which they contracted while nursing the sick and wounded after the Battle of Brandywine. The rest died off because celibacy was required.

From there, drive to Lancaster on Route 272, stopping at the *Landis Valley Museum* (2451 Kissel Road, Lancaster) en route. This is a complex of nearly two dozen original buildings dating back to the mid 1800s.

One of the best ways to explore the town of Lancaster is to take a *Historic Walking Tour*. They depart from the Southern Market at 10 a.m. and 1:30 p.m., Monday through Saturday and at 1:30 p.m. only on Sundays, April through October. Lancaster is the county seat and in fact, back in 1777, for one full day, it was home to the Continental Congress when Philadelphia was captured by the British. Its cobblestone streets are rich in American history, stories of which are well told by knowledgeable guides.

Lancaster's many attractions include *Wheatland*, the last home of President James Buchanan (1120 Marietta Avenue); the *Fulton Opera House* (12 North Prince Street) which is one of the oldest American theaters; and the *Heritage Center of Lancaster County* (Penn Square), which contains examples of early Lancaster arts and crafts and home furnishings. Lancaster is also home to several Georgian churches, Federal-style buildings, and the nation's oldest publicly owned farmers' market, the *Central Market on Penn Square*. The latter is a huge gabled brick structure filled with produce, crafts, and flower stands.

From Lancaster, head west on U.S. 30 to **York**. For several months back in 1777 to 1778, it claims to have been America's first capital. Fleeing the British occupation of Philadelphia, the Continental Congress met here and adopted the Articles of Confederation, using the phrase "United States of America" for the first time. The *Historical Society of York County* maintains a *museum* and several historic sites.

From York, hop on I-83 north to Harrisburg, the state's capital. The name comes from John Harris Jr. who laid out the town in the late 1700s. You can see the mansion he built on the Susquehanna. Take time to see the *Capitol*; it has a 272-foot dome, imitating that of St. Peter's in Rome.

From there, take U.S. 322 east to U.S. 422 to **Hershey**, "Chocolate Town U.S.A." This is home to Hershey Chocolate, which was founded in 1903

Hagley Museum—Wilmington, Delaware

SUNDAY CLOSINGS

If you're traveling in Lancaster during a weekend, keep in mind that many of the family-owned Amish shops and services are closed Sunday.

helpful hints...

by Milton S. Hershey. There are tours and all sorts of amusements in the *Hershey Park* complex.

Next on the itinerary is **Reading**, which you can reach by taking U.S. 422 east (about 38 miles). If you're up for some shopping, you'll find it's rife with outlets. There's also a historic district with several 19th-century buildings.

Carry on to *Hopewell Furnace National Historic Site* which is a restored Early American iron-making village. From Reading, go east for about 10 miles on U.S. 422 to **Birdsboro**, then take Route 345 south. There are tours of the buildings complete with period-costumed interpreters and demonstrations.

Your final stop is Valley Forge. About two miles south of Hopewell Furnace, pick up Route 23 east; it's about 18 miles away. It was here, from December 19, 1777 to June 19, 1778, that the undersupplied troops of Washington's army camped during the American Revolution. More than 2,000 died from the conditions which brought on illness. Today, it's a 3,600-acre memorial with a marked driving route.

From Valley Forge, you can easily pick up I-76 and head eastward into Philadelphia.

Northern Virginia

....

Distance: 263 Miles Round Trip, Washington, D.C.
Time: Allow at least two days
Highlights: Civil War battlesites, George Washington's home and other historic buildings, Shenandoah National Park, underground caverns, wildlife, hiking, and other outdoor activities.

Be prepared to soak up lots of American history in a short time when visiting this part of the country. Though not a large area, it's densely historic. Within the span of two days, you can visit several major Civil War sites and tour many historically significant buildings including George Washington's house. The area is also naturally beautiful, holding one of the country's national parks—*Shenandoah*—which is an Indian word meaning "Daughter of the Stars."

From **Washington, D.C.**, head west on I-66, making your first stop *Manassas National Battlefield Park*. The scene of two major Civil War battles, this 5,000-acre park has several sites to see including *Bull Run*, the creek along which the battles were fought. Stop by the Visitor Center (on *Henry Hill*, just north of I-66 on Route 234), where you can pick up information on self-guided tours (you can take walking and driving tours of the various areas). Be sure to walk to the top of Henry Hill, which was a key spot in both battles; from there, you can see the entire battle area.

Continue west on I-66 to the town of **Front Royal**. Just south of town, you'll find the start of *Skyline Drive*, a two-lane

41

Northern Virginia

[Map of Northern Virginia showing Winchester, Leesburg, Washington, Arlington, Alexandria, Manassas National Battlefield Park, Front Royal, Marshall, New Market, Luray, Luray Caverns, Elkton, Ruckersville, Barboursville, Charlottesville, Gordonsville, Orange, Culpeper, Wilderness Corner, Chancellorsville, Fredericksburg, Stafford, Dumfries, Triangle, Woodbridge, Mt. Vernon, Fort Belvoir, and surrounding highways. Inset map shows PA, MD, NJ, WV, VA, DE, NC, and the Atlantic Ocean. ONE INCH EQUALS APPROX. 25 MILES.]

ZM-5-445M

Shenandoah Mountains, Virginia

scenic highway that runs the length of the *Shenandoah National Park* on the crest of the *Blue Ridge Mountains*. The park, which is 80 miles long and from 2 to 13 miles wide, encompasses some 300 square miles of the Blue Ridge. Along the way, there are about 70 scenic overlooks with outstanding views of the *Shenandoah Valley*. Most of the area is wooded, with over 100 species of hardwood trees that are in full glory during the autumn months. The park is also a wildlife sanctuary with deer, bear, fox, and bobcat plus over 200 varieties of birds.

One especially worthwhile detour off Skyline Drive is the short drive west (turn right onto Route 211 at *Thornton Gap*) to *Luray Caverns*. Here, you can go underground to see rock formations and hear the sounds of a stalacpipe.

If you have extra time, take advantage of the numerous outdoor activities in the park. You can hike, fish, horseback ride, bicycle, bird-watch, picnic, and camp overnight. There are also ranger-led nature walks. Pick up a copy of the *Shenandoah Overlook*, a free newspaper listing daily activities, at the entrance station.

Return to Skyline Drive and head south to U.S. 33, then head east to **Barboursville**. From there, take Route 20 north through **Orange** to **Wilderness Corner**, where you'll turn onto Route 3 which will take you to Chancellorrsville and then on to **Fredericksburg**. Four major Civil War battles were fought between December 1862 and May 1864 in this general area. You can tour the sites by car or foot. They include *Wilderness National Military Park*, *Chancellorsville National Military Site*, *Fredericksburg and Spotsylvania County Battlefields Memorial National Military Park*, and *Fredericksburg National Military Park*.

Plan to spend some time looking around Fredericksburg, which is where George Washington went to school and where his mother and sister lived. Though the city was ravaged during the Civil War, many buildings dating before 1775 still stand and are well preserved. Start by stopping at the Visitor Center (706 Caroline Street) where you can watch an orientation film and then set about on a walking tour. Some of the tour's highlights include the *Hugh Mercer Apothecary Shop* (an 18th-century doctor's office and pharmacy); a tavern that was not only a stagecoach stop, but an important social and political center built by Washington's brother, Charles; the *Masonic Lodge* where Washington was initiated in 1752; and the house he bought for his mother. There are also historic churches, cemeteries, and museums.

From Fredericksburg, head west to I-95 and then north. Get off at U.S. 1

Mount Vernon, Virginia

which is just after **Woodbridge**. Follow signs to *Fort Belvoir*. Go past Fort Belvoir, and then turn right onto Route 235 and follow signs to *Mount Vernon*, the home of George and Martha Washington. You can tour the house and grounds and see George and Martha's tomb.

Alexandria, which was a prosperous tobacco port back in the 1740s, is the last stop before returning to D.C. There are guided walking tours of the cobbled streets of *Old Town* taking in *Robert E. Lee's Boyhood Home*, the *Stabler-Leadbeater Apothecary Museum* (the largest collection of apothecary glass in its original setting in the nation), and other historically significant buildings dating back to the late 1700s.

From Alexandria, it's a seven mile drive to downtown Washington.

Capitalizing on the Capital

Distance: 226 Miles Round Trip, Washington, D.C.
Time: Allow at least two days
Highlights: Hunt Country, Civil War sites, mountain scenery, hiking, fishing, boating, cross-country skiing.

Though the museums and attractions of **Washington, D.C.** could easily keep you busy for weeks, the attractions in the areas around the capital are filled with sights to see. For this tour, we take you from the capital to some of the highlights of Virginia, West Virginia, Maryland, and Pennsylvania all in a matter of a couple of days.

Start by crossing the Potomac River in Washington, D.C. and driving north on the George Washington Parkway. Then get on I-495 southbound, and take Exit 13 for Route 193 West. Follow that for about 4-1/2 miles and then turn onto Route 738 to *Great Falls Park*. Here you can hike up to 15 miles of trails (from easy terrain to somewhat rugged) and see the swirling *Great Falls of the Potomac River*.

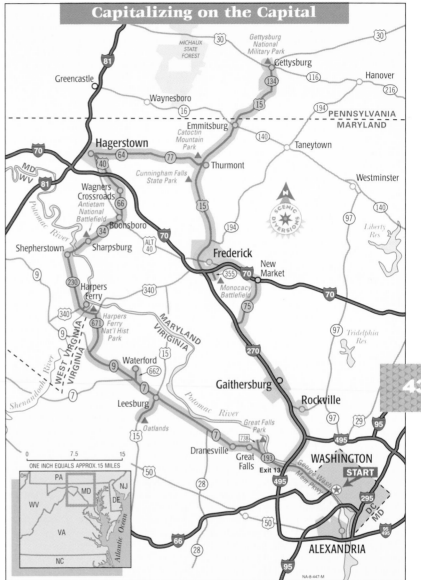

From there, go through the town of **Great Falls**, and then get on Route 7 north at **Dranesville**. Follow that to **Leesburg**, which is in the heart of Virginia's Hunt Country. For a bit of history on the area, have a look around the *Loudoun Museum* (16 Loudoun Street SW) and take a walk around the historic district. Also worthwhile (especially for the horsey set) is the *Museum of Hounds and Hunting* and the *Morven Park International Equestrian Institute* in *Morven Park* about a mile north of town. Morven Park (which sprawls

43

The Capitol—Washington, D.C.

over 1,500 acres) also includes a 28-room mansion, a carriage museum with over 100 horse-drawn vehicles, and boxwood gardens.

The countryside surrounding Leesburg is beautiful in every direction with rolling hills, thoroughbred horse farms, and beautiful rural villages. To the north (Route 662) is **Waterford**, an 18th-century *Quaker Village*, designated a *National Historic Landmark*. Six miles south of town (on U.S. 15) is **Oatlands**, a 261-acre estate that formerly was the center of a 5,000-acre plantation.

Next stop: **Harpers Ferry**, West Virginia, a name you surely know. Because of its strategic location, it was a town that changed hands many times in the Civil War. It was also the site of the U.S. arsenal captured by abolitionist John Brown in 1859. To reach it, take Route 7 from Leesburg, Route 9 to Route 671, then north to Harpers Ferry. You're now at the junction of the Shenandoah and Potomac rivers, where West Virginia, Virginia, and Maryland meet. The whole area (covering more than 2,200 acres) is a *National Historical Park*. There is a Visitor Center just off of U.S. 340 where the tours begin.

From Harpers Ferry, go west on Route 340 for about two miles then turn right onto Route 230 towards **Shepherstown**. Cross the Potomac River into Maryland and follow Route 34 to **Sharpsburg**.

Just north of town you'll find *Antietam National Battlefield*, where one of the bloodiest battles of the Civil War took place on September 17, 1862. At this site, more than 23,000 men were killed or wounded when Union forces blocked the first Confederate invasion of the North. There's a self-guided auto tour of the major landmarks.

Emmitsburg (which is just south of the Pennsylvania line) is your next destination. The drive—through Maryland's Blue Ridge region—is lovely. You pass through mountain scenery (the *Appalachian Trail* cuts through this area). Take Route 34 from Sharpsburg to **Boonsboro**. Then follow Route 66 north to **Wagners Crossroads** and continue north on U.S. 40 to **Hagerstown**. From there, head east on Route 64 and then 77 to Thurmont (consider pausing for a picnic at *Cunningham Falls State Park* or in *Catoctin Mountain Park* just before reaching **Thurmont**). Then turn left onto U.S. 15 and follow it for about nine miles to Emmitsburg.

As you approach Emmitsburg, you'll come to two of the area's most famous attractions. First, the *National Shrine Grotto of Lourdes*, which is a replica of the French shrine (one third the size of the original) and then the *Shrine of*

Gettysburg Battlefield reenactment—Gettysburg National Military Park, Pennsylvania

44

St. Elizabeth Ann Seton, the first American-born saint. Emmitsburg itself is listed in the National Register of Historic Towns. If you're in the market for antiques, check out the *Emmitsburg Antique Mall* (1 Chesapeake Avenue) which has more than 120 dealers displaying their collections.

Continue north on U.S. 15 to Route 134 crossing the Mason-Dixon Line into **Gettysburg**, where the Civil War's most decisive battle was fought between July 1-3, 1863. Gettysburg National Military Park has more than 35 miles of roads through 5,700 acres of battlefield area. You can tour the sites with a Battlefield Guide, licensed by the National Park Service or venture out on your own.

Retrace your steps back to Thurmont on U.S. 15, and then continue south towards **Frederick**. Founded in 1745, this lovely Colonial town is famous for its numerous 18th and 19th-century houses lining tree-lined streets. It's a town rich with history having been the home of Francis Scott Key, author of "The Star Spangled Banner" and Chief Justice Roger Brooke Taney (who issued the famous Dred Scott Decision), and Barbara Fritchie, the ardent Unionist immortalized by Whittier's poem "*Barbara Fritchie.*" Several historic buildings are open for touring including the *Barbara Fritchie House* (154 West Patrick Street); *Schifferstadt* (Rosemont Avenue and 2nd Street), a farmhouse built in 1756; and the *Roger Brooke Taney and Francis Scott Key Museum* (121 South Bentz Street). Also worthwhile: *Trinity Chapel* (where Francis Scott Key was baptized), the *Mt. Olivet Cemetery* (monuments mark the graves of Francis Scott Key and Barbara Fritchie), the *Historical Society of Frederick County Museum*, and *Monocacy Battlefield* (3 miles south of town on Route 355).

About seven miles east of Frederick (take I-70) you'll find the town of **New Market**, which is rife with antiques shops.

Once you've had a look around, take Route 75 south and pick up I-270 southbound to Washington, D.C.

Colonial Virginia

Distance: 249 Miles Round Trip, Richmond.
Time: Allow at least three days
Highlights: Civil War battlefields, plantations, Colonial sites, George Washington's birthplace, Robert E. Lee's birthplace, museums.

Virginia's coast on the Chesapeake Bay, which is popularly called Tidewater Virginia, is one of the most historically rich areas in the United States. It's home to what is known as the "*Historic Triangle*," **Jamestown**, **Williamsburg**, and **Yorktown** as well as several 18th-century plantations.

For this tour, we begin in **Richmond** and then head south to the Historic Triangle, then north, stopping at both Robert E. Lee's and George Washington's birthplaces, before returning to Richmond.

Between 1862 and 1864, several battles

Virginia's Historic Triangle, Virginia

were fought east and south of Richmond. All of these sites (which cover 770 acres in 10 different units) are now part of the *Richmond National Battlefield Park*. Start by getting an overview at the *Chimborazo Park Visitor Center* (from downtown, follow East Broad Street to the park). Then set out to visit one of the battlefields along Route 5.

Route 5 (heading southeast) takes you out on the Virginia Peninsula, which is one of the most historically dense areas in the United States. Not only is it home to Jamestown, Williamsburg, and Yorktown, but there are many old plantation homes and mansions some which were owned by presidents and signers of the *"Declaration of Independence."* Many of these properties (which are referred to as the James River plantations) were the first great houses built in the New World by wealthy Colonists. Take time to visit at least one (keeping in mind that some are open by appointment only). In order, from Richmond, they include *Shirley Plantation* (which has been home to ten generations of the Carter family), *Edgewood* (1849), *Berkeley* (where a thanksgiving feast was held a year before the pilgrims arrived), *Westover* (the finest Georgian mansion in the nation, built in 1730), *Evelynton* (though built in the 1930s,

COLONIAL CHRISTMAS

A delightful place to visit in December is Colonial Williamsburg. Throughout the month, there are plays, concerts, carol-singing, and beautiful lights everywhere.

it's on the sites of a house that was in the Ruffin family since 1847), *Belle Air* (circa 1670), and *Sherwood Forest* (circa 1730, which was owned by two U.S. presidents—William Henry Harrison and John Tyler).

Next stop: Jamestown, which is where America began when John Smith and his group of settlers arrived in 1607, forming the first successful English settlement in America. The National Parks Service operates a park which has a visitor's center with films, exhibits, some crafts demonstrations, and the ruins of the original town. Nearby, at the *Jamestown Settlement*, you can see how the early settlers lived; it's a re-creation of the first settlement with costumed interpreters.

Take the Colonial Parkway north to Williamsburg, which was the Colonial capital of Virginia and is now one of the east coast's biggest tourist attractions. In a 173-acre area, there are scores of beautifully preserved and restored 18th and 19th-century buildings. Costumed role-players (a bootmaker, a gunsmith, a wigmaker) very convincingly recreate life as it was in the city's pre-Revolutionary heyday. Some of the buildings to see include the *Governor's Palace and Gardens* (an extremely elegant Colonial mansion), the *Abby Aldrich Rockefeller Folk Art Center* (one of the country's best collections of American Folk Art), *Raleigh Tavern*, a meeting place for Thomas Jefferson, Patrick Henry and other Revolutionary patriots, and many others. Just east of Colonial Williamsburg, you'll find *Carter's Grove*, another James River plantation, built in 1755.

From Williamsburg, take U.S. 60 to

Colonial Williamsburg, Virginia

Newport News, which has a long tradition of shipbuilding. Take time to have a look around the *Mariners' Museum* and the *War Memorial Museum*.

Carry on to **Hampton** and see the *NASA Langley Visitor Center Museum* (all about space exploration) and the *Casemate Museum*, which is devoted to American history since Independence.

Take I-64 north to U.S. 17 which goes right to Yorktown, where the British surrendered in the final battle of the Revolutionary War. The *Yorktown Battlefield* surrounds and includes part of town. There's a well-marked self-guided battlefield tour.

From Yorktown, take U.S. 17 across the York River, through **Gloucester** up to **Tappahannock**. Pick up U.S. 360 to **Warsaw**, then take Route 3 north for 17 miles to *Stratford Hall*, where Robert E. Lee was born in 1806. A bit to the West (on Route 204), you'll find *George Washington Birthplace National Monument*. Though the original house was destroyed by fire in 1779, there is a *Memorial House* built near the site.

To return to Richmond, continue north on Route 3, then pick up U.S. 301 south and follow it to I-95 which you take southbound into Richmond.

SKIING IN VIRGINIA

Mention skiing and not too many people automatically think of Virginia. Nevertheless, the state provides vacationers with a wide range of ski experiences. Resorts in the highlands offer the finest slopes and ideal snow conditions for both the expert and novice skier. Most of the resorts offer full packages, including lift tickets, lodging,

rentals, and lessons. There are programs designed to fit the needs of families, with infant and child care widely available. Some of the resorts are rustic, others are modeled after the European ski villages.

There are four downhill ski areas in Virginia—*Bryce Mountain*, *The Homestead*, *Massanutten*, and *Wintergreen*. All four are equipped with state-of-the-art snowmaking and lights for night skiing. Snowboarders are welcome. The state's mountain temperatures are 10 to 15 degrees colder than surrounding sea-level areas.

For more details, contact the Ski Virginia Association, P.O. Box 454, Nellysford, VA 22958; (800) THE-SNOW (843-7669).

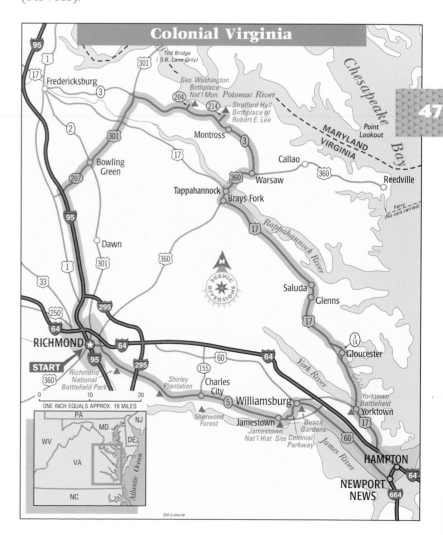

A CHANGE OF PACE

If you want a break from American history, consider visiting Busch Gardens, Williamsburg, a theme park with a 17th century European flavor located just three miles east of Williamsburg on U.S. 60. It sprawls over 360 acres and has more than 100 rides, shows, and attractions.

Great Lakes

*N*othing can quite match the feeling you get watching the Blue Angels soar overhead at the Cleveland National Air Show on Labor Day weekend. This is the land of the red, white, and blue. In these states, you can't help but feel proud to be an American.

Exploring this part of the country is especially rewarding since you not only have the water-related activities associated with the Great Lakes (and thousands of smaller lakes and streams), but the inland forests and farmlands which are dotted with both man-made and natural attractions.

Palisade Head, Minnesota

Minnesota's North Shore Drive

Distance: 227 Miles Round-Trip, Duluth to Grand Portage
Time: Allow at least two days
Highlights: Waterfront attractions, museums, old mining communities, coastal scenery, swimming, fishing, hiking, water sports, wildlife spotting.

Minnesota's North Shore is known for its natural beauty and outdoor diversions. It's also home to a string of inviting little communities. This diversion takes you right up the northern shore of Lake Superior, from **Duluth** to **Grand Portage**, on the Canadian border.

Start by exploring Duluth, which is a world-class seaport with a truly magnificent waterfront that resulted from a $150 million-dollar renaissance. The harbor area has several sights to see including the *Corps of Engineers Canal Park Marine Museum* (devoted to Lake Superior marine history) and the *William A. Irvin*, a former flagship of the U.S. Steel Great Lakes Fleet. The *Downtown Lake Walk* is a two-mile pathway that takes you through a couple of parks from which views of the lake are lovely. The *Depot*, further

Canal Park—Duluth, Minnesota

into town, is a restored train station housing three museums. Other Duluth attractions include the *Lake Superior Zoological Gardens*, the *International Sculpture Garden* in Lake Place, and *Glensheen*, a Jacobean revival mansion.

From Duluth, head north on Route 61, which you'll actually follow for this entire drive. This road clings to the rocky coast of Lake Superior, passing the forested slopes of the *Sawtooth Mountains*.

One of the first towns you'll come to is **Knife River**, which is famous for its smoked fish. **Two Harbors**, a major shipping center for the Iron Range taconite and iron ore industry, is next. Here you can tour the enormous *Duluth and Iron Range Railroad Loading Dock* and watch huge ore boats come into port. To find out more about the iron ore history, take a look around the *Lighthouse Point and Harbor Museum*. Also see the *Lake County Historical Society Museum* where you can learn all about the area's logging, fishing, and railroad heritage.

North of **Castle Danger**, you'll find *Gooseberry Falls State Park*, a 1,675-acre park where you can fish, hike, picnic (and cross-country ski or snowmobile in winter) and then *Split Rock Lighthouse*, the tallest lighthouse on the Great Lakes. Poised high on a cliff, it served as a guiding sentinel from 1910-1968. You can tour the

A ROAD TO FOLLOW

In addition to driving the length of the North Shore, if you have time, consider detouring a bit to follow the *Gunflint Trail*. It starts at the northwestern edge of **Grand Marais** and goes north and west 58 miles to *Saganaga Lake* on the Canadian border taking you through an area rife with lakes. You can camp, picnic, fish, and go canoeing.

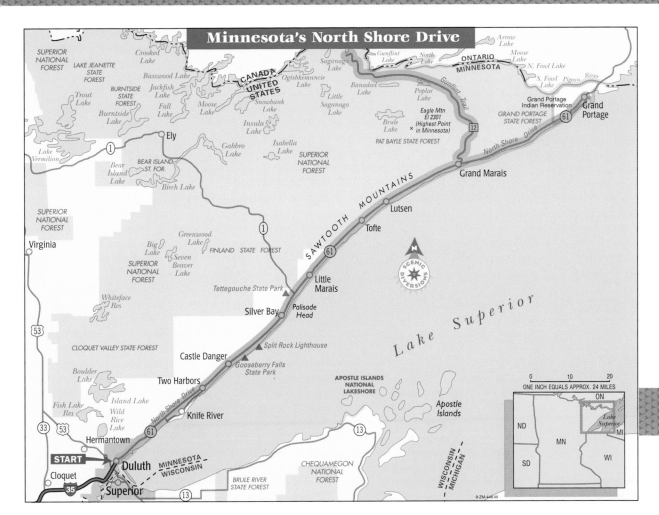

Minnesota's North Shore Drive

lighthouse and outbuildings.

Just up the coast is **Silver Bay**, which got its name from a ship's captain who thought its rocky shores looked like silver. North of Silver Bay, you'll find *Tettegouche State Park*, which is home to the state's highest waterfall. Then you'll come to a string of charming little communities including **Little Marais**, **Tofte**, and **Lutsen**. A little further up the coast is Grand Marais, a major fishing and resort center and starting point for the Gunflint Trail (see "A Road to Follow" on p. 50).

This drive ends just five miles from the Canadian border in Grand Portage. In years gone by the area was a rendezvous point and supply depot for fur traders operating between Montreal and Lake Athabasca. Visitors can see the reconstructed trading post.

Cape Cod of the Midwest

Distance: 546 Miles Round-Trip, Chicago
Time: Allow at least three days
Highlights: Two maritime museums, state parks, beaches, antiques and crafts shops; cross-country skiing and snowmobiling in winter.

Thunderous wave-slapped cliffs, silent small-town harbors, and rolling woodlands paint Door County's picture. "The Door" is a narrow peninsula with **Green Bay** on the west and *Lake Michigan* on the east.

Soldier Field—Chicago, Illinois

It's only eighteen miles across at its widest point, which makes getting around very easy.

To reach the peninsula from Chicago, take I-94 north, which turns into I-43. Stay on I-43 all the way to **Manitowoc**. Stop here to have a look around the *Manitowoc Maritime Museum*, which has a wonderful nautical collection. The highlight is the USS *Cobia*, a full-scale World War II submarine moored outside the museum.

Just north of Manitowoc, pick up Route 42 and continue north to **Sturgeon Bay**, one of the largest shipbuilding ports on the Great Lakes. Just north of Sturgeon Bay, follow Route 57 up the eastern side of the peninsula to reach the next stop: **Baileys Harbor**. Take time to visit *Bjorklunden*, a 325 acre estate with a replica of a wooden Norwegian chapel. Baileys Harbor is the oldest village in Door County and still has operating range lights that were built in 1870 to guide ships into the harbor.

From the lighthouse, return to Route 57 and proceed north to **Sister Bay**, which is known for its deep-water sailing. From Sister Bay, it's a short drive past cherry orchards to **Ellison Bay** which is home to the *Door Country Maritime Museum*, a worthwhile stopover. The northernmost tip of the Door Peninsula is **Gills Rock** from which you can take a ferry ride over to *Washington Island*. The ferry crosses the infamous *"Portes des Morts"* or *"Death's Door"* which is characterized by a rugged coastline of limestone bluffs with offshore shoals and rocky islands. Many vessels have been lost in the passageway's powerful current.

Back on the peninsula, head south, on the west side (Route 42). Along the way, stop at **Fish Creek**, a lovely historic village and **Egg Harbor**, which has several art, craft, and gift shops.

South of Sturgeon Bay, pick up Route 42/57, follow it a short distance to Route 42 south, back to Manitowoc where you can get back on I-43 and return down the coast to Chicago.

Peninsula Players—Fish Creek, Wisconsin

Meandering Around Michigan

Distance: 1033 Miles Round-Trip, Detroit
Time: Allow at least one week
Highlights: Resort communities, beaches, lighthouses, museums, foreign-accented communities, outdoor activities.

Surrounded almost completely by the Great Lakes, the state of Michigan has not just one, but several coastal areas to explore. For this diversion, we take you roughly around the state, visiting small towns, and some cities, as well as resort communities as we go along.

From **Detroit**, take I-75 north past **Flint**. Make your first stop **Frankenmuth** (take Exit 136). Settled by Bavarian immigrants from Germany, this picturesque community offers a host of tourist attractions including *Bronner's Christmas Wonderland* (thought to be the world's largest Christmas store), shops, a brewery, and museums.

ISLE ROYALE NATIONAL PARK

From *Copper Harbor*, on the northernmost tip of Michigan, you can take a ferry to Michigan's *Isle Royale National Park*, a 45-mile-long island in Lake Superior.

Lake Superior's largest island is most famous for its moose and wolves, but it's also a sanctuary for scores of other wildlife species. Among them are beaver, muskrat, mink, weasels, and red fox plus bald eagles, osprey, and more than two dozen kinds of warblers. The island-park also has some ancient Indian mining pits that date back nearly 4,000 years.

Wooden shoe making—Holland, Michigan

Take Route 83 north to Route 46 west and get on I-75 for a short distance. Get off at Exit 164 where you can pick up Route 13 north and follow it up to U.S. 23. This takes you right along the shores of *Lake Huron* passing a number of resort communities including **East Tawas**, **Oscoda**, **Alpena**, **Rogers City**, and **Cheboygan**. There are several very picturesque lighthouses along this coast, in East Tawas, **Presque Isle**, and Cheboygan.

Continue north to **Mackinaw City** and take time to see *Colonial Michilimackinac*, a reconstructed French and British outpost and fur-trading village. From there, head north on I-75 taking the *Mackinac Bridge* over the *Straits of Mackinac*. One of the world's longest suspension bridges, it connects Michigan's Upper and Lower peninsulas.

From **St. Ignace**, you can take a ferry over to Mackinac (pronounced "mackinaw") Island, a resort island that retains the atmosphere of the 19th century, including the absence of automobiles.

Continue north on I-75 to **Sault Sainte Marie**, which lies on the border of Canada. It's home to the *Soo Locks*, the world's largest. Boat tours are available.

Backtrack a bit, and take Route 28 west and then take Route 123 south back to I-75. Return to the Lower Peninsula and follow U.S. 31 south.

This takes you down along the *Lake Michigan* coast, passing beautiful scenery all along the way. Detour a bit to follow Route 37 out to the end of the *Old Mission Peninsula*. **Traverse City** is considered the "Cherry Capital of the World" because of its abundant cherry products. It's also a major resort community situated on *Grand Traverse Bay*.

53

From there, follow Route 22 out to the *Grand Traverse Lighthouse* at the tip of the Leelanau Peninsula and then follow the coastline south. If you have time, consider taking an excursion boat over to North Manitou or South Manitou Islands (from **Leland**), which are part of *Sleeping Bear Dunes National Lakeshore*. This is an intensely beautiful area of the coast with towering dunes, lovely beaches, and walking trails.

As you continue south, you'll pass through several resort communities (with beaches, lighthouses, and tourist facilities) including **Frankfort**, **Manistee**, and **Ludington**.

Continue south on U.S. 31 to **Holland**, which was settled by the Dutch in 1847. The old country flavor has been preserved thanks to its large population of Dutch descendants. Take time to see the *Holland Museum*, the *Dutch Windmill*, and the *Wooden Shoe Factory* (tours are available).

From there, head south to **Kalamazoo** where you can divide your time between the *Kalamazoo Air Zoo*, an aviation history museum with impressively restored World War II aircraft, and the *Gilmore-CCCA Museum*, showcasing over one hundred vintage vehicles.

Continue east on I-94 to **Battle Creek** which owes its fame to two cereal tycoons—W.K. Kellogg and C.W. Post. Of interest here are the *Kingman Museum of Natural History*, the *Kimball House Museum*, the *Kellogg Bird Sanctuary*, and *Sojourners Truth's Grave*.

The city of **Jackson** is next. It's home to the *Michigan Space Center*, where many U.S. space artifacts and memorabilia are displayed.

Before returning to Detroit, make your last stop **Ann Arbor**. The city is famous for being the home of *The University of Michigan*. Campus highlights include the *Museum of Art*, *Natural Science Museums*, an archaeology museum, the *Gerald R. Ford Presidential Library*, and an arboretum.

Continue back to Detroit on I-94.

DID YOU KNOW...

• Michigan has a 3,288-mile shoreline—longer than any other state except Alaska.

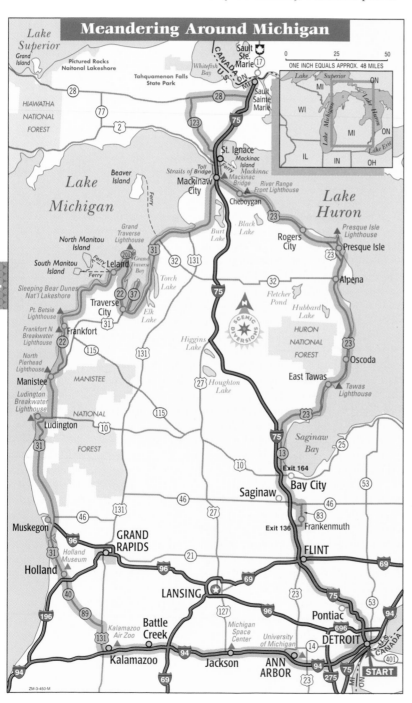

Meandering Around Michigan

ONE INCH EQUALS APPROX. 48 MILES

Ohio's Lake Erie Region

Distance: 185 Miles Round-Trip, Cleveland
Time: Allow at least two days
Highlights: Cleveland's big-city attractions, historic villages, museums, an amusement park, wineries, caves, boating, swimming, fishing.

For this diversion, we combine a visit to **Cleveland** with a drive to the Lake Erie island region, considered "Ohio's Scenic Playground."

If you think you won't need much time to see Cleveland, you'll be very surprised. This increasingly interesting city has lots to do. Start by checking out the shops in the new *Tower City Center*, a three-story shopping complex in the Terminal Tower downtown. Then hit the museums. *The Cleveland Museum of Art* has a top-draw collection of 19th-century French and American Impressionist paintings; the *Cleveland Museum of Natural History* displays the only extant skull of the Pygmy Tyrant; the *Western Reserve Historical Society* which is devoted to the history of Northeast Ohio; and the *Crawford Auto-Aviation Museum*, which houses more than 15 vintage automobiles and aircraft. At the North Coast Harbor, you can visit the brand new *Rock and Roll Hall of Fame and Museum*. Leave yourselves plenty of time to just stroll through the city's neighborhoods including *Public Square* downtown and *The Flats/Warehouse District* just to the west of downtown.

From Cleveland, head west on I-90 to Route 2. Then turn north to get to the coastal town of **Vermilion**. Here you'll find a historic shopping area, some good restaurants, and the *Inland Seas Maritime Museum* which contains Great Lakes ship models, paintings, photographs, and audio-visual displays.

Continue west on U.S. 6 to **Sandusky**, which has one of the best natural harbors in the country. Thanks to its early boat building prosperity, it has a distinct 19th-century look. Take a look around the *Follett House Museum*, a Greek Revival home built in the 1830s. It has an impressive collection of Civil War artifacts. From its widow's walk, there's a great view of the city and the lake. Sandusky is also home to the *Merry-Go-Round Museum*, where you can actually watch a carving demonstration and ride a working carousel.

Rock and Roll Hall of Fame—Cleveland, Ohio

55

Sunset over Lake Erie—Lorain, Ohio

At nearby *Cedar Point* (it's five miles southeast on U.S. 6 to Causeway Drive, then north over the Causeway) you'll find a beach, marina, and an amusement park with more than 50 rides, live shows, a crafts area, and more.

From Sandusky, continue west, crossing the *Sandusky Bay*. When you get on the peninsula, head east towards **Marblehead**, an artist's colony perched on a scenic windswept point. The *Marblehead Lighthouse* has been illuminating the way for more than 170 years. If you want to get away to a laid-back place, consider taking the ferry over to *Kelleys Island*, the largest U.S. island on *Lake Erie*. The entire island is in the National Register of Historic Places. In addition to beaches, the island is most famous for its *Glacial Grooves*, a series of long deep furrows carved by glaciers more than 30,000 years ago. Take time to see *Inscription Rock*, a slab of limestone covered with pictographs.

From Marblehead, backtrack a bit on Route 163, and then turn right onto Route 53 to *Catawba Point*. From here, you can take a ferry over to **Put-in-Bay** on *South Bass Island*. A top spot for fishermen, Put-in-Bay is famed for its small-mouth black bass fishing in spring, walleye in summer, and ice fishing for perch and walleye in winter. On top of

that, there's boating, swimming, biking, golf, and waterskiing. Take time to see *Perry's Victory and International Peace Monument*, a 352-foot-high column that commemorates Commodore Oliver Hazard Perry's victory over the British Naval Squadron at the Battle of Lake Erie, near Put-in-Bay in 1813. Also see *Perry's Cave*, where the commodore is said to have stored supplies before the battle. Nearby is *Crystal Cave*, with numerous deposits of strontium sulphate crystals. *Heineman Winery* is also located on the grounds.

From *South Bass Island*, you can take a ferry to *Middle Bass Island*, where you can tour winery cellars that were carved out of limestone bedrock.

From there, make your way back to Sandusky and then take U.S. 250 south to I-80/90. Then get on I-480 and follow that to I-71 which will take you back to Cleveland.

CURTAIN CALL

When planning your trip to Ohio, consider getting tickets to one of the following performances.

Tecumseh!, **Chillicothe**. All summer long, from mid-June through September, the *Sugarloaf Mountain Amphitheater* offers an outdoor theatrical presentation of the heroic life and the death of

Merry-Go-Round Museum—Sandusky, Ohio

Tecumseh, leader of the Shawnee tribe. Information: Tecumseh, P.O. Box 73, Chillicothe, OH 45601. (614) 775-0700. From March 1 until the end of the season.

Trumpet in the Land, **New Philadelphia**. This outdoor drama is all about life and events in the frontier days. Performances from mid-June through August, about a mile from *Schoenbrunn Village*, a restoration of the settlement where many of the events took place. Information: Trumpet in the Land, P.O. Box 450, New Philadelphia, OH 44663. (216) 364-5111.

Blossom Music Festival, **Cuyanoga Falls**. About eighty musical events are held every year from mid-May through September at this cedar-shingled shell halfway between **Akron** and Cleveland. Information: Blossom Music Festival, P.O. Box 1000, Cuyahoga Falls, OH 44223. (216) 920-8040.

In **Toledo**, every Sunday evening during August, *Music Under the Stars* presents the Toledo concert Band in free performances at the zoo's amphitheater. Concerts start 9 p.m., weather permitting. Each concert has a different musical theme.

OHIO'S AMISH COUNTRY

South of Cleveland, in Holmes, Wayne, and Tuscarawas counties, you'll find the state's Amish Country. About 35,000 plain people (the largest Amish population in the world) live in this area. Originally Swiss Mennonites, the Amish created their own sect. Following Jacob Amman, they came to the United States in 1728 to practice their austere lifestyle undisturbed. For more information on the Amish way of life (and some Amish sights to see), stop by the Mennonite Information Center near Berlin. (216) 893-3192.

Indianapolis & South-Central Indiana

Distance: 130 Miles Round-Trip, Indianapolis
Time: Allow at least three days
Highlights: Museums, contemporary architecture, fall foliage, swimming, horseback riding, hiking, boating, fishing.

If you're looking for a wonderful place to see fall colors in the Great Lakes area, you must visit South-Central Indiana. During autumn, the forested foothills of the Cumberlands offer one of nature's most beautiful extravaganzas. This area—Brown County—is also known as a crafts mecca, with hundreds of shops to explore. This drive (which starts in **Indianapolis**) combines the natural beauty of Brown County with a visit to the university town of **Bloomington** to the west and architecturally-rich **Columbus** to the east.

Mention Indianapolis, and many people automatically think of the famed *Indy 500*, one of the world's largest sporting event. Every year on Memorial Day weekend, auto racing enthusiasts gather at the *Indianapolis Motor Speedway* for the granddaddy of all auto races. If you're in town any other time of year, you can take a bus tour around the 2-1/2-mile track and visit the *Speedway Hall of Fame Museum*.

Other highlights in the state's largest city include the *State Capitol*, the *Indiana State Museum*, the *former homes of Benjamin Harrison* and *James Whitcomb Riley*, the *Children's Museum*, the *Indianapolis Zoo*, the *Morris-Butler House*, the *City Market*, the *Indianapolis Museum of Art*, the *Scottish Rite Cathedral*, and *Union Station*, a former railroad station turned into an entertainment, shopping, and eating complex.

Indy 500—Indianapolis, Indiana

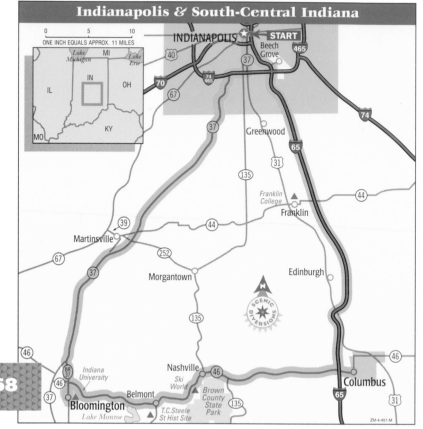

Indianapolis & South-Central Indiana

ONE INCH EQUALS APPROX. 11 MILES

on Route 46. When you enter, you cross a 19th-century covered bridge into an outdoor lover's paradise—woodlands, lakes, and streams. If you want to do an easy hike, consider taking the two-mile trek that starts at the lodge.

Continue east on Route 46 to **Columbus**, which is known for its contemporary architecture designed by famous architects such as Harry Weese, I.M. Pei, and Cesar Pelli. Allow at least half a day to see the buildings here. There's an architectural tour that leaves by minibus from the *Columbus Visitors Center* at Fifth and Franklin streets.

From there, head north on I-65 to return to Indianapolis.

DID YOU KNOW...

- The Raggedy Ann and Andy dolls originated in Indianapolis in 1914.
- The first professional baseball game was played in **Fort Wayne** on May 4, 1871 between the Fort Wayne Kekiongas and the Cleveland Forest Cities—the Kekiongas won.
- Indiana has the only U.S. post office named Santa Claus.
- The Indianapolis Motor Speedway hosted the first long distance automobile race in the U.S. on May 30, 1911.
- The Tippecanoe River's name was applied to an 1811 battle and in turn to William Henry Harrison's presidential campaign slogan, "Tippecanoe and Tyler too," in 1840. Tyler was Harrison's running mate.
- The city of **Gary** was planned and founded by the United States Steel Corporation.
- *Vincennes* was the first permanent Indian settlement.
- Fort Wayne was once an actual fort that protected settlers in the Indiana Territory from raids by hostile Indians.
- The eleven small lakes in *Chain O' Lakes State Park* were formed from the weight and water of enormous blocks of ice left in the ground by retreating glaciers at the end of the last ice age.

Nashville, Indiana

From Indianapolis, head south on Route 37. Follow this to **Bloomington**, which is home to *Indiana University*. There are several good ethnic restaurants in town plus antique malls and a highly regarded opera house. *Lake Monroe*, Indiana's largest body of water, lies south of the city, and offers great fishing.

From Bloomington, it's a scenic drive east on Route 46 through Brown County, a wooded region with log cabins and picturesque hamlets.

About two miles south of **Belmont** (turn right on the county road) you can visit the *home and studio of T.C. Steele*, one of Indiana's most widely praised artists.

Continue east on Route 46 to **Nashville**, a small town rife with boutiques, antique shops, and galleries, so much so that you could easily spend an entire day here.

Brown County State Park, Indiana's largest park (nearly 16,000 acres) is about two miles south of Nashville

LIVING HISTORY

P R A I R I E T O W N

The Village of *Prairietown* at *Conner Prairie* in **Noblesville**, Indiana (about ten miles north of **Indianapolis**) is considered a living museum, but it would be more accurate to call it a living theater—one that deserves a standing ovation. Carrying on exactly as the pioneers might have in 1836, the cast of characters includes Mistress Betsy Birdwhistle who teaches reading, writing, and arithmetic in a one-room log school-house; Ben Curtis, the blacksmith who complains incessantly about the Andrew Jackson presidency while he hammers away; and the village doctor who packs up a bag of terrifying—Medieval looking—medical instruments to take along on house calls. The backdrop is an historically accurate re-creation of approximately thirty 19th-century pioneer buildings, including a general store and an inn where a room goes for 12 and 1/2 cents, or one "bit", a night.

Prairietown, however, is just one area of attraction at Conner Prairie. The others are the *William Conner Estate*, which includes the 1823 Federal-style home of Conner (an early Indiana statesman), and the *Pioneer Adventure Area* where visitors can try pioneer crafts such as weaving, soap making, and wood carving. For more information, call (317) 776-6000.

Golden Eagle Inn—Conner Prairie, Indiana

59

Southeast

*W*ith its sun-bleached beaches, its wildly beautiful Blue Ridge and Smoky Mountains, its multiple man-made attractions (Walt Disney World and the Kennedy Space Center just to name two), and its beautifully preserved plantations and historic cities, the American Southeast is prime vacation territory.

One of the nicest things about exploring this part of the U.S. is that many of its fascinating landscapes are within easy reach of one another. You can easily get from the coast to the mountains, from the excitement of a theme park to quiet horse country. You can visit avant cities such as Miami and Atlanta, and then go back in time to places like St. Augustine and Savannah.

Here is just a sampling of what you'll find.

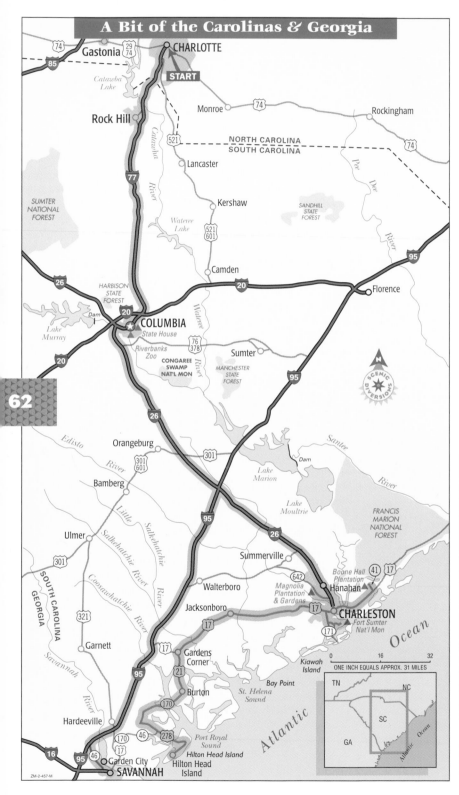

A Bit of the Carolinas & Georgia

Charleston, South Carolina

A Bit of the Carolinas & Georgia

Distance: 856 Miles Round Trip, Charlotte

Time: Allow at least five days

Highlights: Coastal scenery and beaches, mountains, outdoor sports, resorts, golf, tennis, historic cities.

For this tour, we take you from **Charlotte**, North Carolina's largest city, over to the South Carolina coast and then down to **Savannah**, Georgia (just over the border) and back to Charlotte.

En route, you'll visit **Charleston** and Savannah—two historically rich cities—and the offshore island, *Hilton Head*.

From Charlotte, head south on I-77 to **Columbia**, the capital of South Carolina. Spend some time here touring the *Governor's Mansion*, *State House*, *Hampton-Preston House*,

Riverbanks Zoo, and *Trinity Cathedral*.

To reach Charleston and the coast, head east on I-26. Here you'll find Antebellum homes, winding cobblestone streets, and magnificently fragrant gardens. Start your sightseeing with a clip-clopping carriage ride past gracious mansions, antique churches, and oak-studded parks. Historic homes open for touring include the *Nathaniel Russell House,* with its incredible spiral staircase; the *Edmonston-Alston House,* overlooking the harbor; and the *Calhoun Mansion,* which boasts 35 fireplaces—visit at least one. Afterwards stroll along the brightly painted houses on *Rainbow Row* (inspiration for *Porgy and Bess*) and visit *Fort Sumter*, where the first shots of the Civil War were fired. At *Magnolia Plantation and Gardens*, you can bike, boat, or hike through acres of blossoms. And *Boone Hall*, a few miles from town, is where *Gone With the Wind* was filmed. Its mansion and grounds offer well-preserved glimpses of a silver-screen South.

From Charleston, work your way down the coast, taking U.S. 17 to **Gardens Corner** where you'll pick up U.S. 21 south. Then take Route 170 to U.S. 278, which you'll follow right out to Hilton Head Island. A sprawling country club of an island, Hilton Head is home to golf course after golf course, hundreds of tennis courts, and all sorts of clubby facilities, including health spas, marinas (from which you can take boat rides), and yachty *Harbour Town* shops for splurging. On top of all this, the island is surrounded by wide white-sand beaches that are not only wonderful for sunning, but for pedaling bicycles,

Charleston, South Carolina

jogging, and bird-watching.

The coastal city of Savannah, which is well known for its Antebellum buildings and squares, is next on the itinerary. From Hilton Head Island take U.S. 278 to Route 46, following Route 170 and U.S. 17 into town. Here the "Old South" lives on in more than 1,000 restored buildings that are lined up like contestants in a beauty contest.

Founded in 1733 by James Edward Oglethorpe from Surrey, England, Savannah is laid out in a perfect grid. There's a *National Historic Landmark District* covering 2.5 square miles. It's home to numerous Federalist and English Regency houses that were rescued and restored in the mid-1950s by a group of concerned citizens (many of the houses had fallen into disrepair

63

WHAT'S COOKING?

If you love seafood and freshwater fish, you'll be in your glory in this part of the world. You'll find everything from conch fritters cooked in wooden shacks on the beach to scallop mousse with lobster sauce served at a restaurant you'd expect to see on the pages of *Gourmet*. In-between, you'll find gumbos, jambalayas, crabcakes, seafood crepes, fresh fish (broiled, poached, sauteed…you name it), and too many shrimp dishes to mention.

Non-seafood-eaters won't be left out, however. Menus also include Southern Fried Chicken, barbecued spareribs, chateaubriand, pasta dishes—and other perennial favorites.

Victorian District—Savannah, Georgia

when the price of cotton crashed at the turn of the century). The historic district is bordered by East Broad St., Martin Luther King Jr. Boulevard, Gwinnett Street, and the Savannah River. It can best be seen on foot.

Once you've seen Savannah, head back to Charlotte by taking I-95 an then I-26 north to Columbia, then I-77 north to Charlotte.

IF YOU HAVE EXTRA TIME...

Consider detouring a bit to visit *Kiawah Island*. A short drive from Charleston, Kiawah is like a little oasis of perfection. On a typical day the sky is as clear as a pane of glass and the sea, a beautiful blue. Its ten miles of beach, studded with sand dollars, beckons to you with balmy breezes and warming sunshine.

There is a combination platter of resort activities on the island including top-flight tennis, four (yes, four!) 18-hole golf courses, swimming pools, bike trails, and spa facilities. And at the same time, there's lots of nature to see, including over 140 different species of birds, alligators, and loggerhead turtles that lay their eggs on the beach at night between May and August. If you wish to stay in the area try the *Kiawah Island Inn & Villas* with 150 rooms featuring weekend packages. For information, call (800) 845-2471 or (803) 768-2121.

CHARLESTON'S SPECIAL EVENTS

Festival of Houses, mid-March to mid-April. For this event, beautiful historic homes around Charleston are open for touring. For more information, call (803) 723-1623.

Spoleto Festival/USA, late May to early June. This is the American version of the Italian Festival of Two Worlds which was started by Gian Carlo Menotti. All kinds of music is featured including jazz, opera, and classical, plus art exhibitions, dance performances, and theater. For more information, write to: P.O. Box 157, Charleston, SC 29402 or call (803) 722-2764.

Garden Candlelight Tours, mid-September to mid-October. The city's historic homes and gardens are beautifully illuminated by candles during this annual event. For information, call (803) 722-4630.

International Film Festival, late October to early November. Works of film makers from around the world are presented here.

NORTH CAROLINA'S OUTER BANKS

Cape Hatteras Lighthouse, North Carolina

If you're able to spend more time in North Carolina, consider taking a drive to the north end of its coast where you'll find the *Outer Banks*. This string of wind-swept islands stretches 175 miles roughly parallel to the mainland coast.

To reach it from **Norfolk**, Virginia, take Route 168 South to U.S.158. Cross the bridge at **Point Harbor** near the end of U.S. 158 to **Kitty Hawk**. When you first start driving south on this narrow ribbon of islands (connected by bridges and ferries), you may find yourselves saying, "Where's the beach?" You will see lots of honky-tonk attractions, motels, fast-food places, and the like. Ever since the Wright brothers launched the world's first flying machine here, much of the upper Outer Banks have been colonized by tourist facilities. But for vacationers, there's more, especially if you press on—past the busy towns of Kitty Hawk, **Kill Devil Hills**, and **Nags Head**. In fact, go all the way—to *Ocracoke Island* which is ringed by soft-sand—and footprintless—beaches.

En route, you'll find yourself surrounded by the wildly beautiful scenery of *Cape Hatteras National Seashore*: wind-swept dunes, endless stretches of beach, waves breaking in a series of prismatic explosions. Some must-see stops along the way include *Jockey's Ridge* (gargantuan sand dunes), the historic town of **Manteo** (site of Roanoke's Lost Colony—which is performed in an outdoor theater all summer long), and the *Cape Hatteras Lighthouse*—the tallest on the East Coast. Once on Ocracoke Island, you can do some all-out relaxing, beachcombing, clamming, swimming, or bicycling. Consider overnighting in the village of **Ocracoke**, and then catch a ferry back to the mainland.

Land of the Sky

Distance: 723 Miles Round Trip, Charlotte
Time: Allow at least two days
Highlights: Outdoor activities (camping, fishing, hiking, nature walks, bird watching, horseback riding, cycling), beautiful mountain scenery, Cherokee reservation.

In Western North Carolina, you find both the *Great Smoky* and the *Blue Ridge Mountains*, which offer some of the most beautiful scenery in the eastern United States.

From **Charlotte**, head north on I-77. Exit at **Elkin** for U.S. 21 north. Just beyond Cherry Lane, turn left onto the *Blue Ridge Parkway*. All said and done the Blue Ridge Parkway is a 470-mile-long scenic road that runs between *Shenandoah National Park* in Virginia and the *Great Smoky Mountains National Park* in North Carolina. The parkway follows the crest of the Blue Ridge and other ranges, offering many beautiful vistas.

Follow the parkway to **Asheville** which is the center of the mountains' arts and folk culture and the gateway to the state's Appalachian high country region. Take time to see the Vanderbilt's famed *Biltmore*, a 255-room chateau (dating back to the 1890s) that's propped up on 10,000 acres. See, also, the *Asheville Art Museum*, the *Colburn Mineral Museum*, the *Botanical Gardens*, the boyhood home of novelist Thomas Wolfe, and leave plenty of time to explore the town's galleries, especially at *Biltmore Village*, opposite the castle.

From Asheville, follow I-40 west for 23 miles. Just before **Waynesville**, take U.S. 19 west for 27 miles through **Maggie Valley** to the *Cherokee Indian Reservation* at **Cherokee**. Though the town has been heavily exploited for tourism, there is a worthwhile *Museum of the Cherokee Indian* which traces the tribe's history. Also see the *Oconaluftee Indian Village*, which is a re-creation of an early Cherokee village. On summer evenings, the drama "*Unto These Hills*" tells the story of the Cherokee nation.

Smoky Mountains, North Carolina

65

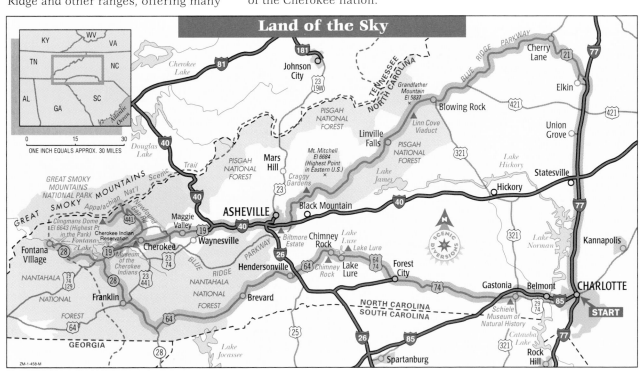

Land of the Sky

Chimney Rock, North Carolina

From Cherokee, drive north on U.S. 441 to the entrance of the Great Smoky Mountains National Park, astride the border of North Carolina and Tennessee. The Smoky Mountains are strikingly beautiful with lofty peaks all around rising above 6,000 feet. In between are green valleys filled with mist from which the mountains derive their name. You can follow self-guided trails, which include the *Appalachian Trail*.

For the most magnificent view, follow U.S. 441 (which is called Newfound Gap Road in the park), then the seven-mile spur road, and then walk a half-mile trail to *Clingmans Dome*, the Smoky's highest point (6,643 feet) which is topped by an observation tower.

Just west of there (take U.S. 19 to Route 28) you'll find **Fontana Village**, which has lodges, rustic cottages, folk dances, and many outlets for family fun.

Backtrack on Route 28, following it south and then east on U.S. 64 which links up with U.S. 74.

En route, be sure to stop at *Chimney Rock*, from which the views are mesmerizingly beautiful (follow the three mile road from the village of **Chimney Rock** to Chimney Rock itself). You can take an elevator inside the rock or climb the strenuous trail to the top. Also consider following one of the trails along the cliffs to the 400-foot

OUTDOOR THEATER

In Boone (which is along the Blue Ridge Parkway), you can see an outdoor drama that tells the story of the town's namesake, Daniel Boone.

Hickory Nut Falls, one of the highest waterfalls in the eastern United States. Next stop: *Lake Lure*, on the edge of the Blue Ridge Mountains. Nearby are the *Bottomless Pools* waterfalls.

Carry on east on U.S. 74, making your next stop **Gastonia**. Take time to see the *Schiele Museum of Natural History*, which sprawls over 30 acres.

Take I-85 back to Charlotte.

A WALK IN THE WOODS

At George Vanderbilt's turn-of-the-century French chateau, *Biltmore House* in Asheville, North Carolina, visitors can not only visit the house and gardens, but the extensive woodlands which surround them. Thanks to the newly developed *Woodland Trails*, paths go through ravines, past a waterfall, and across wooden bridges and stone ledges in the Blue Ridge forests. For more information about Biltmore Estate, contact The Biltmore Company, One North Pack Square, Asheville, NC 28801 or (800) 543-2961.

STONE MOUNTAIN PARK

Just 16 miles east of downtown Atlanta (on U.S. 78), is Stone Mountain Park, which is the third most-visited admission-charging tourist attraction in the United States after Disney World and Disneyland.

The centerpiece of this 3,200-acre recreational area (of lakes, woods, and parkland) is Stone Mountain, the largest granite outcropping on earth. On the north face of the 825-foot high, five-mile

around monolith is the *Confederate Memorial*—the world's largest sculpture.

The mountain sculpture, which took over a half a century to complete, depicts Confederate leaders Jefferson Davis, Robert E. Lee, and Stonewall Jackson galloping throughout eternity on horseback.

The best view of the bas-relief is from below, but you can also follow the walking trail up the slopes. If you'd prefer to sit back

and take it all in, there's a narrated tram ride to the top, running every twenty minutes in both directions. Between April and October, there's a special evening laser show with fireworks, animation, and music. Be sure to see it. In April, September, and October, it takes place on weekends only, at 9 p.m.; from May through Labor Day, it can be seen nightly at 9:30 p.m.

Northeast Georgia Mountains

Distance: 371 Miles Round Trip, Atlanta
Time: Allow at least two days
Highlights: Mountains, lakes, waterfalls, outdoor sports.

The area northeast of **Atlanta** is where many Georgians go to escape the summer heat. It's home to mountains, several lakes, waterfalls, and all-around fresh and invigorating green scenery.

Start by heading north out of Atlanta on I-85, then pick up I-985 north. Just 45 minutes away, you'll find *Lake Lanier* which was formed by damming the *Chestatee*, *Little*, and *Chattahoochee Rivers*. There are four islands, which are actually mountaintops that weren't submerged, called the *Lake Lanier Islands*. These make up a park and recreational resort where there's boating, bicycling, horseback riding, hiking, and camping. There are also two top-of-the-line hotels, *Stouffers* and the *Hilton*.

In the town of **Gainesville**, you'll find the *Georgia Mountain Museum* which highlights the history of the area and the *Elachee Natural Center*, a 1,200-acre nature preserve.

From the Lake Lanier area, continue north (take U.S. 129 to Route 75 to **Helen**, which is a Bavarian-style village tucked away in the Blue Ridge Mountains astride the Chattahoochee River. Here you can settle in for a German meal, poke around the European shops, and hike at nearby *Anna Ruby Falls*.

Follow Route 75 north to Route 180, where you'll turn left to get to *Brasstown Bald*. At 4,784 feet, this is the state's

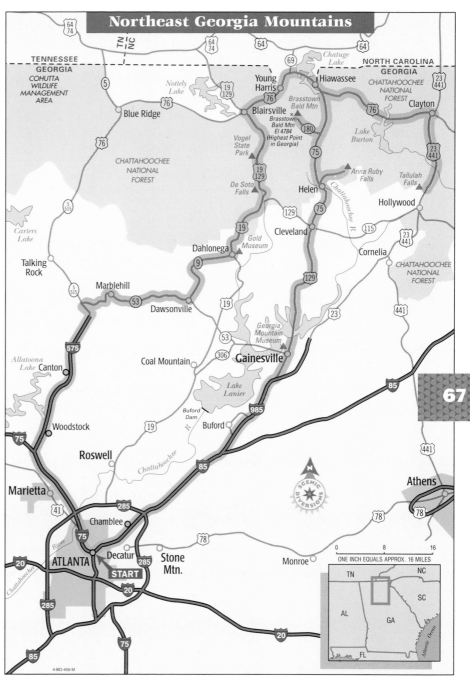

Northeast Georgia Mountains

highest mountain. You can either hike up a steep, paved, half-mile trail or take the shuttle bus to the summit, where there's a visitors center with an observation tower. Retrace your steps back to Route 75 and continue north to U.S. 76 where you'll turn right heading towards **Clayton**. Many consider this

Lake Lanier, Georgia

Balloon Festival—Helen, Georgia

drive—through densely scenic mountains—one of the most beautiful in the state. Clayton is home to several antiques shops and galleries. In fact, you'll find antiques shops beginning on Main Street and along U.S. 441 north for seven miles through **Mountain City** and into **Dillard**. South of Clayton (taking U.S. 23/441) is *Tallulah Falls*, a gorge with falls that have been harnessed for hydroelectric power.

Again retrace your steps again back to Route 75 towards **Hiawassee**, which is on the banks of *Chatuge Lake*. You're in the heart of the *Chattahoochee National Forest* now, and the scenery is stunning in every direction. The drive between **Young Harris** and **Blairsville** (U.S. 76) is especially beautiful.

Continue south on U.S. 19/129, pausing at *Vogel State Park*, and then *De Soto Falls*. Make your last stop **Dahlonega**, which was the site of America's first gold rush in 1828. You can get the whole story in the gold museum before setting out to see the gold mines. The phrase, "thar's gold in them thar hills" was coined here.

From there, take Route 9 to Route 53 west over to Route 5/515. Take Route 5/515 south to I-575 and then follow I-75 back to Atlanta.

READ ALL ABOUT IT

While planning your trip to Georgia, consider picking up copies of the following books.

Gone With the Wind, by Margaret Mitchell

Confederate Georgia, by T. Conn Bryan

Midnight in the Garden of Good and Evil, by John Berendt Grand

Pictorial History of Gone With the Wind, by Gerald and Harriette Gardner

The Legacy of Atlanta: A Short History, by Webb Garrison

Living Atlanta: An Oral History of the City 1914-1918, by Clifford Kahn, Harlan Joye, and Bernard West

Flannery O'Connor's Georgia, by Barbara McKenzie

Atlanta: A Brave and Beautiful City, by Celestine Sibley

WHAT'S IN A NAME?

While visiting Georgia, you may hear it referred to as the Goober State. This comes from nguba, an African word for peanut. Nearly half of the peanut butter consumed in the United States is made from peanuts grown in Georgia.

Lake Lanier, Georgia

Orlando & Environs

....

Distance: 355 Miles Round Trip, Orlando
Time: Allow at least three days
Highlights: Amusement Parks, J.F.K. Space Center, beaches, water sports.

John F. Kennedy Space Center, Florida

If having fun is tops on your vacation wish list, you're in the right area. Central Florida is not home to just one or two major attractions, it's a virtual candy store of amusements. You can easily spend a week hopscotching from one to the next and still not see and do everything.

We'll start with *Disney World* in **Orlando** of course, which is the hub around which much of the state of Florida radiates. We're not going to bore you with pages and pages of history or anything, but it is interesting to note this one story. When Walt Disney first suggested a theme park to appeal to adults as much as children, the idea was ridiculed. Undaunted, he borrowed against both personal and corporate assets to finance the construction of Disneyland in Anaheim, California, in 1954. It was so successful that he was able to embark on an even bigger development: the creation of Walt Disney World in central Florida. But to dwell on that would be a snore, let's move on to today (and, actually, tomorrow, at EPCOT Center).

Walt Disney World stretches across 43 square miles and offers three spectacular theme parks: the *Magic Kingdom*, the *EPCOT Center*, and the *Disney-MGM Studios Theme Park*.

There are also 20 hotels, dozens of restaurants, a total of 99 holes of golf, 15 lighted tennis courts, miles of open waterways, white-sand beaches, and swimming pools galore. On top of all that, the nightlife keeps you going, going, going. At *Pleasure Island*, there are seven night clubs with live music, dance floors, comedy shows, you name it.

Consider starting your Walt Disney World exploration at the Magic Kingdom, which is crowned by the dreamy *Cinderella Castle*. The Kingdom covers 100 acres including *Main Street, U.S.A.* which is a storybook American town with turn-of-the-century buildings and hedges trimmed to look like mouse ears (and other animals). Disney characters wander around merrily greeting visitors. There are several subkingdoms within the Magic Kingdom including *Adventureland* which offers the "Pirates of the Caribbean," an immensely popular animated exhibit. *Frontierland*, a gold-rush town, has one of the Kingdom's newest and most popular attractions, *Splash*

TABLES OF CONTENT

Walt Disney World offers an astonishing selection of foods from around the world including everything from smoked turkey legs, sold from carts in the Magic Kingdom, to elaborate six-course French meals complete with flickering candles, crisp white linen, and fine crystal. The biggest concentration of international restaurants is in EPCOT's World Showcase. You'll need just one phone number to make reservations at all the restaurants in Walt Disney World, EPCOT Center, and Disney-MGM Studios; (407)934-7639.

Mountain. It's a thrill ride that takes you through the Disney movie, "Song of the South," culminating in a five-story drop! By the way, you may get wet. Frontierland is also home to the Magic Kingdom's Big Thunder Railroad which chugs through the desert to the town of *Tumbleweed*. If you prefer a roller coaster to a train, you can soar through space at *Tomorrowland's Space Mountain*—another thrilling Disney attraction.

Tomorrowland also features a new sensory thriller called The ExtraTERRORestrial Alien Encounter which looks like a city imagined by sci-fi writers and movie-makers of the 1920s and 1930s.

EPCOT (Experimental Prototype Community of Tomorrow) consists of two main areas: *Future World* and the *World Showcase*. Inside that enormous white thing—the Spaceship Earth—that looks like a golf ball, visitors can take a time-travel journey through the story of civilization and then experience a simulated ride around the AT & T Worldwide Information Network. INNOVENTIONS, one of the hottest new attractions at EPCOT is a showcase of technology of the near future. Guests can try out wrist phones, interactive videos, CD-ROM, and virtual reality. Travel the Motorola Information Skyway is a virtual reality/3-D ride that shows how wireless communications are transmitted and received.

Another wonderful new attraction at EPCOT Center is a high-tech 3-D "misadventure," called "*Honey I Shrunk the Audience.*" This wildly amazing and amusing 20-minute experience happens in *Kodak's Journey Into Imagination Pavilion*, where audiences (wearing 3-D goggles) shrink into their seats.

The World Showcase at EPCOT is a living gallery of international cultures. Eleven nations from around the world share their cultures in shows, attractions, restaurants, and shops. Time it so you can have at least a meal or two here; you can take your pick of cuisines from around the world.

If you've always wanted to experience the excitement of movie-making, you can go behind the scenes, take a screen test, or learn animation techniques at Disney-MGM Studios, where movies and TV shows are made. But there's more here including attractions such as *The Twilight Zone Tower of Terror* which sends audiences on a visit to a long-abandoned Hollywood hotel where they meet some of the long-lost guests.

Orlando & Environs

9-BO-454-M

As wonderful as Disney World is, there's a lot more to see in the Orlando area. Right nearby, you'll find *Sea World of Florida* (home to Shamu and Baby Shamu), *Gatorland Zoo* ("The Alligator Capital of the World"—home to more than 5,000 alligators and crocodiles); *Universal Studios Florida* (with more than 40 movie-themed rides), and *Cypress Gardens* (see human pyramids on water skis among other amphibious acts).

Over on the coast (take Route 528 east), you can visit the *John F. Kennedy Space Center* and *Spaceport U.S.A.* which is the launch site for all United States manned space missions. You can tour the Space Center and *Cape Canaveral Air Force Station* and watch IMAX movies like "The Dream is Alive" and "Blue Planet" on giant screens. In nearby **Titusville**, take a walk through the *Astronaut Hall of Fame*.

Follow U.S. 1 or I-95 to reach **Daytona Beach**, one of Florida's oldest resorts. This famous beach town lives a carnival-atmosphered life on its lively boardwalk where the sounds of bowling balls trundling down alleys, the ringing and dinging of pinball machines, and the smacks of cue sticks hitting pool balls can always be heard. Drive right up on the beach; it's all part of the scene.

To return to Orlando, take I-4. If you want to detour to **Ocala** take Route 40 west (just north of Daytona Beach).

IF YOU HAVE THE TIME...

Consider visiting *Amelia Island.* Just 30 miles north of **Jacksonville**, this offshore island has dune-covered beaches, a lovely Victorian town named **Fernandina Beach**, and a pair of impressive resorts. When you're not golfing, biking, playing tennis, or horseback riding, take a stroll or carriage ride around the town, which has more than 30 restored gingerbread houses. Then stop in for a drink at the oldest bar in the state, the *Palace Saloon*. You might also take a ride over to *Amelia Island Lighthouse* and *Fort Clinch*, surrounded by 1,000 acres of well-tended parkland. For staying, the *Amelia Island Plantation* offers a sports scene almost too good to be true, and private villas for lovers of solitude. Its neighbor, the *Ritz-Carlton*, is atop a bluff of dunes and has golf, tennis, a fitness center, dining, and dancing, as well as ocean views from each and every room.

Daytona Beach, Florida

71

ANOTHER WORLD
FLORIDA'S HORSE COUNTRY

If you thought Florida was all palm trees, sand, and amusement parks, you'll be delightfully surprised to discover Ocala, which is about an hour and a half drive north (and slightly west) of the Orlando area.

Here you'll think you're in Kentucky, Virginia, or even the English Cotswolds. White-fenced pastures stretch out in every direction. Statuesque thoroughbreds stretch their long necks as they yank clumps of grass out of the earth. Women with perfect French braids rigorously currycomb ink-black stallions. Several decades ago, thoroughbred horse breeders found that Ocala's combination of steady sunshine, mineral spring water, and limestone-based soil would be ideal for race horses. Today, there are over 450 thoroughbred farms in the Ocala area (especially along Route 40 and U.S. 27). Some are open for touring. For information on which ones are open when, contact the Florida Thoroughbred Breeders' and Owners' Association, (904) 629-2160 or the Ocala Marion Chamber of Commerce, 110 East Silver Springs Road, Ocala; (904) 629-2160.

Highlights of Southern Florida

Distance: 996 Miles Round Trip, Orlando
Time: Allow at least a week
Highlights: Beaches, grand old Floridian architecture, amusement parks, golf and tennis, water sports, resorts, city attractions, history.

What comes to mind when you think of Florida? Sunshine and oranges? Sweeps of perfect beach? Mickey Mouse and Donald Duck? Golf and tennis year round? Mega-resorts? Caribbean rhythms? Palm trees clicking in the breeze?

Though it is only one state, Florida is made up of about a hundred different worlds—which makes it a fascinating state to explore. Here's just a sampling of what you'll find.

Orlando is a delightful place to begin. So go ahead. Put on the Mickey Mouse ears and throw your sophisticated image to the wind. *Walt Disney World* is not only a dream come true for the younger-set, but can also be the biggest thrill of your adult lives. (Actually, Walt Disney designed it for both kids and grown-ups). Today's visitors find three separate constellations of entertainment on the 28,000 acres including the fantastic *Magic Kingdom*, the eye-poppingly progressive *EPCOT Center*, and the new *Disney MGM Studios Theme Park*.

If you don't go overboard on fun at Disney World, you'll find there's lots more nearby including *Universal Studios Florida* where the thrills of motion pictures come to life before your eyes with rides through movie sets; *Sea World of Florida* (home to Shamu and Baby Shamu); *The John F. Kennedy Space Center*, over on the coast; and thoroughbred horse country inland around **Ocala**.

From Orlando head south on Florida's Turnpike towards the coast. Once there, make your first stop **Palm Beach**. The scene here is a far cry

from Disney World. In fact, it looks like the pages of a slick magazine come to life: Socialites in silk-toed pumps step from sleek limousines, distinguished gentlemen concentrate on croquet balls, polo players accept trophies that glisten in the sun. Still, Palm Beach is not reserved for the rich and famous. To do as the locals do, take time out to work on your tennis serve or golf swing, lounge around your hotel's pool or the beach, and people-watch and window-shop along *Worth Avenue*. Be sure to take a drive along mansion-lined *Ocean Boulevard* and don't miss the *Henry Morris Flagler Museum*.

From there, carry on south to **Boca Raton**. The architect Addison Mizner saw Boca Raton as the perfect site for a society retreat by the sea. The Depression stopped most of his dreams before they started. But his *Cloister Inn* made it just under the wire, opening to one of the greatest society bashes ever. Just months later, Mizner went broke, yet the town has gone on to become one of the nation's wealthiest communities.

Fort Lauderdale is next. Here you'll find a year-round party spirit, enough yachts to stretch for miles, and many multi-million-dollar homes.

Continue down the coast to **Miami Beach** and **Miami**, which are separated by the blue waters of *Biscayne Bay*, offer a wonderful mix of city excitement, and seaside resort life. You'd need months to take it in, but start with a day strolling around the *Art Deco District*.

Bayside Market—Miami, Florida

72

The square-mile area in *SoBe* (short for South Beach) is not only chockablock with Easter-egg colored deco buildings, but is now a magnet for the young and hip and artsy with its alfresco cafes and fast-forward night clubs.

For exploring elsewhere in the Greater Miami area, consider taking the *Old Town Trolley* which starts off at the *Bayside Marketplace*, a sprawling outdoor plaza in downtown. The two-hour trip takes you to *Coconut Grove*, which is rife with cafes, galleries, and shops; to *Coral Gables*, a wealthy neighborhood of old-money Cuban families; and to *Calle Ocho*, the nucleus of *Little Havana* where you can drink Cuban-style coffee. For shopping—or window-shopping— make your way to the designer shops of *Bal Harbour* or the *Miracle Mile*.

All over Miami and Miami Beach, you'll find clubs where you can hear jazz, dance to be-bop, tap your toes to reggae—you name it. An especially fun after-dark area is the Art Deco District with its collection of outdoor bars, cafes, and clubs. In addition, all the big hotels have bars and discos.

Continue south to U.S. 1 which will take you over the *Florida Keys* out to *Key West*. All too often, travelers skim over the northernmost keys on their way to Key West. But the real key here is to take your time. These islands (45 are linked by the *Overseas Highway*) are little destinations in themselves.

Working your way southwest, the Overseas Highway (U.S. 1) takes you over one stray puzzle-piece of an island after another, and slowly introduces you to a different world. This is more Caribbean than Floridian, with water the color of green apples spreading on one side, and the deep blue Atlantic rolling in on the other.

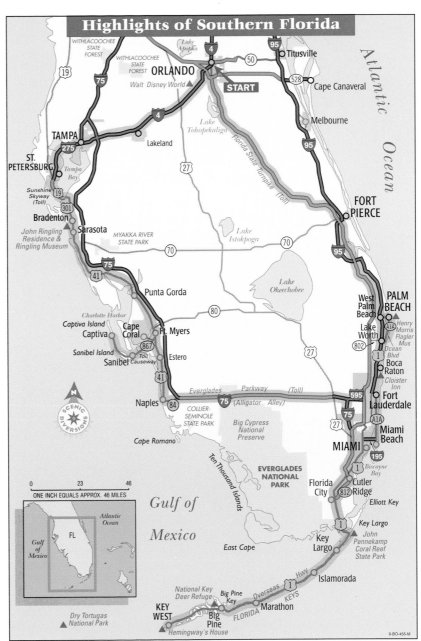

73

First stop is **Key Largo** where parts of the movie by that name were filmed. Though Bacall and Bogart hardly set foot on the island, some locals talk about them as if they were family. Running parallel to the key is the country's only underwater state park and the only living coral reef in the continental U.S. The park (*John Pennekamp Coral Reef State Park*) is derigueur for snorkelers and divers.

Bottle-Nosed Dolphins, Florida Keys

There are also sailing trips and glass-bottom boat rides for less amphibious types. And for the open-minded, there's *Dolphins Plus*, a research center where you can swim with dolphins.

Islamorada is another worthwhile stop, especially if you want to don masks, snorkels, fins, and get wet. It's home to two coral deposits and the wreck of a Spanish galleon. Consider trying some "nouvelle Key cuisine" at the *Cheeca Lodge* afterwards. Further along, **Marathon** is on a serious fishing island and has been commercialized quite a bit. However, it still has its original fishing town character in tact and should not be skipped over.

The star attraction on *Big Pine Key* is a colony of tiny white-tailed deer, appropriately named Key Deer. Follow the signs for the *National Key Deer Refuge* for a glimpse of these fragile creatures.

Year after year, the heart of Key West remains the same with its pastel clapboard houses, its hibiscus and bougainvillaea plants, and its souffle of "come what may" residents. You've come all this way, so be sure to see the standard attractions such as *Hemingway's House*, *Sloppy Joe's Bar*, and *Mallory Pier*, where the locals (known as "Conchs") congregate daily to watch horizon-filling sunsets. And don't you dare leave Key West without trying the key lime pie.

For eating out in Key West, don't miss the *Half Shell Raw Bar* for stone crab claws and *Louie's Backyard* (a Key West landmark) for fresh local seafood. For apres-dinner drinks, stop by Sloppy Joe's, where Papa Hemingway used to drink with Sloppy Joe. It's a full-of-character (and characters) place.

Retrace your steps up the keys, back to the Fort Lauderdale area, where you'll then head west on I-75, which is known as *Alligator Alley*. This shoots you right from the Atlantic to the Gulf Coast and cuts through the northern end of the *Big Cypress National Preserve*.

At **Naples**, head north on U.S. 41, detouring to see *Sanibel* and *Captiva Islands*. These two "sister" islands are linked by a causeway to **Fort Myers**. For years, they've been known for the wealth of shells that are washed in with the tide. But there's lots more that make these Gulf gems prime vacation territory. Between the two, you'll find miles of wide, secluded beaches, breezy sailing waters, top-notch sport setups, small shops, and an impressive selection of restaurants.

Continue on up the coast to **Sarasota**, which the circus made famous. See the elegant John Ringling residence, *Ca'd'zan*, as well as the *Ringling museums*. Also see the botanical gardens and the bird sanctuary.

PEEKING AT THE PANHANDLE

Florida's Panhandle is lined by a 100-mile-long sweep of paper-white beach that stretches from **Pensacola** to **Panama City**. And though its pristine sands (often footprintless) and emerald green waters are—undeniably—the area's main attraction, there's some sightseeing too. In Pensacola, visit the *Naval Museum of Aviation* (one of the largest air and space museums in the world), *Seville Square* (the city's historic district), and *Fort Pickens*, where the great Native American hero Geronimo was imprisoned. In **Fort Walton Beach**, inspect the *Indian Temple Mound Museum*, *Eglin Air Force Base*, and the fascinating *Gulfarium*. And in **Destin**, stroll around the "Gone With the Wind" grounds of *Eden House*, a spacious old Southern mansion.

Carry on north to **St. Petersburg** (visit the sunken gardens, the historical museum, the planetarium, seabird sanctuary, and *Fort De Soto Park*), and sister city **Tampa** (highlights include *Old Ybor city*, an art museum, *Busch Gardens Dark Continent* theme park, *Adventure Island* water theme park, and the *Museum of Science and Industry*).

From there, it's a quick drive back to Orlando via I-4.

NATIONAL PARKS IN FLORIDA

Florida is home to three of the nations national parks: *Biscayne National Park, Dry Tortugas National Park,* and *Everglades National Park.*

■ BISCAYNE NATIONAL PARK

Biscayne National Park was established to protect the fragile ecology of a living coral reef that extends for 150 miles just off the Florida coast. It encompasses 181,000 acres of reef, water, keys, and shoreline.

The reef—which can be seen by snorkeling, diving, or by gliding over it in a glass-bottom boat—is an exceedingly beautiful submarine world teeming with phosphorescent fish. On the shore, mangrove jungles provide nesting and feeding grounds for snakes and turtles, and numerous sea birds (pelicans, egrets). The keys are small coral islands covered with tropical flowers.

Fresh-air activities: Year-round boating, snorkeling, diving, fishing, and birdwatching.

For more information: Biscayne National Park, Box 1369, Homestead, FL 33090. (302) 247-7275.

■ DRY TORTUGAS AND EVERGLADES NATIONAL PARKS

Sprawling over 2,000 square miles, these parks are teeming with wild animals and rare birds.

As many as 30 endangered or threatened species have found refuge here including bald eagles, Florida panthers, manatees, American crocodiles, and alligators. In addition, there are hundreds of marine birds and dozens of plant varieties.

Boat and seaplane provide the only access to Dry Tortugas National Park.

Fresh-air activities: Naturalist programs, guided airboat tours, boating, camping, fishing, hiking, nature walks, and birdwatching.

For more information: Everglades National Park, Box 279, Homestead, FL 33030. (305) 242-7700.

Art Deco District—Miami, Florida

Mid-South

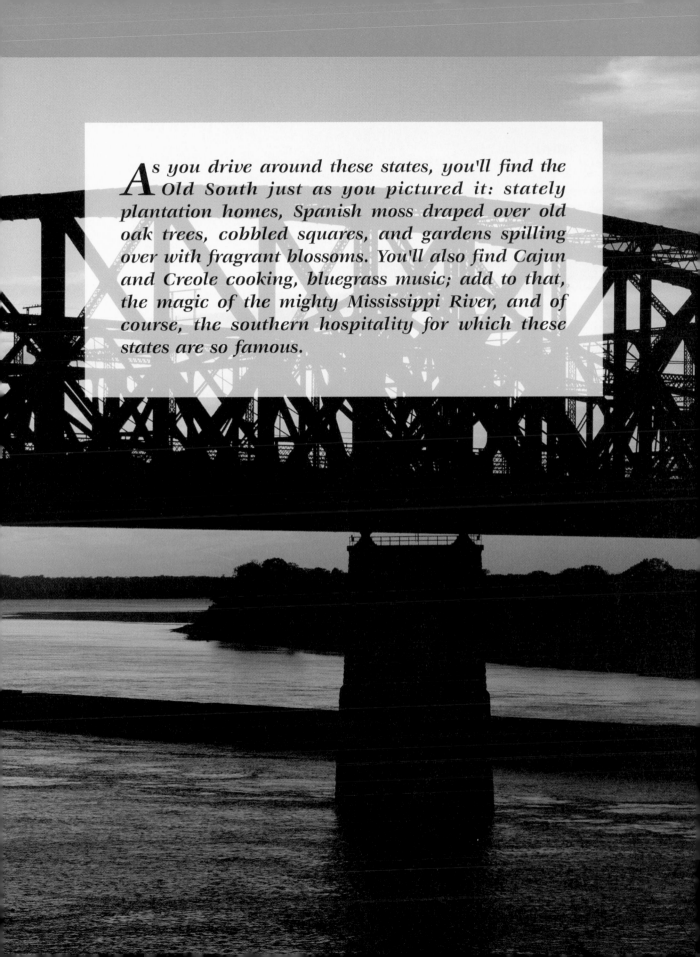

As you drive around these states, you'll find the Old South just as you pictured it: stately plantation homes, Spanish moss draped over old oak trees, cobbled squares, and gardens spilling over with fragrant blossoms. You'll also find Cajun and Creole cooking, bluegrass music; add to that, the magic of the mighty Mississippi River, and of course, the southern hospitality for which these states are so famous.

Bluegrass Country

Churchill Downs—Louisville, Kentucky

Distance: 190 Miles Round Trip, Louisville
Time: Allow at least one day
Highlights: Historic homes and buildings in Louisville, Lexington, and Frankfort, old cemeteries, horse farms, race tracks.

You don't have to be a horse lover to appreciate Kentucky, but if you are, you'll be in your glory. The "Horse Capital of the World" has been a mecca of sorts for thoroughbred horse owners, breeders, and racers since the state was first settled. For this short drive, we take you to the heart of horse country.

Situated on the Ohio River, **Louisville** (pronounced LOU-uh-vul) is where the famed Kentucky Derby takes place each May. If you can't be in town for that, at least visit *Churchill Downs* where the horse races take place. Also see the *Kentucky Derby Museum* (at Churchill Downs) which not only fills you in on the history, but gives betting tips on what makes a horse a "sure thing." Elsewhere in Louisville: wander around the *Riverfront Plaza*, see the *Museum of History and Science*, the *Louisville Zoo*, and the *Zachary Taylor National Cemetery*, where the 12th President of the U.S. is buried.

From Louisville, head east on I-64 to **Frankfort**, Kentucky's capital. Back in 1792, Frankfort was chosen as the state capital as a compromise to settle the rival claims of Louisville and **Lexington**. See the *State Capitol* overlooking the Kentucky River (there are guided tours) and the *Governor's Mansion* which was styled after the Petit Trianon, *Marie Antoinette's villa* at **Versailles**. Also visit the *Old Capitol Building* which was used between 1829-1909 (inside, there's a museum devoted to the history and development of the Commonwealth). Other attractions include *Daniel Boone's Grave* (in Frankfort Cemetery), the *Kentucky Military History Museum*, and *Liberty Hall*, a beautiful Georgian building.

Lexington is about 23 miles east of Frankfort, via I-64. The state's second-largest city and horse capital of the world, it lies in the heart of Bluegrass Country surrounded by sprawling horse farms. You can take a walking, driving, or horse-drawn carriage tour of the city's main attractions including several stately homes that antebellum plantation owners built as summer retreats in milder Lexington. Most of them are a few blocks northeast of the town center in the *Gratz Park* area. Among the most noteworthy are the *Hunt Morgan House*, *Mary Todd Lincoln's childhood home*, and *Henry Clay's Ashland Estate*. At the *University of Kentucky*, there's an *Art Museum* and a *Museum of Anthropology*.

Throughout Lexington-Fayette County, there are more than 400 horse

Bluegrass Country

farms. Though the majority are Thoroughbred farms, there are other breeds including American Saddle Horses, Arabians, Morgans,Quarter Horses, and Standardbreds.

Six miles north of Lexington (take I-75 to exit 120), you'll find the *Kentucky Horse Park*, a thousand-acre state park with facilities for equestrians, a museum devoted to horses, and the *Man O' War Monument*.

Head west out of Lexington on U.S. 60. If you're interested in horse racing, visit the *Keeneland Race Track* (just west of Lexington). This is where the final prep race for the Kentucky Derby takes place every April.

Carry on west through rolling horse farm countryside to Versailles (pro-nounced Ver-SALES) continue on U.S. 62 to U.S. 127 north, then to Route 151 north which will take you back to I-64. Take that west to return to Louisville.

ATTENTION KENTUCKY-BOUND CORVETTE LOVERS

You can't help but get a charge walking around the newly-opened *National Corvette Museum* in **Bowling Green**, Kentucky. Among its fleet of 50 cars, is the original model from 1953, the 1990 ZR1 racing Corvette that set a world record by going 175 miles an hour for a full 24 hours, and the world's only Corvette with an aluminum body. The museum is located a quarter-mile from the world's only Corvette plant, at 350 Corvette Drive. For more information, call (502) 781-7973.

DID YOU KNOW

- *Transylvania University* was the first college west of the Alleghenies.

Bluegrass Thoroughbred horse farm—Lexington, Kentucky

- Kentucky leads the U.S. in bourbon whiskey production.
- The Kentucky Derby is the oldest con-tinually run horse race in the U.S.
- The *Fort Knox Bullion Depository* con-tains more than $6 billion in gold bullion.
- The world's first free-flowing oil well was drilled in **Burkesville**.
- Kentucky tobacco growers lead the world in burley tobacco production.
- The two opposing presidents in the Civil War, Abraham Lincoln and Jefferson Davis, were both born in Kentucky.
- Kentucky is called "the Bluegrass State" because of the blue blossoms on the grass of the region around Lexington.
- Cheeseburgers are a Kentucky invention.
- The world's largest privately owned Coca-Cola collection is in Kentucky.
- **Covington** has the world's largest stained glass window.

MAMMOTH CAVE NATIONAL PARK

About 90 miles south of Louisville, you'll find Mammoth Cave National Park, where there are more than 300 miles of underground corridors, making it the longest known cave system in the world. A variety of tours are offered, lasting anywhere from an hour to half a day. The park also preserves the river valleys of the Green and Nolin rivers and a sec-tion of the hilly country north of Green River. A wide variety of birds and wildflowers can be spotted throughout the forests.

Tooling Around Tennessee

Distance: 542 Miles Round Trip, Nashville
Time: Allow at least four or five days
Highlights: Nashville, Chattanooga, Knoxville, plantation houses, horse farms, battlefields and historic sites, museums, Great Smoky Mountains National Park, white-water rafting, canoeing, swimming, hiking.

Mention Tennessee and country music comes to mind. Not only is it the home state of many popular performers (including Elvis Presley's Graceland Estate in Memphis), but **Nashville's** recording studios are world-renowned for producing some of the most enduring performers and beloved songs. But good old country music is just part of the Tennessee picture. For this drive, we start you off in Nashville and then head south to **Chattanooga** and east to the craggy terrain of the *Great Smoky Mountains*. We then visit **Knoxville** and head back west to Nashville.

If you're not into country music, you'll be happy to know that Nashville's musical repertoire includes a lot more than banjo strumming. In fact, the city is a virtual candy store of music including symphony, rock and roll, and folk. Start by visiting *Music Row*, the center of the city's most famous industry. See the *Country Music Hall of Fame* and the *Recording Studio of America* where you can try out your own vocals with pre-recorded country and popular tune backgrounds. Also check out the *Hank Williams, Jr. Museum*. A short walk west of Music Row, in *Centennial Park*, is the *Parthenon*, an exact-size replica of the Greek original (hence, the nickname "Athens of the South"). Other sights to see include the *Ryman Auditorium*, which was the home of the *Grand Ole Opry* from 1943-1974; the *Tennessee State Capitol*, a Greek-Revival structure; and the *Tennessee State Museum*.

From Nashville, head southeast on I-24, making your first stop in **Smyrna**. Here you'll find the *Sam Davis Home*, which has been described as "the most beautiful shrine to a private soldier in the U.S." The house and working farm have been preserved as a memorial to the Confederate scout who was caught behind Union lines and tried as a spy.

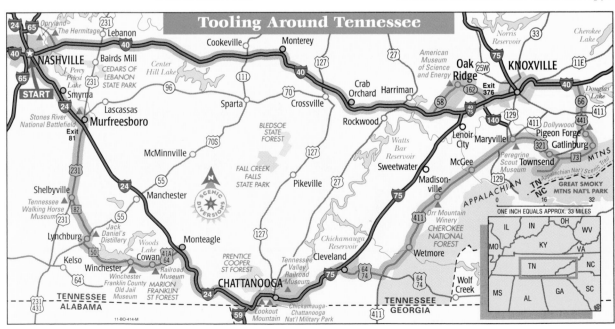

Tooling Around Tennessee

Rather than reveal the name of his informer, Davis chose to be executed. His impeccably restored boyhood home stands in perpetual memory of him.

In **Murfreesboro** (south of Smyrna), you can tour the *Stones River National Battlefield*. The Battle of Stones River took place from December 31, 1862 - January 2, 1863 leaving 10,000 Confederate and 13,000 Union soldiers dead.

Continue south to Exit 81. From there, head south on U.S. 231 to **Shelbyville**, which is where the *Tennessee Walking Horse National Celebration* takes place every August–September. Find out all about this noble horse in the *Tennessee Walking Horse Museum*. There are 50 *Tennessee Walking Horse farms* within a 14-mile radius of town.

From Shelbyville, head south on Route 82 to **Lynchburg**, where you can tour the *Jack Daniel Distillery*. Take Route 58 to **Winchester** where you'll find an operating water-powered *grain mill and museum* that was built in 1873 and the *Winchester Franklin County Old Jail Museum*. Continue east on U.S. 41A/64, stopping to see the *Railroad Museum* in **Cowan**, especially if you're a railroad buff.

Then get on I-24 heading south to Chattanooga, which is surrounded by mountains on three sides. Attractions here include *Lookout Mountain*, *Chickamauga-Chattanooga National Military Park*, *Chattanooga Choo-Choo*, *Creative Discovery Museum*, *Hunter Museum of Art*, and the *Tennessee Valley Railroad Museum*.

Continue east on I-75 to **Cleveland**, a town steeped in Cherokee history and then continue east on U.S. 64/74 and then north on U.S. 411. Consider stopping in **Madisonville** to tour the *Orr Mountain Winery* and then stop in **Maryville** to have a look around the *Peregrine Scout Museum* and the *old schoolhouse where Sam Houston taught*.

From there, head east to **Townsend** and follow Route 73 into the *Great Smoky Mountains National Park*. The lofty *Appalachian Mountains* stand in this 800-square-mile park which is divided between North Carolina and

Music Row—Nashville, Tennessee

Tennessee. To reach one of the visitor's centers, follow Route 73 five miles southeast of Townsend, then eight miles southwest on an unnumbered road. The park is threaded with hiking trails including the *Appalachian National Scenic Trail* which follows the state line for 70 miles. In addition to the wraparound beautiful alpine scenery, the Great Smoky Mountains National Park is home to many descendants of the Cherokee Indian Nation, whose ancestors were driven out of the area over the "Trail of Tears" to Oklahoma.

Continue on to **Gatlinburg**, where you'll find lots of mountain crafts shops to peruse and **Pigeon Forge** a family-focused town with a water park, an amusement park, and *Dollywood*, a theme park devoted to Dolly Parton and homespun mountain fun.

Carry on to Knoxville (U.S. 441 to Route 66 to I-40 west) where you can stroll around the beautifully restored *Old City Historic District* and then move along to **Oak Ridge** (take Route 162 off of I-40) which was once the production center for the atomic bomb. Now a major energy research center, it's most celebrated attraction is the *American Museum of Science and Energy*.

Take Route 58 to I-40 which you can follow back to Nashville.

MAKE A NOTE

helpful hints...

Every June, in the town of Ozark, the Original Ozark Festival takes place. Ozark crafters teach visitors how to weave baskets, churn butter, and make soap. There's lots of music including country, bluegrass, and gospel, and of course, home-cooked and baked treats. For more details, call (800) 951-2525.

About thirteen miles east of Nashville, you'll find *The Hermitage* (Exit 221), Andrew Jackson's manor house situated on 625 acres.

On the eastern outskirts of the city, (north on Briley Parkway) is *Opryland*, a 120-acre entertainment showpark. It's home to the *Grand Ole Opry* (a live radio show) and *TNN* (The Nashville Network), a cable television network.

DID YOU KNOW

- The first guide dog for the blind in the United States was a dog named Buddy, who was trained in Switzerland in 1928 and lived in Nashville with her owner.
- **Kingston** was the capital of Tennessee for one day in 1807.
- In Tennessee in 1886 two brothers competed in a gubernatorial election for the first time.
- The first publications wholly devoted to abolishing slavery were written by a slaveholder in Tennessee.
- From 1784 to 1788 there was a region called Franklin, named after Benjamin Franklin. It became part of Tennessee when it became a state in 1796.
- More Civil War battles were fought in Tennessee than in any other state except Virginia.
- Tennessee's loyalty was so divided during the Civil War that it was the last Confederate state to secede from the Union and the first to return.
- Davy Crockett grew up in Tennessee.
- Tennessee's name is taken from the Cherokee Indian village of Tanasie.
- Tennessee's nickname—the "Volunteer State"—comes from its devoted military traditions.
- The world's largest underground lake is in **Sweetwater**.

Camping near Gatlinburg, Tennessee

BOAT TRIPS

A great way to see and experience Nashville is to climb aboard a riverboat on the Cumberland River. The *Music City Queen* and *Captain Ann* are two boats run by the Belle Carol Riverboat Company that offer daytime sightseeing tours and nighttime party cruises. Call (800) 342-2355 or (615) 244-3430.

Northwest Arkansas

Distance: 574 Miles Round Trip, Little Rock
Time: Allow at least four or five days
Highlights: Museums, Civil War site, Hot Springs National Park, spring waters, swimming, boating, hiking, water skiing, fishing.

A vacationer's playground, the rivers and hills of the Ozark Mountains stretch across Arkansas' northern reaches. Separated by the Arkansas River Valley, the Ouachita Mountains range a bit to the south. Between the two, you'll find plenty of fresh-air diversions, a handful of worthwhile sites to see (including an important Civil War battle site) and the state capital, **Little Rock**.

Start by having a look around Little Rock, which got its name from French explorers who called the site on the Arkansas River, "La Petite Roche" to distinguish it from larger rock outcroppings up the river. See the *State Capitol*, a scaled-down replica of the nation's capitol; the *Quapaw Quarter Historic Neighborhoods* (where more than 60 buildings are listed in the National Register of Historic Places), the *Decorative Arts Museum* and the *Arkansas Art Center*. And don't miss the Clinton exhibit at the *Old Statehouse* with its re-created Oval Office and a Clinton saxophone.

From Little Rock, head north on I-40 to Exit 125. Follow U.S. 65 to Route 25 north toward **Heber Springs**, and then turn left on Route 16. This skirts around *Greers Ferry Lake*, a 50-mile-long lake that was impounded by a dam built by the U.S. Army Corps of Engineers and dedicated by President John F. Kennedy shortly before his assassination. It's now a huge recreation area with swimming, water skiing, scuba diving, boating, hiking, and camping. There's a visitor center about 3 miles northeast of Heber Springs on Route 25 where you can find out all about tours of the dam and powerhouse, nature walks, and learn a little about the history and culture of the southern Ozarks.

Continue north on Route 16, then turn right on U.S. 65. Follow that north and then turn right onto Route 27. Then turn left onto Route 14. Follow this north

to **Yellville**, where you'll turn right on U.S. 62/412, then left onto Route 178. This area is known for its two big lakes: *Bull Shoals* and *Norfolk*. Both lakes are great for canoeing, swimming, and water skiing. They're both also famed for their bass, crappie, catfish, stripers, and rainbow trout. At *Bull Shoals State Park* (on Route 178), you can fish for bass, crappie and trout; go boating, hiking, and picnic.

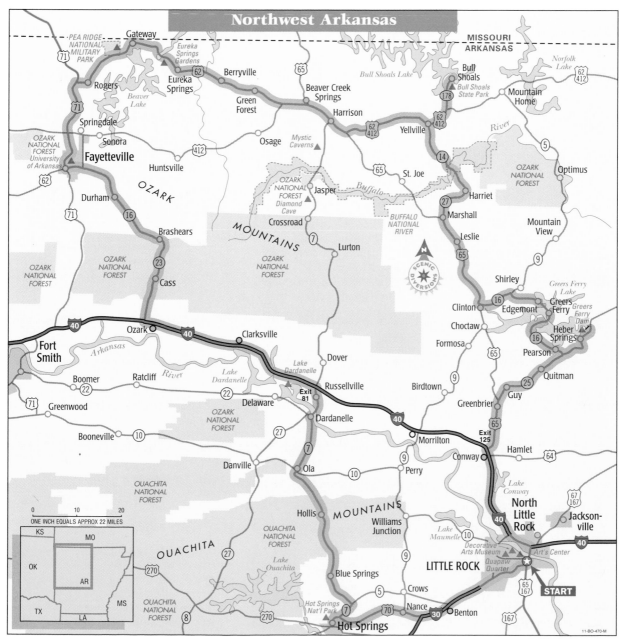

Retrace your steps to Yellville, and then head west for **Harrison**. This is an especially beautiful resort area. If you have time, consider driving south on Route 7 (though we do pick up the southern part of it later in this tour).

Between Harrison in the north and **Hot Springs** in west-central Arkansas, the scenery is consistently lovely with rolling hills and deep green valleys punctuated with small towns.

Continue west on U.S. 62 to **Eureka Springs**, a lovely Victorian town which was a health spa in the 1880s. Within the city limits, there are 63 natural springs.

Follow U.S. 62 as it skirts around the north shore of *Beaver Lake*. You'll soon come to *Eureka Springs Gardens*, a 33-acre park full of blossoms. Continue on west and then south on U.S. 62 to *Pea Ridge National Military Park*. It was the site of an important 1862 Civil War battle which secured Missouri's status with the Union.

Follow U.S. 62 west and then take U.S. 71 south to **Fayetteville**, a resort center in the *Ozark Mountains* and home to the *University of Arkansas*.

From there, head south on Route 16 and then turn right on Route 23. Then head east on I-40 for a bit, and take Exit 81 following Route 7 south to Hot Springs. *Lake Dardanelle* (just west of Russellville) is a popular spot for swimmers, fishermen, and boaters. Route 7 takes you through some of the most densely scenic landscapes of the *Ouachita Mountains*. Follow it to Hot Springs, which is one of the country's most popular spas and resorts. It surrounds portions of *Hot Springs National Park*, where approximately one million gallons of thermal water flow from some 47 springs scattered throughout the wooded landscape. These spring waters were recognized as having extraordinary healing powers by Native Americans and continue to attract visitors seeking treatment for rheumatic and nervous conditions.

Return to Little Rock by heading east on U.S. 70 and then taking I-30 north.

ARKANSAS: DID YOU KNOW

- The thermal water from the springs within Hot Springs National Park has an average temperature of 143° F.
- A shot was fired on a Union boat in the Arkansas River several days before the Southern attack on *Fort Sumter* prompting the local belief that the Civil War started here, not in South Carolina.
- Petit Jean Mountain is named after a French girl who disguised herself as a boy and accompanied her sweetheart sailor to America.
- Hot Springs was considered neutral ground by warring Indian tribes, whose members smoked a peace pipe as they bathed together.
- The Ouachita Mountains stretch from east to west, as opposed to most of the U.S.'s ranges, which run from north to south.
- One out of five Arkansans has a fishing license.
- *Gann Museum*, in **Benton**, is the only known building made of bauxite.
- The water from *Hot Springs Mountain* is so pure that NASA used it to protect the moon rocks collected during the Apollo missions from bacteria.

HS *Belle*—Hot Springs, Arkansas

Hot Springs, Arkansas

Around Mobile Bay

Distance: 97 Miles Round Trip, Mobile
Time: Allow at least one day
Highlights: Antebellum mansions, gardens, bird watching, historic forts, gulf beaches, water sports.

Situated on the Gulf of Mexico, **Mobile** (pronounced mo-BEEL) is one of the South's best-kept secrets. In Alabama's oldest city, you'll find stately Antebellum mansions (many adorned with "iron lace"), oak-lined streets, and azaleas everywhere. Combine a visit here with a drive along Alabama's gulf shores (broken up with visits to forts, historic houses, and other attractions), and you have a perfect introduction to the South.

In Mobile, see the *Bragg-Mitchell Mansion*, which is the most photographed building in the city; the *Carlen House Museum* (a Creole cottage dating back to 1842); the *Conde-Charlotte Museum House* built in 1822; the *Eichold-Heustis Medical Museum* (filled with antique medical instruments); the *Exploreum Museum of Discovery* (hands-on science exhibits); the *Fine Arts Museum of the South*, the *Museum of the City of Mobile*, and *Fort Conde* which was the headquarters of the French colony in Mobile built

between 1724-35. And don't miss *Oakleigh*, the city's official Antebellum period house museum. Built in 1833 on the highest point of what was known as Simon Favre's Old Spanish Land Grant, it's one of Mobile's finest homes.

From Mobile, head southwest on I-10 to Route 59 south. You'll find *Bellingrath Gardens and Home*, an 800-acre estate where over 250,000 azaleas bloom along with hundreds of other varieties of flowering plants. The centerpiece of it all is a stunning antiques-furnished home where tours are offered daily.

Continue south on Route 193 to **Dauphin Island**. Steeped in history, the island was visited by Spaniards in the 16th century. There also was a battle here—The Battle of Mobile Bay—back in 1864. Visitors can tour *Fort Gaines* at the east end of the island, which was manned by Confederate forces from 1861 until it was captured by the Union land troops in 1864. Dauphin Island is a favorite playground for Mobile's residents. It's also home to a 60-acre *bird sanctuary*.

Gulf Coast, Alabama

85

MARK YOUR CALENDAR

If you're planning to visit Mobile in March or early April, you're in luck. Every year the Azalea Trail Festival takes place around this time, when the azaleas are in bloom. A 35-mile-long driving tour winds through the streets in and around Mobile, taking you through the floral extravaganza.

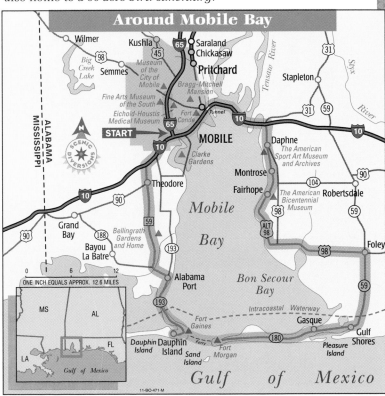

Around Mobile Bay

ONE INCH EQUALS APPROX. 12.6 MILES

0   6   12

MS   AL
LA   FL

Gulf of Mexico

Gulf of Mexico

A ferry service to *Fort Morgan* (just across the opening to Mobile Bay) operates year round. This area was also explored by the Spanish back in 1519. After that, it was held by Spain, France, England, and finally the United States. The fort endured two battles during the War of 1812. There's a museum filled with military artifacts.

Continue east on Route 180 to **Gulf Shores**, the center of a hugely popular beach area on *Pleasure Island,* which is separated from the mainland by the Intracoastal Waterway. There are a total of 32 miles of white sand beach excellant for swimming and fishing.

From Gulf Shores, head north on Route 59 to **Foley** where you can do some outlet shopping at the *Riviera Centre Factory Stores* or look for antiques in *The Gas Works Antique Mall*.

Follow U.S. 98 west to Alt 98 north along Mobile Bay. In **Fairhope**, stop to have a look around the *American Bicentennial Museum* (thousands of items from America's 200th birthday are on display), the *Eastern Shore Art Center*, and the *Marietta Johnson Museum*.

Then carry on to **Daphne**, where you can wander through *The American Sport Art Museum and Archives*. From there, return to I-10 and head west to Mobile.

FISHING IN THE MOBILE AND GULF COAST AREA

Fishing is really big in this area. In Gulf Shores, head for the *Gulf State Park* where you can fish from an 825-foot pier. There are also deep-sea fishing charters and flat-bottom boats available to rent for lake fishing. From Gulf Shores, you can go out on the *Moreno Queen*, (334) 981-8499, for a four or six-hour-long fishing trip. *Orange Beach* has several charter boats to pick from. Fishing licenses can be obtained at most bait shops. For more details, contact the Department of Conservation and Natural Resources, (334) 242-3829.

ALABAMA: DID YOU KNOW

- It was from **Montgomery** that the telegram, "Fire on Fort Sumter," announcing the April 1861 Southern attack on Union troops was sent. Thus began the Civil War.
- The torch held by the statue of *Vulcan*, which towers over **Birmingham**, always burns green, except on days when there has been a traffic fatality—the flame is then red.
- The small town of **Demopolis** was settled in 1817 by the "French Emigrants for the Cultivation of the Vine and Olive," exiles from Napoleon's France who were given four townships by Congress.
- DeSoto Caverns were the first officially recorded caves in the country (1776).
- Horton Mill Covered Bridge, in Gadsen, is the highest covered bridge above the waterline in the U.S. (70 feet).
- The paint used by the "Red Stick" Indians of the early 19th century on their faces and weapons, turned out to be hematite iron ore, which became the foundation of Birmingham's wealth.

Fort Morgan, Alabama

The Old South

Distance: 546 Miles Round Trip, New Orleans
Time: Allow at least four or five days
Highlights: New Orleans, Cajun country, museums, bayou cruises, Indian burial mounds, gardens.

Moss-draped plantations, *Mardi Gras*, heavenly food—there must be a million reasons to visit this part of the world. Here we take you from Louisiana's much loved city of **New Orleans**, through Cajun Country and up to **Natchez**, Mississippi.

Jazz Musicians call it the *"Big Easy."* Locals refer to as "N'Awlins." New Orleans is a city you'll want lots of time to explore. Start in the *French Quarter*, called the "Kaw-tuh" by New Orleanians, and spelled out in French—"Vieux Carre"— on most signs. It's easy to get around on foot. Within a couple of hours, you should know the main streets: Bourbon, Royal, and Chartres (pronounce it "Charters"). To get the most out of your visit, pick up a copy of the *French Quarter Walking Tour* from the tourism booth at 529 St. Ann Street (right on Jackson Square). It will take you past the most significant historical buildings as well as scores of candy-colored houses adorned with wrought-iron porches, gates, and windows. In between, you can peek through fences at tidy little gardens dotted with statues and fountains. Be sure to go to the *French Market* (a two-block-long farmers' market), the *Moon Walk* (a riverside promenade), the *St. Louis Cathedral* (tours given daily), and *Cafe du Monde*, which feels a lot like Paris, where you can sip cafe au lait and feast on beignets (like doughnuts, without holes, smothered

Jackson Square—New Orleans, Louisiana

in confectioner's sugar) as you watch the New Orleans characters stroll by.

While the French Quarter is the city's most romantic district, you might want to see something more: the *New Orleans Museum of Art* (NOMA) in *City Park* and *the Garden District*, which is most fun to see aboard the 150-year-old *St. Charles Avenue streetcar*, clanging up the tree-lined street, passing one mammoth 19th-century mansion after another.

On menus all over New Orleans, you'll find lots of seafood (crab, shrimp, redfish) cooked Creole style, a spicy blend of French, Spanish, and Caribbean influences. After dinner, everybody moves on to *Bourbon Street*, one big open-air party that happens year-round, 24 hours a day. This famous boulevard is lined with jazz clubs, night spots, and bars you may have to queue up for. One of the biggest lines gathers at *Pat O'Brien's*, where everyone goes to sip Hurricanes (watch out!). And there's always a crowd huddled outside *Preservation Hall*. That's where you can hear some of the Big Easy's best jazz musicians strum, toot, and tap out tunes that will give you the chills.

87

Mardi Gras—New Orleans, Louisiana

Once you've had your fill of New Orleans, cross the Mississippi River on either the *Greater New Orleans Bridge* or *Huey P. Long Bridge* and follow U.S. 90 west to Route 1 towards **Thibodaux**, passing bayous and sugar plantations as you go along. Make your first stop the *Laurel Valley Village and Rural Life Museum*, a turn-of-the-century plantation complete with a schoolhouse, general store, boarding house, and the remains of an old sugar mill.

From there, go south on Route 24 and pick up Route 20 southwest. Follow that to **Gibson** and then take U.S. 90 then Route 14 north to **New Iberia**. The center of Louisiana's sugarcane industry, there's a handful of sights to see here. Take a walk around its downtown *Historic District* and don't miss seeing *Shadows-on-the-Teche Plantation*, a red brick and white-pillared Greek revival

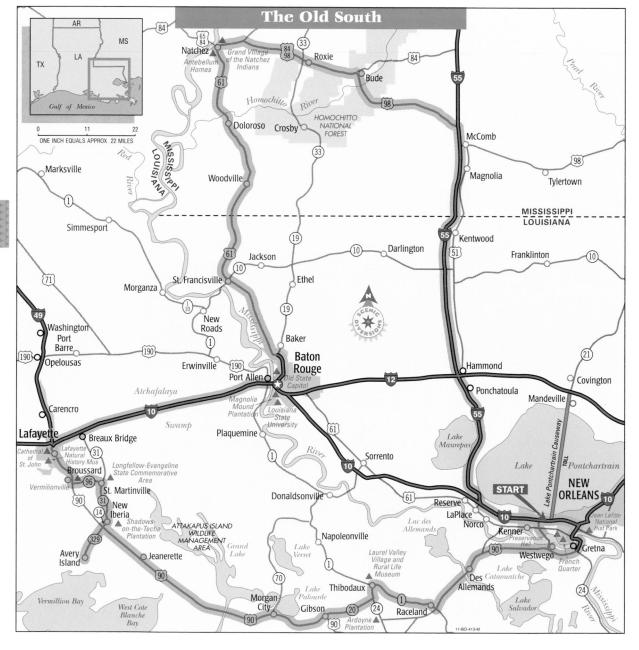

The Old South

house built on the banks of *Bayou Teche*. Nearby, you can find out all about how Tabasco brand pepper sauce is made on *Avery Island* (reached by toll bridge, 7 miles southwest of New Iberia, via Route 14 and 329) at the McIlhenny Company.

From New Iberia, follow Route 31 for about ten miles to **St. Martinville**. This is where Longfellow's heroine Evangaline, (in real life, Emmeline Labiche), ended her journey from Nova Scotia in the 1760s along with many other Acadians. You can see her grave, the *Evangeline Oak* (where she and her lover supposedly met), and a 157-acre *Longfellow- Evangeline State Commemorative Area*. Other attractions in town include the *St. Martin de Tours Church* and the *Petit Paris Museum*. You can also climb aboard the *Cajun Queen* at *Evangeline Oak* for a one-hour cruise on the bayou.

Take Route 96 out of St. Martinville and pick up U.S. 90 northbound to **Lafayette**, Cajun Country's biggest city. Take time to see the *Old City Hall*, the *Cathedral of St. John the Evangelist*, the *Lafayette Museum*, and the *Lafayette Natural History Museum and Planetarium*. Don't miss the *Acadian Village* southwest of town, which is a reconstruction of a small 19th-century Cajun community or Vermilionville, a museum village of crafters, cooks, fiddlers, and storytellers.

From there, head east on I-10, crossing the *Atchafalaya Swamp* and the Mississippi River to **Baton Rouge**, a major river port, with historic homes and tree-lined streets. See the *Old State Capitol* and the newer 34-story Capitol Building which was constructed during the tenure of Governor Huey Long (you can go to the top for a view of the city). Other attractions include the *Old Arsenal Museum*, an arboretum, *Magnolia Mound and Mt. Hope Plantations* (two 19th-century houses), the *Rural Life Museum* and the preserved *Indian mounds* at *Louisiana State University*, and steamboat excursions. The *Old Governor's Mansion*, which resembles The White House, offers weekend tours (by appointment).

From Baton Rouge, head north on U.S. 61 to Natchez, Mississippi, where the Old South is very much alive. There are lovely Antebellum and Victorian mansions (many listed in the National Register of Historic Places), tree-shaded streets, manicured gardens and grounds. Many of the houses are open for touring. See also the *City Cemetery* which dates from the early 1800s, *Emerald Mound* (an Indian mound constructed about 1300 AD), the *Grand Village of the Natchez Indians*, the *Natchez Museum of African-American History and Culture*, and *Natchez Under-the-Hill*, the historic waterfront district.

Stanton Hall—Natchez, Mississippi

From Natchez, head east on U.S. 98 to I-55 which you can follow south back into the New Orleans area.

MARDI GRAS AND MORE

New Orleans is certainly a good place to be for Mardi Gras, but the rest of the year, the city always has a tipsy air of carnival with its profusion of festivals, parades, and celebrations. In March alone there's a Black Heritage Festival, an environmental festival called Earth Fest, a St. Patrick's Day Parade, St. Joseph's Day Festivities, and a Tennessee Williams Literary Festival. For a complete calendar of events, write: New Orleans Metropolitan Convention and Visitors Bureau, 1520 Sugar Bowl Drive, New Orleans, LA 70112. (504) 566-5005

INN-SIDE INFORMATION

For staying in New Orleans' French Quarter, consider the Soniat House on Chartres Street. It's a perfect Southern inn, with high-ceilinged rooms filled with canopy and four-poster beds, Victorian love seats, and antique furnishings that would look at home in a palace.

You'll fall in love with breakfast: still-warm biscuits accompanied by homemade strawberry preserves, just-squeezed orange juice, and rich Creole coffee served in your room, on your patio, or in the courtyard. For more information, call (504)522-0570.

Prairie States

You always hear how young America is as a country. However, spend a week or two exploring these states, and you'll be bombarded with images of how old this country really is. You'll see land that was shaped by erosion over the past half-million years, fossils of prehistoric animals, and caves that go on for miles. There are also numerous signs of recent events, such as, Indian reservations, pioneer sites, and historic landmarks. Thanks to the laws governing national parks and forests, these historical treasures live on, bringing the past into the present and preserving it for the future.

Walnut Hill, Living History Farms
Urbandale, Iowa

America's Heartland

Distance: 1630 Miles Round Trip, St. Louis
Time: Allow at least one week to ten days
Highlights: Museums, historic houses, churches, boating, camping, swimming, and horseback riding.

On this diversion, we take you back to the days of the pioneers by exploring Missouri, Kansas, and Iowa.

Missouri's largest city, **St. Louis**, near the confluence of the *Missouri* and *Mississippi rivers*, was the gateway to the West back in the pioneer days. This era is memorialized by the *Gateway Arch*, a 630-foot-high stainless steel structure that was designed by Finnish-American architect Eero Saarinen. Among the city's other attractions are the *Museum of Westward Expansion*, the *Sports Hall of Fame*, cathedrals, the *National Museum of Transport*, an art museum, a science center, and a botanical garden.

From St. Louis, head west on I-70 to **Fulton**. On the campus of *Westminister College* where Winston Churchill gave his "Iron Curtain" speech in 1946, you'll find a 17th-century *Christopher Wren church* that was brought here from England and reassembled.

Take U.S. 54 south to **Jefferson City**, which, like many state capitals, nobody ever guesses right on a name-the-capitals trivia quiz. Named after Thomas Jefferson, it is locally known as "Jeff City." Attractions here include the *State Capitol*, the *Governor's Mansion*, the *Cole County Historical Society Museum*, and the *Missouri Veterinary Medical Foundation Museum*.

About 54 miles southwest of the capital on Route 54 is *Lake of the Ozarks State Park*. The lake itself was formed by the *Bagnell Dam* constructed across the Osage River. It's a popular recreation area with boating, camping, swimming, and horseback riding.

Springfield is the next stop (follow I-44). This city is known as a the "Gateway to Ozark Mountain Country" and is close to some of the state's most beautiful scenery. See the *History Museum*, the *Art Museum*, and the *National Cemetery* (where both Union and Confederate soldiers are buried).

From Springfield, detour south (on U.S. 65) to **Branson**, a resort town in the Ozarks featuring more than 40 music/variety shows. *Table Rock Dam* is on the *White River* about six miles southwest of Branson, an excellent fishing spot.

ON THE ROAD AGAIN

Here's a real find: *American Dream Safari* offers 7 and 14-day escorted tours through select American landscapes in classic 1950 cars and trailers. Tours include a 3 - 5 day *Prairie Tour* through the Kansas area, a *Desert Southwest trip* (through parts of Arizona and New Mexico), and a *Blues Pilgrimage* (including New Orleans, The Delta Region, Memphis, and more). Tours are designed for small groups (2 - 6 travelers) in order to be flexible and spontaneous. If you don't want to go on an extended trip, you can take the two-hour sunset Prairie Cruise from Kansas City. You'll explore the prairie countryside in a beautifully restored two-ton wheat truck. Contact American Dream Safari, P.O. Box 556, McPherson, KS 67460-0556. (800) 552-2397.

America's Heartland

(map of America's Heartland — Prairie States, showing Iowa, Nebraska, Kansas, Missouri, and parts of Illinois, Wisconsin, Oklahoma, Arkansas, with cities including Sioux City, Waterloo, Dubuque, Des Moines, Omaha, Lincoln, Kansas City, St. Joseph, Topeka, Wichita, Springfield, St. Louis, and route markers. Scale: ONE INCH EQUALS APPROX. 70 MILES)

93

Backtrack to Springfield and then go west on I-44 and then north on U.S. 71. At the town of Nevada, turn left onto U.S. 54 and cross the border into Kansas. Right at the junction of U.S. 69 and U.S. 54, you'll find the *Fort Scott National Historic Site*, a frontier military post that saw action during the Civil War. There are some restored buildings, a museum, and a visitor center.

Continue on to **Wichita**, the largest city in Kansas. Take time out to see the *Old Cowtown Museum*, which is a 40-building historic museum village. Also see the *Indian Center Museum*, the *Omnisphere and Science Center*, the *Wichita Art Museum*, and the *Allen-Lambe House Museum and Study Center*, which is considered the last of Frank Lloyd Wright's prairie houses.

At Exit 34, take Route 15 north to **Abilene**, which was once famous as a Kansas "cow town." Back in 1867, it was the terminal point of the Kansas Pacific

Gateway Arch—St. Louis, Missouri

Railroad and the nearest railhead for the shipment of cattle brought over the Chisholm Trail. Take a walk around "*Old Abilene Town*" which includes original buildings of the town's cattle boom days. Also see the *Eisenhower Center*, where Dwight Eisenhower and his five brothers were raised. The grave sites of Ike and Mamie, his wife, are also here.

Take I-70 east to **Kansas City**. The greater Kansas City metropolitan area is comprised of both Kansas City, Kansas and Kansas City, Missouri. Most of the attractions are on the Missouri side, but the Kansas side has its share with an Indian cemetery, *1857 Grinter House* (Grinter was the first permanent white settler in Wyandotte County) and a 20-acre wildlife preserve.

On the Missouri side, visitor highlights include the *Kansas City Museum*, the *Liberty Memorial Museum*, the *Toy and Miniature Museum*, the *Arabia Steamboat Museum*, the *Nelson-Atkins Museum of Art*, and *Crown Center* (a "city within a city" with shops, theaters, restaurants, and hotels).

Nearby **Independence**, Missouri is best known as the home of President Harry S Truman. It used to be the jumping-off point for pioneers heading west along the Santa Fe, California, and

Pony Express

Oregon trails. See the *Harry S Truman Library and Museum*, the *Harry S Truman Courtroom and Office Museum*, the *Harry S Truman National Historic Site*, and the *Truman Farm Home*. Other attractions include the *Bingham-Waggoner Estate* (where the Missouri artist George Bingham lived from 1864-1870) and the *1859 Marshal's Home and Jail Museum*.

Take I-29 north to **St. Joseph**. Once the starting point of the Pony Express, the town is now home to the *Pony Express Museum* and several other historical houses and museums.

From there, take U.S. 36 east and then I-35 north, crossing the border into Iowa. The state's largest city and capital, **Des Moines**, is next. Attractions here include the *Science Center of Iowa*, the *Polk County Heritage Gallery*, the *Botanical Center*, *Blank Park Zoo*, the *State Capitol* with its gold-leaf dome, *Salisbury House*, the Victorian mansion *Terrace Hill* and the *Living History Farms* in nearby **Urbandale**.

From Des Moines, head east on I-80 to U.S. 151 north, stopping at the *Amana Colonies*.

These seven villages (west of **Iowa City** and south of **Cedar Rapids**) are Iowa's leading tourist destination. The history of the communities goes back more than 250 years when a Lutheran separatist group from Germany settled here. Attractions include general stores, wineries, bakeries, a woolen mill, furniture and clock shops, and hearty German family-style restaurants.

Continue on U.S. 151 through Cedar Rapids to **Dubuque**. Situated along the Mississippi River where Iowa, Illinois,

Harry S Truman's House—Independence, Missouri

94

and Wisconsin meet, Dubuque was once a lead mining center. Of interest are the *Fenelon Place Elevator*, the *Mathias Ham House Historic Site*, the 130 year-old *farmers' market*, *General Zebulon Pike Lock and Dam*, and the *Old Shot Tower* where Civil War cannonballs were fashioned from molten lead.

Cross the Mississippi on U.S. 20 and take Route 84 south, the *Great River Road*, through the Quad Cities metropolitan area. Go back across the river on I-280 and then continue south on U.S. 61 to **Hannibal**, which was Mark Twain's boyhood home.

Return to St. Louis via U.S. 61.

Nebraska and the Dakotas

Distance: 2107 Miles Round Trip, Omaha
Time: Allow at least one week to ten days
Highlights: Pioneer museums and landmarks, natural wonders, two national parks, historic houses, camping, fishing, and bird watching; cross-country skiing in winter.

If you're interested in seeing some of America's most astounding natural and man-made wonders, head to this part of the country. For this diversion, we take you from **Omaha**, Nebraska, through many towns steeped in pioneer history. We travel up to South Dakota, where the faces of U.S. presidents Washington, Jefferson, Roosevelt, and Lincoln survey the *Black Hills* and we visit the southwestern corner of North Dakota, which is home to the *Theodore Roosevelt National Park*, before meandering slowly back to Omaha.

In Omaha, Nebraska's largest city, you can take your pick of museums: the *Joslyn Art Museum*, the *Great Plains Black Museum*, the *Omaha Children's Museum*, the *Union Pacific Historical Museum*, and the *Western Heritage Museum*. Then plan to spend some time strolling around the *Old Market* which is a revitalized warehouse district. Also see the *Henry Doorly Zoo* and nearby **Boys Town**.

Missouri River

From Omaha, head south on I-80 to **Lincoln**, the state's capital. Here you'll find a magnificent capitol building designed by Bertram Goodhue and once voted the "fourth architectural wonder of the world" by a nationwide poll of architects. Other attractions in Lincoln include the *University of Nebraska State Museum*, the *Museum of Nebraska History*, and the *National Museum of Roller Skating*.

Continue west to **Grand Island**, where you'll find the *Stuhr Museum of the Prairie Pioneer*. It includes a restored prairie town and railroad.

North Platte is next on the itinerary as you continue west on I-80. This railroad town was once the home of Buffalo Bill, who originated his first public rodeo here. You can see his home and ranch, the *Lincoln County Historical Museum*, *Cody Park*, and *Fort McPherson National Cemetery* where soldiers and scouts of Indian and later wars are buried.

Take exit 126 to U.S. 26 north. *Chimney Rock National Historic Site* is about 13 miles west of Bridgeport off of U.S. 26. Chimney Rock rises almost 500 feet above the bank of the North Platte River. For early travelers, this rock marked the end of the prairies. A local museum offers exhibits devoted to pioneer history. Another pioneer landmark is *Scotts Bluff National Monument* which is just three miles west of **Gering**. This 800-foot bluff was spotted by many a pioneer who traveled the California/Oregon Trail by wagon train.

Turn right onto Route 29 and follow that north stopping to see the fossils of prehistoric beasts at *Agate Fossil Beds National Monument* before continuing on to U.S. 20 where you'll turn right. Consider pausing awhile in *Fort Robinson State Historical Park*, which stands on what was once the site of a

Red Cloud's Grave
Pine Ridge Indian Reservation, South Dakota

IN NEARBY WYOMING

While visiting all the natural wonders of South Dakota, consider cruising over the border on I-90 into Wyoming to see Devil's Tower National Monument. Rising 1,267 feet above the banks of the Belle Fourche River in Wyoming's neck of the Black Hills, this fluted rock monolith is a sight to behold.

frontier army post. The army settlement has been completely restored with officers' quarters, a museum, and a parade ground where staffers in uniform re-enact 19th-century roles. There are stagecoach and Jeep rides, cookouts, and horseback riding.

To the east, in **Chadron**, you'll find the *Museum of the Fur Trade* which recreates the trading posts of the early 19th century. *Chadron State Park* offers lakes, trails, and campsites.

Continue east on U.S. 20, and then turn left at **Merriman** to cross the border into South Dakota. Route 73 takes you right through the *Pine Ridge Indian Reservation*. When you reach I-90, head west to get to *Badlands National Park*. Take Exit 131 to follow Route 240 which winds through the northern part of the park taking you by some of its most spectacular scenery. A lonesome landscape of canyons, wind-carved spires and buttes, and prairie grasslands—the Badlands were slowly shaped by erosion over the past half-million years. The whole area was once submerged beneath an extensive sea that spanned the Great Plains.

On the *Fossil Exhibit Trail* you can see remains of fleet-footed rhinos and predecessors of the horse that roamed the area 23 million to 37 million years ago.

From the Badlands, continue west on I-90 and pick up Route 79 south at **Rapid City** if you want to visit **Hot Springs**. Follow that to U.S. 385 north and around to the town of Hot Springs where waters bubble at a constant 82 degrees Fahrenheit. Nearby is the *Wind Cave National Park*. Though this park is clearly named after its underground cave, its above-ground appeals are also very noteworthy. It is largely prairie land colonized by prairie dogs, small herds of bison, and pronghorn sheep. It is also home to a wide variety of plants and trees including ponderosa pines, cacti, and cottonwood. Below the surface, the limestone Wind Cave goes on and on for about 52 miles.

The *Black Hills National Forest* is an enormous nature preserve—1,236,000

Black Hills, South Dakota

acres—with forests, mountains (the highest east of the Rockies), ghost towns, and the famous profiles of *Mount Rushmore*. Take your time exploring. Be sure to see the *Crazy Horse Memorial*, which is the world's largest statue, currently being carved by sculptor Korczak Ziolkowski, from a 563-foot mountain about five miles north of **Custer**. The statue will depict Crazy Horse, the Sioux Indian Chief who defeated Lieutenant Colonel Custer and the U.S. 7th Calvary. Also see the *Jewel Cave National Monument*, where there are over 78 miles of cave passageways, making it the second largest in the United States. And plan to spend some time in Custer, an old gold mining town. See the *Custer County Courthouse Museum* and the *National Museum of Woodcarving*. The Needles Highway (Route 87) takes you right through *Custer State Park*, which is home to one of the largest remaining bison herds in the U.S. Just 14 miles long, it follows the hiking route that Peter Norbeck, a former governor of South Dakota, loved to travel. It takes you past towering rock formations and captures the haunting essence of the Black Hills.

And of course, Mount Rushmore, where the president's faces measure 60 feet from forehead to chin. Led by sculptor Gutzon Borglum, America's "*Shrine of Democracy*" took 14 years to complete.

North of the Black Hills National Forest, get on U.S. 85 north, crossing the border into North Dakota. Turn left on I-94 to reach the south unit of the *Theodore Roosevelt National Park*. This park is a monument to

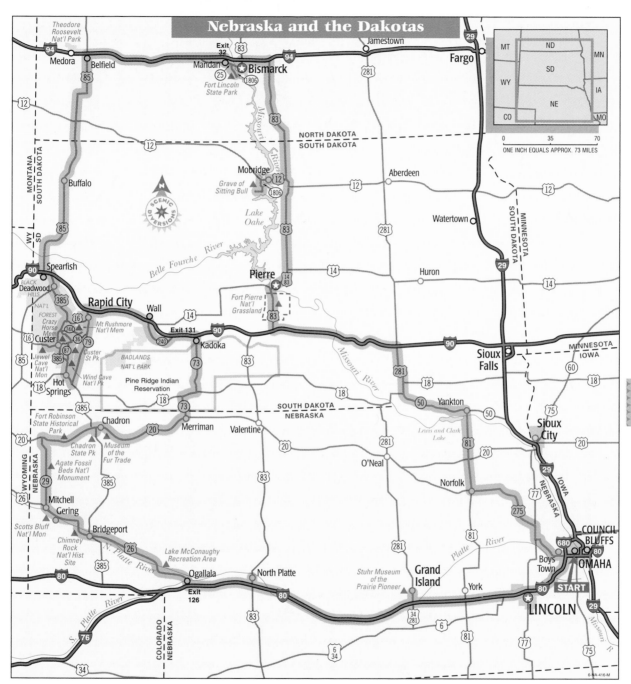

Nebraska and the Dakotas

Theodore Roosevelt who first came to North Dakota in 1883. Much of the landscape—rugged Missouri River Badlands—is preserved as he first saw it. There are virgin prairies, deep canyons, and a petrified forest. Wildlife seen in the park includes buffalo, deer, elk, wild horses, prairie dogs, and bighorn sheep.

From there, head east on I-94 to **Mandan**, which is located across the Missouri River from **Bismarck**. It is named after the Indians who lived here. To the south, *Fort Lincoln State Park* features the restored home of George Armstrong

Custer and a reconstructed earth lodge Indian village.

Bismarck, the state capital, is next. Sights to see here include the *North Dakota Heritage Center* with its Plains Indian artifacts, the *State Capitol*, the former governor's mansion, and *Camp Hancock State Historic Site*.

East of Bismark, take U.S. 83 south, detouring three miles west on U.S. 12 and then four miles south on county road 1806 to see the *burial site of Sitting Bull*. Korczak Ziolkowski sculpted the bust for this monument. From the burial ground, it's a lovely view of the Missouri River and surrounding countryside.

Take U.S. 83 south to **Pierre**, South Dakota's capital. See the *State Capitol*, the *Cultural Heritage Museum*, and the *State National Guard Museum*.

From Pierre, head south through the *Fort Pierre National Grassland*, and then go east on I-90, then south on U.S. 281 then turn left on Route 50. Follow that around to **Yankton**, and then continue south on U.S. 81 to **Norfolk**. Then take U.S. 275 south back into Omaha.

NATIONAL PARKS

■ *BADLANDS NATIONAL PARK*

Wall, South Dakota

A lonesome landscape of canyons, wind-carved spires and buttes, and prairie grasslands—the Badlands were slowly shaped by erosion over the past half-million years. The whole area was once submerged beneath an extensive sea that spanned the Great Plains.

Though at first glance a seemingly inhospitable place, the Badlands have been home to humans for more than 12,000 years, The earliest inhabitants were mammoth hunters, The *Fossil Exhibit Trail* offers glimpses of fossil bones left by predators and scavengers of even earlier times, more than 30 million years ago.

Fresh-air activities: Nature walks and talks, camping, fishing, hiking, and bird watching year round.

For more information: Badlands National Park, Box 6, Interior, SD 57750. (605) 433-5361.

■ *THEODORE ROOSEVELT NATIONAL PARK*

Medora, North Dakota

This sprawling 70,447-acre park, a tribute to Teddy Roosevelt, is com-

Badlands, North Dakota

Mt. Rushmore National Memorial, South Dakota

prised of two units. The *North Unit* straddles the Little Missouri River. A 15-mile scenic drive has turnouts which provide panoramic vistas. Trails wind through river woodlands and badlands. The *South Unit* can be reached via I-94 at Medora, It features a 36-mile scenic loop road with interpretive signs describing the park's cultural and natural history.

Fresh-air activities: Hiking, horseback riding, bird watching, camping, and canoeing from May to October; snowmobiling in winter.

For more information: Theodore Roosevelt National Park, Box 7, Medora, ND 58645. (701) 623-4466.

■ *WIND CAVE NATIONAL PARK*

Hot Springs, South Dakota

Located in the Black Hills, the park can be reached by several scenic roads. Though originally created to protect the cave, protecting the wildlife—prairie dogs, bison, pronghorn sheep, and coyotes—is also part of the park's mission. The park is also home to a variety of common plant species such as ponderosa pines, American elms, and prairie grasses. To experience the wonders of the underground, there are ranger-guided tours of the more than 70 miles of known passages in Wind Cave. Be sure to wear non-slip shoes. Because of the cool temperature of the cave, bring along a light jacket or sweater.

Fresh-air activities: Ranger-led cave trips, naturalist programs, camping, hiking, nature walks, and bird watching year round.

For more information: Wind Cave National Park, Hot Springs, SD 57747. (605) 745-4600.

DID YOU KNOW

• The geographic center of North America is located near the town of **Balta**, North Dakota.
• Nebraska, now a leading farming state, was once part of the *"Great American Desert."* Through early irrigation systems and scientific farming, 95% of the state is now made up of farms.

THE DAYS OF OLD

By visiting the Living History Farms in Urbandale, Iowa, a suburb of Des Moines, you can rewind American history and watch 300 years of agricultural history evolve.

This 600-acre open-air museum is home to four working farms, including an early 1700 Iowa Indian encampment, an 1850s farmstead (an oak cabin as its centerpiece), a 1900 farm complete with a clapboard house and windmill, and the Farm of Today and Tomorrow with a solar-heated dome.

Interpreters, dressed in clothing of various times, bring the past into the present by carrying out their various farm tasks with methods and tools that were used in their respective periods. For more details, call (515) 278-5286.

The Rockies

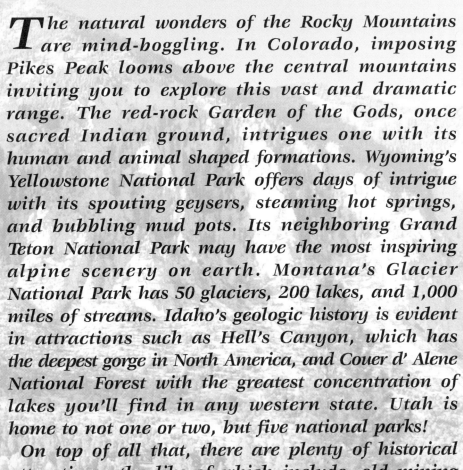

*T*he natural wonders of the Rocky Mountains are mind-boggling. In Colorado, imposing Pikes Peak looms above the central mountains inviting you to explore this vast and dramatic range. The red-rock Garden of the Gods, once sacred Indian ground, intrigues one with its human and animal shaped formations. Wyoming's Yellowstone National Park offers days of intrigue with its spouting geysers, steaming hot springs, and bubbling mud pots. Its neighboring Grand Teton National Park may have the most inspiring alpine scenery on earth. Montana's Glacier National Park has 50 glaciers, 200 lakes, and 1,000 miles of streams. Idaho's geologic history is evident in attractions such as Hell's Canyon, which has the deepest gorge in North America, and Couer d' Alene National Forest with the greatest concentration of lakes you'll find in any western state. Utah is home to not one or two, but five national parks!

On top of all that, there are plenty of historical attractions, the like of which include, old mining settlements, restored Victorian villages, ghost towns, even Indian cliff dwellings.

Glacier National Park & Environs

Distance: 626 Miles Round-Trip, Coeur d'Alene
Time: Allow at least five days
Highlights: Glacier National Park, lakes, boating, rafting, hiking, bird-watching, horseback riding, camping, fishing.

GO FISHING

Every summer there are fishing derbies at *Coeur d'Alene Lake* including "Catch The Big One" where the fisherman pulling in the largest Chinook salmon can win cash and prizes.

102

For this drive, we take you through two mesmerizingly beautiful landscapes—Idaho's lake country and Montana's glacier country.

Tucked away in the northern corner (the panhandle) of Idaho is *Coeur d'Alene Lake*, one of several lakes for which the area is known. In fact, this area has the greatest concentration of lakes you'll find in any western state. The lake—which is backdropped by mountains and stunning alpine scenery—is a magnet for outdoor lovers who come to go swimming, boating, waterskiing, fishing, and bird-watching (it's home to the largest population of osprey in the

Swiftcurrent Lake—Glacier National Park, Montana

Western U.S.). On the northern shore is the city of **Coeur d'Alene** which is home to the *Museum of North Idaho* (where you can learn all about the lake's steamboat era) and *Fort Sherman* and the *Fort Sherman Museum*.

From Coeur d'Alene, head north on U.S. 95 to **Sandpoint**, a resort town on the shores of *Lake Pend Oreille*, the largest lake in the northern lakes (43 miles long and over a thousand feet deep) completely encircled by mountains. While in town, check out *The Cedar Street Bridge*, a marketplace on a bridge. Also see the *Vintage Wheel Museum*, with its collection of vintage vehicles.

North of Sandpoint (continue on U.S. 95), is **Bonners Ferry**, a scenic little community. A short distance west of town is the *Kootenai Tribal Mission*, where the Kootenai Tribe of Idaho has an experimental sturgeon hatchery. Nearby is the *Kootenai Wildlife Refuge* with hiking trails and self-guided auto tours.

Head east on U.S. 2 and cross the border into Montana. Known as *Glacier Country*, this part of the state is sensationally scenic. As you drive along, you'll see magnificent peaks, meadows carpeted with wildflowers, powerful rivers, and wildlife (keep an eye out for eagles, marmots, and mountain goats).

One of the first towns you'll come to is **Troy**. At its *Ross Creek Cedar Grove Scenic Area*, you can walk among cedars that are more than 500 years old and 250 feet high. Carry on to **Libby** where you can find out a little about the area's history in the *Heritage Museum* and then head east on U.S. 2 to **Kalispell**. Stop to have a look at the *Victorian Conrad Mansion*, which was built in 1895 as the home of C.E. Conrad, a Montana pioneer, Missouri River trader, and founder of Kalispell. Also stop in at the *Hockaday Center for the Arts* to see some regional and national artwork.

Continue north on U.S. 2 which skirts the south end of *Glacier National Park*. The park's west entrance is directly off this highway at **West Glacier**. Lying on the U.S./Canadian border, Glacier National Park joins

Waterton Lakes National Park in **Alberta**, Canada to create *Waterton-Glacier International Peace Park*.

When you get inside, follow the *Going-to-the-Sun Road*, the park's number one attraction. With its panorama of craggy peaks and glistening lakes, this road has been described as one of the most magnificent drives in the world. The best way to really see this park, however, is on foot.

Exit the park at **St. Mary** and head south on U.S. 89. Then turn right onto Route 49 and follow that to U.S. 2. This will take you along the edge of the southern end of the park. At Route 206, turn left and follow that to Route 35, which takes you along the eastern shore of *Flathead Lake*, the largest natural freshwater lake west of the Mississippi. There's fishing, boating, and swimming available.

In **Polson**, get on U.S. 93 and follow it west to Route 28 which will take you to **Plains** where there is a log schoolhouse right on Main Street. Turn left onto Route 200, go through **Paradise**, and then turn right onto Route 135. At

St. Regis, get on I-90 heading west to get back to Coeur d'Alene.

TRAVELING WITH CHILDREN IN NATIONAL PARKS

When traveling with children in the National Parks, its important to be as self-sufficient as possible. Be sure to take along diapers, formula, and any special medications or food your child might need. Don't forget to pack a complete first-aid kit (see page 106). Also take along your pediatricians phone number, and if you have one, a cellular phone. In the National Parks, you can be driving through dense wilderness for long periods of time. If you do any hiking, there's always the chance of someone twisting an ankle or having some other accident. For long car trips, it's a good idea to have your children pack their own car bag with their favorite books and toys to play with en route. Pack snacks, too. Your not always going to find yourselves near a grocery store.

Glacier National Park, Montana

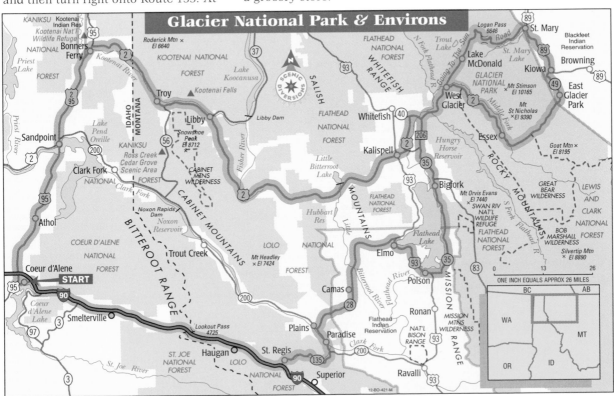

Glacier National Park & Environs

Skiing the Rockies in Idaho

MUSIC IN THE AIR

Throughout the summer months, the Idaho Shakespeare Festival takes place at the amphitheater in Boise. For program and ticket information, call (208)336-9221.

Inside Idaho

Distance: 351 Miles Round-Trip, Boise

Time: Allow at least three or four days

Highlights: Boise attractions, mountain scenery, old mining towns, air force base, hiking, white-water rafting, fishing, skiing, skating, and other winter sports.

M onumental mountains, thundering rivers, alpine lakes... Idaho is heart-poundingly beautiful. For this drive we take you to the capital, **Boise** and then to the *Sawtooth Wilderness Area* and nearby *Sun Valley*, a world-famous ski resort. From there, we guide you back to Boise, making a stop at *Mountain Home Air Force Base.*

Established during the gold-rush days, Boise is both the capital and the largest city in Idaho. It's known as the "City of Trees," and is beautifully situated against the foothills of the *Rocky Mountains*. The open-air *Boise Tour Train* (which starts at Julia Davis Park) is a fun way to see the city during the warm-weather months. Pulled by a replica of an 1890 puff-belly

Five Nations Indian Powwow—Boise, Idaho

engine, it chugs along taking you by all the major sights.

Many of the city's attractions are located in and around *Julia Davis Park*. There's the *City Zoo*, the *Boise Art Museum*, the *Idaho State Historical Museum*, and *The Discovery Center of Idaho* which offers interactive exhibits for all ages. Boise also has an impressive *State Capitol Building* and an old penitentiary (one of only four territorial prisons still in existence). See also the *Idaho Botanical Gardens* and the *Morrison-Knudsen Nature Center*. For a far-reaching view of the entire valley area, head north to *Bogus Basin Ski Area* (it's about a 45-minute drive) where there are picnic areas at about 7,590 feet.

From Boise, follow Route 21 northeast (it's known as the *Ponderosa Pine Scenic Byway*) to **Idaho City**, a beautifully restored gold rush town. In fact, the area surrounding the community is said to have produced more gold than all of Alaska. You can try your hand at panning for gold here in the area's creeks. For about $5, the *Idaho City Hotel* provides you with a pan and instructions.

With your new-found fortune, continue heading north through **Lowman** and on to **Stanley**, the gateway to the *Sawtooth National Recreational Area* and headquarters for float trips down the *Salmon River*. At the ranger station, you can pick up a pre-recorded, mile-post tour of scenic highway 75 which cuts through the mountains, and return it at the south end. The drive here is sensationally scenic with peaks in every direction competing for your attention. There are also 300 lakes, plus

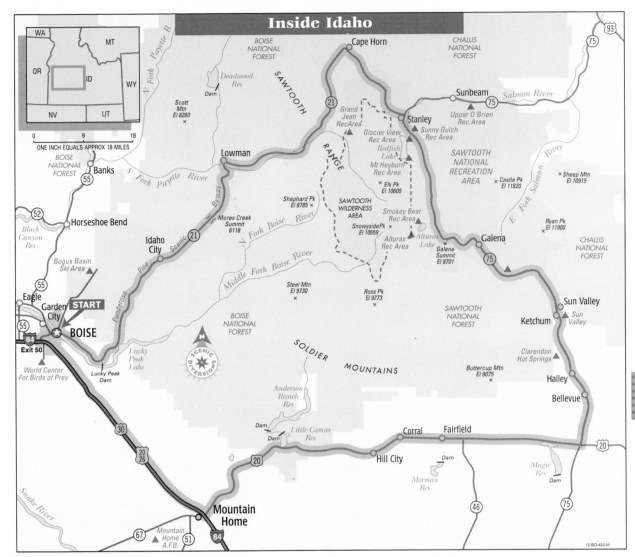

Inside Idaho

the nation's highest elevation hatchery (which you can tour).

Ketchum and **Sun Valley** are just south of the Sawtooths. These well-known ski resort areas are actually year-round vacation destinations. There are alpine golf courses, plenty of tennis courts and pools, and an extensive trail system that can be used for biking, in-line skating, running, and walking. You can also go fishing and horseback riding in impossibly beautiful landscapes.

In Ketchum, take time to see the *Ernest Hemingway Memorial*. The Nobel prize winning author lived here near the end of his life and was buried in the *Ketchum cemetery*.

Head south on Route 75 and then turn right onto U.S. 20 towards **Mountain Home**. This is where the Mountain Home Air Force Base is located. It's home of the nation's air intervention composite wing. The annual air show is held every October, and is open to the public.

From there, you can cruise back to Boise on I-84, making your last stop at the *World Center for Birds of Prey* (exit 50) on the outskirts of town. Here you can get an up-close look at birds of prey and their environments.

Panning for Gold—Idaho City, Idaho

FIRST AID KITS

If you're going to be visiting the National Parks—or any other wilderness area—be sure to take along a first aid kit. Here are suggested items to include:

- Adhesive bandages
- A first-aid manual
- A needle
- Antibiotic ointment
- Antihistamines
- Antiseptic cream
- Any necessary prescriptions
- Aspirin
- Butterfly bandages
- Calamine lotion
- Elastic bandage
- Insect repellent
- Matches
- 1" wide adhesive tape
- Razor blades
- Scissors
- Sterile gauze pads (2"x2" and 4"x4")
- Sunscreen
- Tweezers

Yellowstone and the Grand Tetons

Distance: 622 Miles Round-Trip, Billings
Time: Allow at least five days
Highlights: Yellowstone National Park, Grand Teton National Park, outdoor activities (hiking, biking, bird and wildlife watching, boating, fishing, horseback riding, rock climbing, rafting, skiing)

Ask anyone who has been to this part of the world to describe what they saw and they'll inevitably respond, "You have to see it to believe it." It's hard to capture in photos, and I hesitate to say, even in words.

The warm-weather months are the most popular time to visit. That's when the sky is typically a strong blue, the sun soothingly warm, and mountain meadows are spangled with wildflowers of every color. Add to that, the spectacular scenery (rugged peaks,

GOOD NIGHTS

Jenny Lake Lodge is magnificently situated in the *Grand Tetons*. Guests stay in log cabins which are comfortably furnished with hand-made quilts and braided rugs. Activities include hiking, biking, and trail riding. For more information, call (307) 543-2855.

Grand Tetons, Wyoming

waterfalls spilling over cliffs, painted canyons, hot springs, shiny lakes) and the wildlife sightings (moose, bear, elk, bighorn sheep), and in a couple of days, you'll see and experience more than most people do in a lifetime.

For this tour, we take you south from **Billings**, Montana, through the fabled *Beartooth Pass*, which straddles the Wyoming-Montana border, and then slowly meander through both *Yellowstone* and *Grand Teton National Park*, before heading back north to Billings.

Montana's largest city, Billings, is not only a great stepping stone to Yellowstone (and other alpine wilderness areas), but has some worthwhile sights of its own. See the *Yellowstone Art Center*, the *Western Heritage Center*, and the *Yellowstone County Museum*. At the *Boothill Cemetery*, you can see the final resting place of many Billings' gunmen who died with their boots on. From there, drive the *Chief Black Otter Trail*, which goes up *Kelly Mountain*, offering excellent views of the city itself.

From Billings, head south on U.S. 212 (known as the *Beartooth Highway*) which crosses the Wyoming border and happens to be the most beautiful entry into Yellowstone National Park. In fact, CBS correspondent Charles Kuralt described it as "the most beautiful drive in America." It takes you over the 10,947-foot Beartooth Pass, an awesome sight, and past snow-capped peaks, glaciers, alpine meadows, and plateaus.

The world's first national park is a place of awesome beauty renowned for its geysers, mud caldrons, canyons, rivers and lakes, waterfalls, and wildlife. It encompasses 2.2 million acres and has a 142-mile-long loop road that passes nearly every major attraction in the park. For this drive, we suggest taking in some of its sights as you work your way south towards Grand Teton National Park. Then, once you've visited Grand Teton, return through

Yellowstone, visiting the rest of the attractions. There's an admission charge that's good for both parks for seven full days.

Some of its highlights include *Old Faithful*, the *Grand Canyon of the Yellowstone*, *Mammoth Hot Springs*, *Norris Geyser Basin*, and *Yellowstone Lake*. The park is also a sanctuary for wildlife and is famous for its bears (both black and grizzly), elk, buffalo, moose, pronghorn antelope, bighorn sheep, coyotes, lynx, dozens of species of birds...the list goes on.

From Yellowstone, it's a short drive south on the *John D. Rockefeller, Jr. Memorial Parkway* to Grand Teton

MUSIC IN THE MOUNTAINS

Musicians from around the world perform at the *Grand Teton Music Festival* in Grand Teton National Park, a summer music festival with programs that include chamber and orchestral concerts. For more information, call (307) 733-3050.

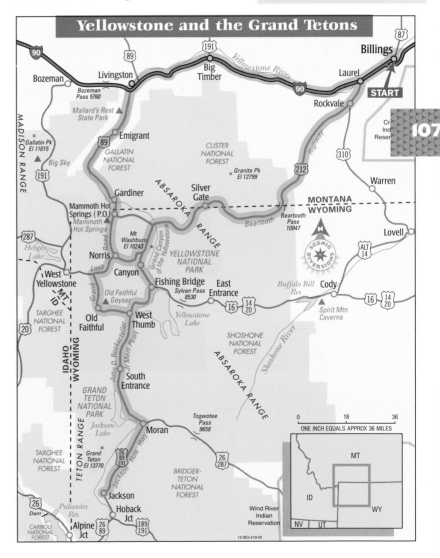

107

National Park. The parkway, which extends from *West Thumb* in Yellowstone to the south boundary of Grand Teton (near **Jackson**), was established on August 25, 1972 as an Act of Congress and is administered by the National Park Service. It was dedicated as a memorial to the many contributions made to national park conservation by John D. Rockefeller, Jr.

Perhaps the most inspiring alpine scenery on earth, Grand Teton National Park is a sudden 40-mile-long wall of skyline-dominating summits. It is a stunningly beautiful place—with dense forests, moraine lakes, serrated peaks, and deeply cut canyons.

Though you certainly see the majestic mountains by driving, there are more than 200 miles of hiking trails that take you to and through some of the park's most astoundingly beautiful landscapes. You can also rent canoes and boats on *Jackson* and *Jenny Lakes* or launch your own.

Head south to Jackson, which is twelve miles south of the park on the *Jackson Hole Highway*. This is the key town for the 600-square-mile valley of Jackson Hole (one of the most famous ski areas in the country). Once a town of real cowboys, it's now a popular spot for camera-toting visitors trying to look Western. Nevertheless, there are still many true Westerners here.

Check out the *Million Dollar Cowboy Bar* where saddles serve as bar stools. If you're in town during the summer, you can see the *Jackson Hole Rodeo* and the prestigious *Grand Teton Music Festival* in *Teton Village*.

From Jackson, head back north through Grand Teton National Park and continue on back through Yellowstone. Then get on U.S. 89 heading north through the *Gallatin National Forest* to I-90 east which will take you back to Billings.

READING MATERIAL

Whether you're a serious birder or you can't tell the difference between a Robin and a Cardinal, there are plenty of bird-watching opportunities in the western national parks. Consider taking along a copy of *Peterson Field Guide to Western Birds*. Other field books to consider packing are the *Peterson Field Guide to Rocky Mountain Wildflowers and Western Butterflies*. The Audubon Society also publishes a *Field Guide to Western Birds, Western Trees, and Western Wildflowers*.Two other handy books are *The Traveling Birder* (Doubleday), by Clive Goodwin and *Wild Plants of America: A Select Guide for the Naturalist and Traveler* (John Wiley & Sons), by Richard M. Smith.

Old Faithful—Yellowstone National Park, Wyoming

Otherworldly Utah

Distance: 744 Miles Round Trip, Salt Lake City
Time: Allow at least one week
Highlights: Salt Lake City, the Great Salt Lake, Zion and Bryce Canyon National Parks, hiking, swimming, bird watching, boating, fishing, rock climbing, white-water rafting, mountain biking, four-wheel drive adventures and snowmobiling, snowshoeing and ski touring in winter.

Looking around at the rugged landscape that characterizes most of southern Utah, it's not hard to picture the dinosaurs who once roamed this land. It's a world of redstone canyons, deep gorges, and naturally sculpted rock formations. Our route begins in **Salt Lake City** and then continues south to visit two of the state's national parks before returning to Salt Lake City.

Founded by Mormon pioneers in 1847, Salt Lake City lies over 4,300 feet above sea level between the *Great Salt Lake* and the *Wasatch Mountains*. Start by seeing the main Mormon buildings in *Temple Square* (the symbolic center of the Mormon religion) including the *Temple* and *Tabernacle*. See also the *Beehive House* (which belonged to Brigham Young who

MUSICAL NOTE

Throughout the summer months, Shakespeare is presented on an outdoor stage at the *Utah Shakespearean Festival* in Cedar City, Utah. For program and ticket information, call (801)586-1970.

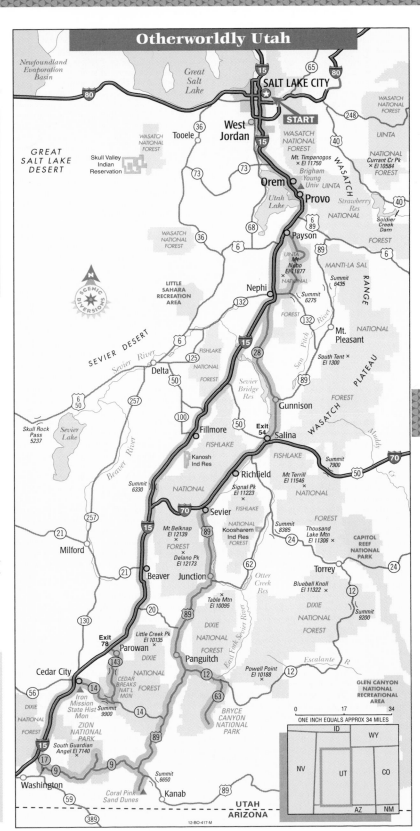

109

Autoroute through Zion National Park, Utah

led the Mormon pioneers); the *Utah State Capitol*; the super-modern *Delta Center* (a sports and cultural center); and *Pioneer State Park* which has a reconstructed Mormon settlement and monument commemorating the Mormon's arrival.

From Salt Lake City, head south on I-15 to **Provo**, which is home to *Brigham Young University*. At the university itself, there are several attractions including the *Harris Fine Arts Center*, the *Eyring Science Center*, the *Monte L. Bean Life Science Museum*, and the *Museum of Peoples and Cultures*. Elsewhere in the city, you'll find the great *Pioneer Memorial Museum* filled with relics from early Utah settlers; the *McCurdy Historical Doll Museum*, the *Springville Museum of Art* (devoted to Utah's art history), and the *John Hutchings Museum of Natural History*.

From Provo, take I-15 south. If you're in no big hurry to get to the national parks and other attractions in the southern part of the state, consider taking a small detour just south of Provo in **Payson**. There's a 45-mile drive around the eastern shoulder of *Mt. Nebo* (11,877 feet). The road goes to *Santaquin Canyon* and then climbs Mt. Nebo, offering a view of *Devil's Kitchen*, an exquisitely colored canyon. This loop takes you to Route 132. Follow Route 132 west to Nephi and back to I-15.

Take I-15 all the way south to Exit 78, towards **Parowan**. Follow Route 143 south to *Cedar Breaks National Monument*, where you'll find a spectacular natural amphitheater at an elevation of 10,000 feet. Shaped like a coliseum, it's 2,000 feet deep and more than three miles in diameter. It's carved out of the *Markagunt Plateau* and surrounded by the *Dixie National Forest*. You can follow the *Rim Drive*, a five-mile scenic road through the Cedar Breaks' high country, getting a good look at this astounding natural monument.

About 23 miles to the west (via Route 14) is *Cedar City*, which is a tourist center close to *Bryce Canyon* and *Zion national parks*. Both of these parks are geologically part of the area that includes the Grand Canyon.

Get back on I-15 and head south to reach Zion National Park, which is made up of multi-colored gorges and canyons, sandstone towers, chasms, and rock formations. The park, which sprawls over 229 square miles, was named by a 19th-century Mormon. To the Mormons—or Latter Day Saints—Zion means "a heavenly resting place."

To enter the park, take Route 17 off I-15 a short distance to Route 9. Take Route 9 right through the southern end of the park. Make your first stop at the *Zion Canyon Visitors Center* where you can have a look around the museum and actually see the extraordinarily colored Zion Canyon right from the lobby. Though you can view the wonder of Zion from your car by driving the 30 mile distance on Route 9 (called the *Zion-Mt. Carmel Highway*) plan to do some hiking. There are many hiking trails that range from simple flat foot paths to strenuous climbs.

In addition to driving on Route 9, be sure to follow the seven-mile *Zion Canyon Scenic Drive*, from the Visitor Center at the south entrance. It's one of the most beautiful drives in the entire state. It takes you to the *Temple of Sinawava*, where you can follow the two-mile trail (on foot) through hanging gardens.

Follow Route 9 east out of the park and then detour a bit by turning right onto U.S. 89 and then right again to reach the *Coral Pink Sand Dunes*. A sight to behold, there are six square miles of very coral pink sand dunes. In the nearby town of **Kanab**, there are over a dozen motels and many restaurants.

From there, head north on U.S. 89 and then turn right onto Route 12 and then south on Route 63, which leads directly into Bryce Canyon National Park. The iridescent colors you see here, combined with the mind-boggling shapes (castles, cathedrals) are truly hard to believe. Start by stopping at the Visitor's Center and then follow the rim road. There are 13 major overlooks allowing a great view of the canyon. If you have time, do try to get out and walk a bit. There's an 11-mile *Rim Trail* that you can follow for short stretches.

Backtrack a bit to reach U.S. 89 north and follow that to I-70 where you'll head east. Take Exit 54 to Route 28 north which will take you back to I-15 and then to Salt Lake City.

RESPECTING THE ENVIRONMENT

While out and about enjoying our country's natural beauty, do keep in mind that with the increased number of visitors to the national parks, there is stress on wildlife and plantlife. Take great care as you explore. Never leave garbage behind. Unless you've obtained passes for hiking in the backcountry, stick to the trails. Never sneak up on any animals or birds. Don't try to touch them or remove them from their habitat. And for your own safety, never

HORSING AROUND

Even if the last time you got in a saddle was on a coin-operated steed outside your childhood home-town supermarket, you can have a wonderful time at a dude ranch. All of them welcome beginners. Besides, giddy-upin' is only part of the picture. In addition to a combination platter of daytime activities (trail rides, rodeos, fishing, swimming), there are wonderful Western treats at night including chuck wagon dinners, foot stompin' square dances, yodeling contests, and campfires around which wranglers tell stories as eager listeners roast marshmallows. For more information, call The Dude Rancher's Association in Colorado at (303) 223-8440.

stand between animal parents and their young.

If you build fires, keep the following in mind. Keep fires small. Always build fires away from anything that could burn including dry leaves. Never build a fire in a tent or poorly ventilated place. Use a fireplace or fire grate if one is available. Throw used matches into the fire. Never, ever leave the fire unattended. Always have a pot of water or sand handy. Before leaving your camp, make sure the fire is completely out—meaning you can touch it with your hand.

Bryce Canyon National Park, Utah

Falls River—Rocky Mountain
National Park, Colorado

Rocky Mountain National Park

Distance: 261 Miles Round-Trip, Denver
Time: Allow at least three days
Highlights: Denver's museums, restaurants, historical attractions, mountain scenery, hiking, bird watching, fishing, boating, hunting, horseback riding, mountaineering; skiing and snow sports in winter months.

The Colorado Rockies, famed for their winter skiing, offer a world of warm-weather diversions as well. On this tour, we take you from **Denver**, up through **Boulder**, to *Rocky Mountain National Park* and then back to Denver.

Though most visitors to Colorado are eager to get out and see the countryside, Denver (the mile-high city) offers lots of things to do. Stroll about the arcades and courtyards of 19th-century *Larimar Square*, see the *United States Mint*; inspect the Western art collection at the *Denver Art Museum* and the *Museum of Western Art*.

From downtown Denver, take I-25 northbound, and at exit 217, get on U.S. 36 to Boulder. Situated on the edge of the Rockies, Boulder is the only U.S. city that gets part of its water supply from a city-owned glacier (*Arapaho Glacier*, 28 miles west). It's considered the technical and scientific center of the state and is home to the *University of Colorado*. There are several worthwhile sites to see including the museum, the planetarium, science center, and observatory at the university; the *Boulder Art Center* (lots of good regional art); the *National Center for Atmospheric Research*, and the *Boulder Museum of History*. You can also take a tour of the *Boulder Laboratories* of the *National Institute of Standards and Technology*.

Continue north on U.S. 36 to **Estes Park**, a resort area surrounded by mountains. There's a historical museum in town that provides a good background on the park and environs. Check out the *Stanley Hotel*, a landmark building. For a peak experience, ride the *Aerial Tramway* to the top of *Prospect Mountain* (8,700-feet). The views from the top are, well...top-notch.

Follow U.S. 34 west for about two miles to Rocky Mountain National Park. Over 65 peaks exceed 9,600 feet in this gaspingly beautiful mountain range. There are also beautiful lakes set into the mountains as if precious jewels, rushing streams, thick forests, and meadows sprinkled with wildflowers.

Once inside the park, U.S. 34 becomes the noted *Trail Ridge Road*, which follows the route of an ancient Native American trail, cutting right through the park (across the *Continental Divide* and into **Grand Lake**), immersing you in the spectacular scenery all the way. Like most of the national parks, you can see quite a bit when traveling by car, but you always get more when you do some hiking. There are trails everywhere.

Once you've stuffed yourselves on the beauty of the park, exit the same way you came in and go through Estes Park, heading east on U.S. 34. This takes you right through *Big Thompson Canyon*, one of the prettiest drives in the state.

When you reach I-25, head south to get back to Denver.

ACCOMMODATING ACCOMMODATIONS

One of the nicest things about visiting Colorado is that there are all sorts of wonderful places to stay. You can spend a week at a dude ranch, dividing your time between trail rides and rodeos. You can step back in time by staying a few days in a grand historic resort hotel or an old robber barons mansion. You can choose to luxuriate in a mountain spa or settle into a ski lodge. Of course, you'll also find the usual combination platter of affordable chain hotels and motels and plenty of campsites to go around. Here are some of our favorite Colorado accommodations.

■ BED AND BREAKFASTS

You will find many bed and breakfasts throughout Colorado. Usually they're very reasonably priced. They also offer wonderful opportunities to feel at home when away and in some cases, meet and get to know a local family. There's a nice casualness about staying in a bed and breakfast. Also, a good home-cooked breakfast is part of the deal. In many bed and breakfasts, it can be the highlight of your stay.

B & B's are not for everyone however. One of the biggest drawbacks is that the bath is most likely down the hall and to be shared with fellow guests. If you must have a bathroom of your own, make sure it's possible ahead of time. Another drawback—only in some cases—is that you may have to walk through somebody's living room (or other private areas) to get to your room. Very often a family shares the house with the guests. If having a phone in your room (and TV) is important, you may want to rule out a B & B. You also don't have the services one gets at a hotel—such as room-service, dry cleaning, and all that.

For a directory of B & B's in Colorado, contact Bed & Breakfast Innkeepers of Colorado Association, P.O. Box 38416, Colorado Springs, CO 80937; (800) 83-BOOKS (832-6657).

You'll be required to send $3 for shipping and handling.

■ HISTORIC HOTELS AND INNS

Colorado is home to some lovely historic inns and hotels. Heres a sampling of what you'll find.

Over a hundred years old, the *Brown Palace* in Denver is a masterpiece building—both inside and out. Designed by architect Frank Edbrooke, it is triangular in shape. All of the rooms are elaborately decorated in Victorian style. 321 17th Street; (800) 321-2599 or (303) 297-3111.

Also in Denver, *The Oxford Hotel* was built at the crest of the silver bonanza. Inside, there are stained-glass windows, marble walls, and frescoes. 1600 17th Street; (800) 228-5838 or (303) 628-5400.

The Broadmoor in **Colorado Springs** opened its doors in 1918 and is a grand old resort with hand-painted ceilings, brass chandeliers, and an elegant marble staircase. Lake Circle at Lake Avenue; (800) 634-7711 or (719) 634-7711.

University of Colorado football game—Boulder, Colorado

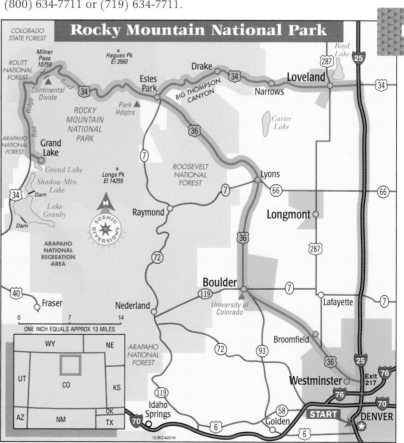

113

Trail Ridge Road—Rocky Mountain National Park, Colorado

The *Strater Hotel* in **Durango** was built in 1887 by Henry H. Strater, a prominent druggist in this gold and silver boom town. An excellent example of American Victorian architecture, it's a showcase not to be missed. 699 Main Avenue; (800) 246-4431 or (303) 247-4431.

For more information on these and other properties, contact the Association of Historic Hotels of the Rocky Mountain West, 1002 Walnut, #201, Boulder, CO 80303; (303) 546-9040.

■ COLORADO SPAS

Many resorts in Colorado have small spas or beauty centers where you can book a facial, a massage, or some other beauty treatment. Some also have health clubs with exercise classes, weight rooms, and a menu of instructor-led physical fitness activities. There are a couple of places, however, that have full-fledged spas where you can spend your time in a terry cloth robe shuffling from seaweed wrap to salt glow body scrub, from pedicure to facial, and a whole array of other treatments designed to revive, replenish, and beautify the body.

Here are two real winners that offer all the pleasures of mountain ski resorts combined with top-of-the-line spa facilities.

The Peaks at Telluride have a wonderful selection of treatments including a special high altitude massage to help alleviate the symptoms associated with high altitude, an Alpine hydrotherapy bath made with local botanicals, and a Colorado clay treatment that leaves your skin soft and smooth. In addition, there are first class steam rooms, saunas, whirlpools, and exercise equipment, plus yoga classes, snowshoeing or hiking (depending on the season) instruction, daily fitness classes...you name it. For information: The Peaks at Telluride, 136 Country Club Drive, P.O. Box 2702, Telluride, CO 81435; (800) 789-2220 or (303) 728-6800.

The Lodge & Spa at Cordillera in Vail Valley has a long list of spa treatments including a variety of massages, a body polish, body wraps, and much more. There's also computerized workout equipment, steamrooms, saunas, an indoor heated lap pool, and indoor and outdoor Jacuzzis. For information: The Lodge & Spa at Cordillera, P.O. Box 1110, Edwards, CO 81632; (800) 877-3529.

■ CAMPING OUT

With nature as big as it is in Colorado, of course, camping out is extraordinarily popular. For information on campgrounds, contact one of the following:

Colorado Association of Campgrounds, Cabins, and Lodges
5101 Pennsylvania Avenue
Boulder, CO 80303
(303) 499-9343

KOA (Kampgrounds of America)
P.O. Box 30558
Billings, MT 59114-0558
(406) 248-7444

Larimar Square—Denver, Colorado

Colorado Tour

Distance: 1037 Miles Round-Trip, Denver
Time: Allow at least one week to ten days
Highlights: Denver, Colorado Springs, ski resorts, old mining towns, Indian cliff dwellings, museums, mountain scenery, outdoor activities.

If you have the time, do yourselves a favor and see as much of Colorado as you can. Here's a tour of some of the state's highlights.

You don't have to drive far from **Denver** to completely immerse yourselves in spellbindingly beautiful alpine scenery. Head west on I-70 and no sooner do you leave behind the mile-high city, you're in the mountains of the *Arapaho National Forest*.

Some of the state's oldest mining towns are in this area including **Central City**, propped up on *Gregory Gulch* (turn off I-70 onto Route 119, then turn onto Route 279) where the first major discovery of gold was made in 1859. Today, visitors can wander about the Victorian buildings such as the *Opera House* which was impeccably restored in the 1930s. Another impressive—and very famous—Victorian gold-rush town is **Georgetown**, further along on I-70. It's home to more than 200 19th-century structures including the *Hotel de Paris*, an elaborately decorated building that was built and operated by a Frenchman. If you're visiting between early June and early October, don't miss out on riding the *Georgetown Loop Railroad* (Exit 226 from I-70). It takes visitors on a seven-mile tour through jaw-droppingly beautiful scenery.

Continuing west, I-70 climbs up as it approaches the *Continental Divide*. At the summit, you can actually park your car and walk along the ridges. After you've had plenty of time to soak in the view, carry on to **Dillon**, which is a year-round resort town set in the mountains.

Vail, the glamorous ski resort is next. If it's not ski season, you'll find plenty to keep your muscles working. There's tennis, golf, biking, hiking, river rafting, and some ambitious pursuits as well, including Jeep tours and scenic gondola rides.

Keep going west and you'll come to **Glenwood Springs**, which has some wonderful mineral pools and baths to dip into.

From there, head south on Route 82 to **Aspen**, another "beautiful people" resort area. Aspen—and its neighboring **Snowmass**—is known as a celebrity retreat year round, and it's easy to see why. Together, Victorian-charmed Aspen and handsomely contemporary Snowmass have everything an active-minded person could ever want. During the winter, there's top-notch skiing and other snow sports. The rest of the year, you can join in the local fitness craze on tennis courts and golf courses. You can hike, bike, or go horseback riding.

Maxwell House—Georgetown, Colorado

You can go white-river rafting, canoeing, or kayaking. There are also plenty of low-keyed diversions such as gallery hopping and cafe-sampling. On top of that, there are some great restaurants and plenty of shops to explore.

If you have time, consider going a little further southeast of Aspen on Route 82 to *Independence Pass*. At 12,095 feet, the view is unparalleled. Keep in mind that it's open only between June and October.

Then head back on Route 82, turning left onto Route 133, all the way, soaking in the sensational mountain scenery.

Turn left onto Route 92 at **Hotchkiss**.

Follow it around to U.S. 50 heading west. Take that to **Montrose** and go south on U.S. 550. Just three miles south of Montrose, stop to see the *Ute Indian Museum*.

Many who have driven it agree that U.S. 550 between **Ouray** and **Durango** (through the *San Juan Mountains*) is Colorado's most spectacular driving route. Words cannot do justice to the extraordinary beauty of this high country as the road passes through it, hugging the sheer mountain slopes, twisting and turning over passes and down into valleys where historic towns nestle below the awesome peaks. This

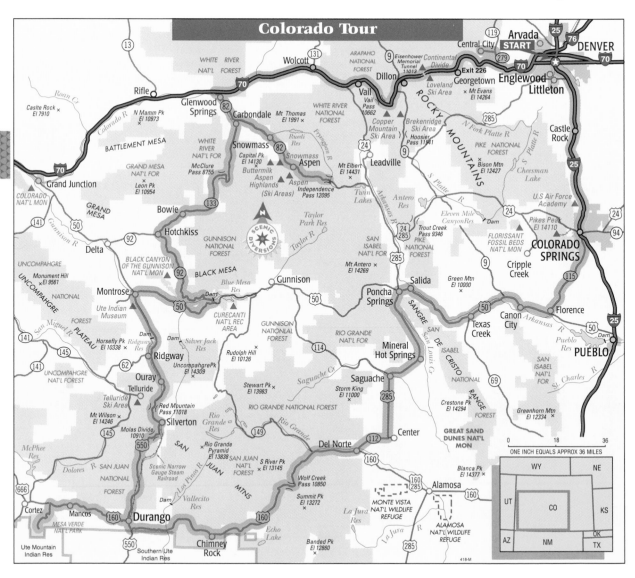

road must be traveled to be believed. Open year-around, this highway can be treacherous in winter with sudden weather changes and should only be driven with a four-wheel drive vehicle.

Tucked away in Southwestern Colorado, Durango feels like another world, another time. In this old mining-town, even little old ladies drive pick-ups, one-syllable words stretch to sound like two (well is pronounced way-el), and cowboy boots and hats are normal streetwear.

Explore the historic district where restored Victorian buildings, old-fashioned shops, and an 1882 railroad tell you the past is still alive. If you have time, take the bumpy train ride through the thick forest and along the steep wildflower-covered cliffs to the old mining town of **Silverton**.

From Durango, head west on U.S. 160 to visit *Mesa Verde National Park*. Here you'll find remarkable cliff dwellings, including *Cliff Palace* (with more than 200 rooms) and *Spruce Tree House* (the best preserved). There are two self-guided six-mile loops from the *Chapin Mesa Archaeological Museum* that pass a series of scenic overlooks and short trails leading to mesa-top ruins.

Then retrace your steps, heading east on U.S. 160 back through Durango and keep going. You'll go through *Wolf Creek Pass* and when you reach **Del Norte**, turn left onto Route 112 and then turn left onto U.S. 285.

At **Poncha Springs**, turn right onto U.S. 50 and take that to **Canon City** (Canon is pronounced like Canyon), which is located on the mouth of the *Grand Canyon of the Arkansas River*. Take time to have a look around the *Canon City Municipal Museum*, which includes a reconstructed pioneer's cabin and a stone house that was built in 1881.

Just beyond Canon City, turn left onto Route 115 and follow that to **Colorado Springs**, where the plains meet the Rockies. When gold was discovered in nearby **Cripple Creek** back in 1891, Colorado Springs became a millionaire's city practically overnight. Today, people flock here for its spas, its Victorian history, and its wonderful way of life—

all backdropped by *Pikes Peak*, looming above the clouds. Don't forget to see the *Garden of the Gods*, the *Air Force Academy*, the *Cave of the Winds*, and *Wood Avenue* (where the millionaire homes are). If you have time, take a drive over to Cripple Creek (west of town); also, take the *Cog railroad* up to the top of Pikes Peak.

From there, you can easily get back to Denver, via I-25.

Denver, Colorado

SKIING COLORADO: THE PEAKS OF PERFECTION

With over 25 alpine ski areas and more than 25,000 acres of skiable terrain and 259 lifts, Colorado offers every kind of ski experience imaginable. Conditions are almost always ideal, with knee-deep champagne powder, bright sunshine (300 days of the year), and gaspingly beautiful scenery. Most of the ski areas are easily accessible from several major airports and a network of centrally located highways. Here we introduce you to just some of them.

■ THE ASPENS

Skiing in Aspen sounds like something only the exceptionally privileged get to do. You picture them as extraordinarily wealthy, well-traveled, beautiful, frightfully fit, and famous (or at the very least, related to some bold-faced name). Indeed, Aspen and nearby Snowmass— is a glitzy resort duo where you probably will see spandex-clad socialites effortlessly zigzagging

117

TRAVEL SMART: FOOL WOULD-BE THIEVES

All too often, tourists—especially families—drive around advertising the fact that they're out-of-towners. They openly read maps, have travel brochures visible, and do eyebrow-raising maneuvers (like pulling a "U-ie" in the middle of a major intersection).

helpful hints...

Though crooks may be street smart, you can outsmart them anywhere you go. Fool them into thinking you're locals by having a local newspaper clearly visible in your car. Also, study your route before setting out so you don't draw attention to yourselves by sitting on the side of the road reading the map or turning on the car light to see it.

down trails and you might just find yourself seated next to somebody you last saw on the cover of *People* magazine on a chair lift.

An historic mining town, Victorian **Aspen** draws the rich and famous with its varied cultural offerings and beautiful mountains just begging to be skied. Its four ski mountains and more than 3,000 skiable acres together offer fine powder skiing with runs to match every ability. Off the slopes, Aspen is a happening, party kind of place, particularly during the Christmas holidays, when the town is jumping.

■ ASPEN MOUNTAIN

Aspen Mountain, or *Ajax* (after a defunct silver mine), is exciting and often challenging for advanced skiers, but with no green runs it is too difficult for the less accomplished skier. (The three mountains, *Buttermilk*, *Aspen Highlands* and *Snowmass* offer a wide range of slopes. Lift tickets that are good at all four areas are available, as is transportation between areas.)

Aspen Mountain is a long narrow area that extends along the sides and tops of two long ridges that run down into the *Roaring Fork Valley*. The six-passenger *Silver Queen gondola* takes skiers from the base up the mountain in 13 minutes and high-speed quad lifts service some-

what easier blue runs at the top. (The gondola and other chairs have cut lift lines dramatically.) There are steep moguled slopes, backcountry terrain, and long cruising runs. You'll also enjoy the four on-mountain restaurants.

■ SNOWMASS

Snowmass, by some accounts, provides the best all-around skiing in the Aspen area. Though there are places to stay, Snowmass is not much of a town, and it is an easy 20-minute ride from Aspen. Its real attraction is the variety of long runs for everyone from beginners to daredevils on its vast acreage. It is truly a mountain for every member of the family, with excellent high-speed lifts and skier services such as trail condition reports at the bottom of the lifts.

Snowmass has more expert-level slopes than any other mountain in the area, yet there is more gentle learning terrain than the percentages indicate. There are plenty of broad expanses for graceful cruising through big turns, such as the *Big Burn*, and an abundance of big thrills in the high alpine terrain of the *Cirque and Hanging Valley*.

■ TELLURIDE

Many of those who have traveled through the Rockies consider the *Telluride Valley* the most beautiful place in the state and easily one of the most beautiful spots in the world. Surrounded by the rugged thirteen and fourteen-thousand-foot peaks of the *San Juan Mountains*, this turn-of-the-century mining town is perfectly enchanting with its mix of pastel and brick Victorian buildings and tumble-down wooden shacks that are all a part of this carefully preserved historic tradition.

Rising directly above the town, the ski mountain is known for its steep and bumpy expert slopes, its gentle wide

HIKE WITH CARE

One of the most common problems with hikers is altitude sickness, which is a result of ascending to heights over 8,500 feet without properly acclimating themselves. The symptoms include headache, nausea, vomiting, shortness of breath, weakness, and sleep disturbance. If any of these occur, it's important to retreat to a lower altitude. Altitude sickness can develop into high altitude pulmonary edema (HAPE) and high altitude cerebral edema (HACE). Both can be permanently debilitating or fatal.

Do yourself a huge favor. Before setting out on mountainous trails, take the following three things into consideration:

1) How long is the trail?
2) How steep is it and how quickly does the elevation gain?
3) How acclimated are you to the altitude at the start and finish?

flats, and two exceptionally long, dreamy runs from the top also make it a delightful place for the novice and intermediate skier. From the back side of the mountain on a clear day you can see all the way to Utah, and on your way down the front face—by ski or lift— you'll be awestruck by the panoramic view of the town and surrounding peaks.

The town of **Telluride** is a treasure trove of shops for the apres-ski browser and a food-lovers paradise. Have a drink at the magnificently restored bar of *The New Sheridan Hotel*.

■ VAIL

The other capital of skiing in Colorado offers more skiable terrain and high-speed quad chairlifts than any other ski area in North America. Its world-famous *Back Bowls*, tucked away behind *Vail Mountain*, offer the states finest powder skiing for average to expert skiers. These bowls are ungroomed and on fresh-snow days, there is nothing better.

Vail has the broadest range of ski options in the country for every level skier—and more skiable terrain than the four areas of Summit County put together. Its exceptionally wide runs were originally cut by World War II veterans of the 10th Mountain Division, men who had skied the Alps after the war.

The *Vail Ski School* is the largest in the world. There is a special ski program for children ages three to six, a school for children six and up, and separate classes for teenagers. Children ski through re-created gold mines, bear caves, and Indian villages and are treated to many other special mountain attractions.

Founded in 1962, the young town of Vail is an imitation Tirolian Village, quaint in its own way, but without the historic charm of Aspen and other resorts. Its a town that works well and, to the pedestrians delight, allows no cars in its center.

Vail Village and the newer *Lionshead* are chock full of pricey shops, restaurants, and lodges.

FAMILY TRAVEL TIP: STAY TOGETHER, PLAY TOGETHER

No sooner do you pass through the gates of an amusement park or some other big attraction and your children want to run off in every direction. To avoid getting separated, consider the following:

• Have your child wear a name tag or write down your name, local address and telephone number on a slip of paper and put it in his/her pocket.

• Agree on a very specific meeting place in the event you do get separated. Rather than say something general like "at the Cinderella Castle," be more specific. For example, "on the steps of City Hall in the Magic Kingdom."

• Consider dressing your family members in color-coordinated bright clothes. You might also have each member wear a baseball cap or a straw hat.

Mesa Verde National Park, Colorado

119

Southwest

S ometimes the Southwest feels like another country with its unique cultures and dramatic landscapes. Giant mesas loom on the horizon, real live cowboys compete in daredevil rodeos, and the scenery is so awesome—cloudless skies, enormous red rocks, forests of towering cacti—it could knock the boots off anyone. There are all sorts of distinctly Southwestern things to do: riding horses down multi-colored canyons, kicking up your heels in Texas saloons, and visiting Native American pueblos. Even the food is out of this world—Mexican, New Mexican, and Tex-Mex specialties, juicy T-Bone steaks, and saucy bar-b-que'd ribs so messy you'd think they were illegal.

On the following pages, we take you to some of the Southwest's most remarkable places from Native American cliff-dwellings, that date back to prehistoric times, to Arcosanti, a prototype of a futuristic city. We'll show you around historic villages, cosmopolitan cities, and then take you out into the wilderness, where the landscape can be anything from sprawling prairie lands to rugged mountains.

The End of the Trail by James Earl Foster, National Cowboy Hall of Fame and Western Heritage Center—Oklahoma City, Oklahoma

Discovering Oklahoma

Distance: 619 Miles Round-Trip, Oklahoma City
Time: Allow at least three days
Highlights: Native American sites, cowboy history, museums, lake recreation areas, mountains.

If you're interested in Native American history, you've got to go to Oklahoma. Until it achieved statehood in 1907, Oklahoma was designated "Indian Territory." Five tribes— the Choctaw, Chickasaw, Creek, Seminole, and Cherokee Indians—were forced by the U.S. Army to relocate here from the Southeastern states during the period 1828-1846.

As the nation expanded west, white settlers increasingly wanted the land for themselves. On April 22, 1889, it became *Oklahoma Territory* at the sound of a gunshot. This sent thousands of pioneers, some of whom literally jumped the gun to get a head start on staking their claims. They became known as "sooners" and today, the state is nicknamed, "the Sooner State."

As you drive around, you'll find all sorts of Native American and early pioneer sites. In this diversion, we take you to many of them as well as through some of the state's most scenic lake and mountain regions.

Start in **Oklahoma City**, a city that

Cherokee Heritage Center—Tahlequah, Oklahoma

grew from a barren prairie to a population of 10,000 in one day. See the *Crystal Bridge at Myriad Gardens*, *Enterprise Square, U.S.A.* (exhibits celebrating the free enterprise system), and the *National Cowboy Hall of Fame and Western Heritage Center*, where you can find out all about the early pioneers and see John Wayne's collection of Pueblo kachina dolls. The center was built by 17 western states to memorialize the American cowboy. There's also an impressive zoo with walk-through aviaries, a herpetarium, and safari tram. If you'd like to see a cattle auction, head over to the *Oklahoma City Stockyards*, where you can watch the bidding take place.

From Oklahoma City, drive east on I-44 about 100 miles to **Tulsa**, which lies in the heart of Green Country, a region known for its many lakes, wooded hillsides, and farmlands. Called the "*Oil Capital of the World*," Tulsa is home to more oil company headquarters than any other city. Back in its boom days, when oil was discovered here, wealthy oil barons built several eccentric buildings which remain today including art deco skyscrapers, French villas, and Georgian mansions.

There are three outstanding museums here: the *Thomas Gilcrease Museum* (which contains the world's largest collection of American art), the *Philbrook Art Center* (a former oil baron's villa, now housing a collection of native American artifacts and some Renaissance artwork), and the *Museum of Jewish Art*, with collections dating back to 2,000 B.C.. Tulsa is also home to *Oral Roberts University* (ORU), a Christian university, which has some interesting buildings regardless of your religious affiliation.

Also in town is the *Boston Avenue United Methodist Church*, an art deco building reminiscent of the witch's castle in *The Wizard of Oz*. From its tower, you can get a great view of downtown Tulsa.

Continue east on I-44 towards **Miami**, and pick up Route 10 which is a beautiful drive right through the Grand

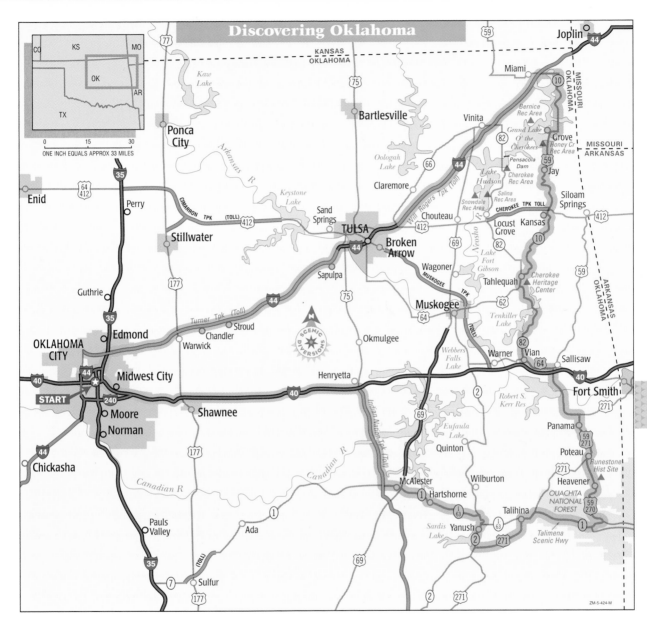

Discovering Oklahoma

Lake area. *Grand Lake*, which is also called *Grand Lake O' the Cherokees*, is a 66-mile-long lake above *Pensacola Dam*. A major source of electric power, it's also rife with recreational areas where you can swim, fish, camp, and go boating. **Grove** is the major hub in the area.

Tahlequah is next. Back in 1839, tribal branches of the Cherokee met here to sign a new constitution forming the Cherokee Nation. Don't miss the *Cherokee Heritage Center* and, if it's summer, consider staying for a performance of *Trail of Tears*, a musical drama depicting the history of the Cherokee Tribe.

From Tahlequah, head south on Route 82 to U.S. 64 east to U.S. 59 south. Follow this to **Heavener** (stop to see the *runestone*), and then on to Route 1 west. You're right in the heart of the Ouachita National Forest and the drive (known as the *Talimena Scenic Highway*) is lovely. It takes you by pine-covered peaks and shimmering lakes to Talihina.

Oklahoma Air Space Museum
Oklahoma City, Oklahoma

barren prairie, but by nightfall it had a population of over 10,000.

- The Oklahoma State Capitol is the only statehouse in the U.S. with working oil wells on its grounds.
- The name Oklahoma is a combination of two Choctaw Indian words—okla means "people" and homma means "red."
- Oklahoma became known as the "Sooner State" because, when the government first opened Oklahoma to white settlement in the late 1880's, some settlers were there "sooner" than it was opened.
- In 1909 Oklahoma organized the world's first Boy Scout Troop.

Spellbinding New Mexico

Distance: 455 Miles Round-Trip, Albuquerque
Time: Allow at least five days
Highlights: Native American sites (including cave dwellings), ghost towns, museums and art galleries, arts and crafts, forest-clad mountains, prairie lands, historic Spanish towns.

Writers and artists have been moved to create great masterpieces about the landscape in this part of the world. Indeed, its beauty is breathtaking. There's an incredible spaciousness of earth and sky, mountains and mesas loom up dramatically, cattle-dotted grasslands stretch off in every direction, the *Rio Grande* snakes through the landscape. Scattered around are a handful of urban hubs, several ghost towns, the ruins of cliff dwellings, and over half a dozen Indian pueblos.

You could easily spend days in **Albuquerque**. Start by seeing *Old Town* which was the original settlement, and is now a popular shopping area. Then head for the museums which interest you the most. At the *University of New Mexico*, you'll find

Carry on from there on U.S. 271 south and then turn north on Route 2. Follow that to Route 1/63 which you'll take west towards **McAlester** and then head north on the Indian Nation turnpike to pick up I-40 back to Oklahoma City.

DID YOU KNOW...

- Tulsa claims to have the highest percentage of Native American population of any U.S. metropolitan region.
- The Oklahoma City Stockyards are the busiest in the world.
- Oklahoma has more than 200 lakes.
- The first automatic parking meter was installed in Oklahoma City on July 16, 1935.
- In the morning of April 22, 1889 Oklahoma City was nothing but

VICTORIAN JEWEL

Just north of Oklahoma City—on Route I-35—is the town of Guthrie, which was settled in just a few hours during the great land rush. Today's visitors find a smashing collection of restored Victorian buildings. About 1,600 acres of the city is listed in the National Historic Register.

MUSIC IN THE AIR

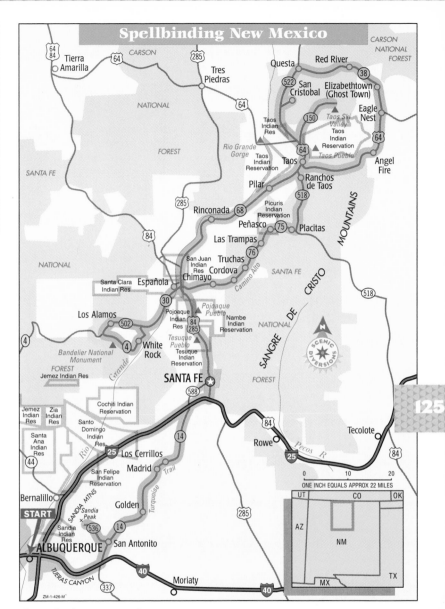

Spellbinding New Mexico

Spellbinding New Mexico

During the summer months, visitors to Santa Fe can seize the opportunity to see the famed Sante Fe Opera perform in the foothills of the Sangre de Cristo mountains. For program and ticket information, write Santa Fe Opera, P.O. Box 2408, Santa Fe, New Mexico 87504-2408 or call (505) 986-5900.

a fine arts center, an art gallery, the *Maxwell Museum of Anthropology*, and the *Museum of Geology* and *Institute of Meteoritics*. The *Albuquerque Museum* showcases regional art and history. There's a *New Mexico Museum of Natural History*, the *Telephone Pioneer Museum* (displays the evolution of the telephone from 1876 to the present), the *National Atomic Museum*, and the *Indian Pueblo Cultural Center* (featuring the story of Pueblo Indians).

From Albuquerque, head east on I-40 for about 15 miles through *Tijeras Canyon* and then turn north on Route 14, the *Turquoise Trail*. This is the most beautiful route between Albuquerque and **Santa Fe**. It takes you through mesa country east of the *Sandia Mountains*. You can drive up to the area's highest peak (follow Route 536). At 10,678 feet, you won't be able to take your eyes off the view. Back on Route 14, continue north and you'll pass through some old mining towns including **Golden**, **Madrid**, and **Los Cerrillos**. From Los Cerrillos, continue north on Route 14 and I-25 then pick up U.S. 285 north for 24 miles to Santa Fe.

With its narrow, cobblestoned streets, low adobe buildings, and unique art galleries, Santa Fe is a place of inexhaustible vitality. To get a historical lay-of-the-land, check out the *Palace of the Governors* (the oldest public building in the U.S.), the *Museum of Fine Arts* (there's also a quartet of Native-American museums), and the *San Miguel Mission*,

dating back to 1610. In between, shop for Indian pottery, jewelry, and basketry in dozens of small shops; *Canyon Drive*, the soul of Santa Fe (a.k.a. the Arts and Crafts Road) is where you'll find the biggest concentration of galleries.

Nothing can quite prepare you for the sensational scenery you will drive through between Santa Fe and **Taos** and north. Head north out of Santa Fe on U.S. 84/285 past several Pueblo

Rafting on the Rio Grande, New Mexico

Old Catholic Chapel—Santa Fe, New Mexico

The Museum of Fine Arts—Santa Fe, New Mexico

Indian settlements and then turn east on Route 76.

This is the High Road to Taos, the *Camino Alto*. As the road ascends the *Sangre de Cristo Mountains*, you'll find yourself passing through sun-bleached Spanish villages such as **Chimayo** which has been a center of Spanish weaving for centuries. It's also home to a small chapel which was built on land that is reputed to have miraculous healing powers and attracts pilgrims from around the world. Just east of Chimayo is **Cordova**, which is known for its woodcarving. **Truchas**, another weaving center, offers beautiful views of the mountains and desert. **Las Trampas** has a Spanish Colonial chapel, *San Jose de Gracias*, that was built in the eighteenth century.

At **Penasco**, take Route 75 east to Route 518 which takes you north into Taos. Taos is the kind of place people fall in love with and hesitate to tell anybody about. A combination artists' community, winter ski resort, and ancient Indian pueblo, it's always bustling with energy. The historic plaza is the heart of it, bordered by festive shops and galleries in terra-cotta adobe buildings. Visit the *Kit Carson Home and Historical Museum*, the *Governor Charles Bent House*, and the *Hacienda de Don Antonio Severino Marinez*. North of town, you'll find the *Taos Pueblo*, a 900-year-old Native American community known for its multistory adobe buildings.

From Taos, take U.S. 64 and Route 522 north to **Questa**, turn east on Route 38 and go through **Red River** to **Eagle Nest**. En route be sure to pull over and take a look at the *Rio Grande Gorge* from the bridge on U.S. 64. Also stop to see *D.H. Lawrence's shrine* at **San Cristobal** (off Route 522). Red River is a popular ski resort area as well as summer family vacation center. **Elizabethtown** is a ghost town; Eagle Nest, a popular summer destination.

Follow the road around and back to Taos, then head south on Route 68 towards **Española**. Allow yourself plenty of time to drive slowly and soak in the view. From there, it's a short drive west to **Los Alamos**, which was made famous as the birthplace of the first atomic bomb. See the *Bradbury Science Hall* to find out more about the history of the bomb and the *County Historical Museum* for some fascinating local lore.

One of the state's most fascinating cliff-dwellings is nearby. Look for the sign on Route 4 for *Bandelier National Monument*. Here you can wander through the landscape and see one mile of cave dwellings.

From there, make your way back to Santa Fe (via U.S. 84/285) and then back to Albuquerque on I-25.

BELIEVE IN UFOS?

Supposedly, in 1947 a spaceship crashed in **Roswell**, New Mexico. Four aliens apparently were found dead at the site. Several local residents were aware of what happened. However, shortly after the crash, supposedly, the government hushed those who had any information and said it was only a weather balloon. Years later, in 1995, a film (shot by an army officer) surfaced showing an autopsy on what is said to have been one of the aliens. This whole story broke on a Fox-TV documentary called *Alien Autopsy: Fact or Fiction*. What really did happen? You decide. In addition to the film which has been made into a video, books have been written on the Roswell incident.

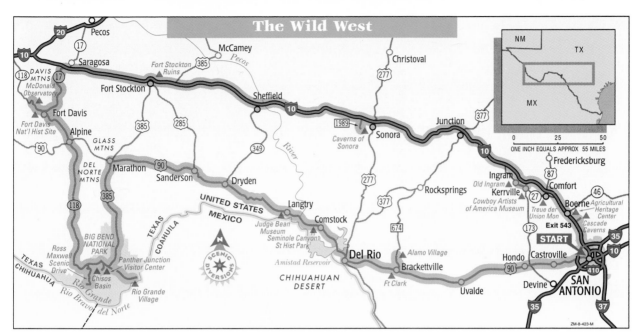

The Wild West

Distance: 1044 Miles Round-Trip, San Antonio
Time: Allow at least four days
Highlights: Big Bend National Park, caverns, canyons, caves, pictographs, mountain scenery, pioneer villages, museums, hiking, horseback riding, white-water rafting, water sports.

If you want to get an idea of what the pioneers saw when they moved across the nation, head for *Big Bend National Park* in the southwestern pocket of Texas. Though much of the wild, untamed landscape remains unchanged and contained in the park itself, it actually sprawls out well beyond the park's boundaries.

For this drive, we start you off in the lively city of **San Antonio**, then head west to the "Big Bend" of Texas. From there, we take you north through the mountains and then east through desert country and finish up the tour by cutting through the *Texas Hill Country*.

San Antonio is a historically rich city, combining Western and Mexican cultures. The *Paseo del Rio* (or *River Walk*) along the gently moving San Antonio River is the happening part of town with small shops and boutiques, outdoor cafes, mariachi bands, and lively night spots. But there are other sights to see including the history-laden *Alamo*; *La Villita*, a restored city block that dates back to the mid-1700s; and *El Mercado*, a Mexican-style market where you can buy piñatas and terra-cotta figurines. Also see the old *San Fernando Cathedral* and the *Spanish Governor's Palace*.

From San Antonio, head west on U.S. 90. Just twenty miles outside the city, you'll find the community of **Castroville**, which is sometimes called "The Little Alsace of Texas" because of its mixture of many cultures (including Alsatian). It was founded by a Frenchman Henri Castro who made an agreement with the Republic of Texas to bring settlers from Europe. Many of those who did come over were Alsatian and, in fact, the Germanic dialect is used among the community's older residents. You can find out more about the early European immigrants at the *Landmark Inn and Museum*.

127

Retama Race Track—Selma, Texas

Mission San Jose, one of the five Spanish missions —San Antonio, Texas

Continue west on U.S. 90 to **Brackettville**. Here you'll find *Fort Clark*, which was built by the U.S. Cavalry in 1852 to protect the frontier settlers from the Indians. At one point, General George S. Patton was stationed here. Seven miles north of Bracketville (on Route 674) you'll find *Alamo Village*, a theme park located on a ranch that's often used as a movie set. Though there are no rides, there's a *John Wayne Museum*, and Old West jail, blacksmith's shops, a chapel, and a bank.

Del Rio, 32 miles to the west of Brackettville and right on the border of Mexico, is your next stop. In addition to being a stepping stone to Mexico, it has its own share of attractions including a museum, some historic sites, and plenty of outdoor activities especially those that involve water. The town is right on the *Rio Grande* and is actually an oasis at the edge of the *Chihuahuan Desert*. West of town on U.S. 90 is the *Amistad Reservoir*, with more than 850 miles of shoreline. You can go swimming, boating, and fishing and play golf on lush green courses shaded by tall palm trees (an uncommon sight for a Mexican/US border town). There's also a winery with tours and tastings, and some archaeological sites to see.

If you're archaeology buffs, don't miss seeing the *Seminole Canyon State Historical Park* (nine miles west of the town of **Comstock**). On cave and canyon walls there are prehistoric pictographs that date back as much as 8,500 years.

Continue west to **Marathon** and then turn left onto U.S. 385 south. This will take you right down into Big Bend National Park, on the United States/ Mexican border. Named for the bend in the Rio Grande where the park is located, Big Bend National Park sprawls over 1,252 square miles. There are a variety of terrains here from flat desert plains to mountain forests.

Start by driving to the *Panther Junction Visitor Center* at the center of the park where you can pick up additional visitor information. Then continue on to *Chisos Basin*. Bear in

mind that this is a steep climb through canyon country and though only seven miles long, the sharp turns can be challenging. Once you reach the basin, you can get out and do a little exploring on foot. There are several hiking trails including the moderate 5-1/4-mile-long round-trip *Window Trail* (so named because you can look out through a "window" formed by the canyon walls and see the desert below), the 5-mile round-trip *Lost Mine Trail*, and the challenging 14-mile-long *South Rim Hike*.

Afterwards, consider driving southwest on the *Ross Maxwell Scenic Drive*, a 30-mile road that takes in some of the park's most magnificent scenery or heading over toward the *Rio Grande Village* where there are several overlooks, some hot springs, and another visitor center.

In addition to the beautiful scenery, scattered around the park are some historic ranches, cavalry outposts, and farming and mining communities—all listed in the National Register of Historic Places.

Though you really can see a lot when exploring by car in Big Bend, there are plenty of other activities to try including hiking, horseback

Paseo del Rio, the River Walk—San Antonio, Texas

Boot Canyon—Big Bend National Park, Texas

riding, fishing, rock climbing, and river rafting. There are also guided tours covering a range of topics including birds, nature photography, and wildflowers.

When you're ready to move on, take Route 118 north on the western side of the park towards **Alpine**, which sits in a high valley. This route continues to be very scenic taking you through the *Del Norte*, the *Glass*, and then the *Davis Mountains*. Keep going past Alpine on Route 118 and you'll come to **Fort Davis**, the highest town in Texas (5,050 feet). Just outside of town is the *Fort Davis National Historic Site*, the restored ruins of a frontier outpost. Carry on to the *McDonald Observatory*, located atop *Mt. Locke*.

Backtrack to Fort Davis and turn left onto Route 17 north. Take this right to I-10, heading east. Consider stopping to see the fort ruins at **Fort Stockton** and then carry on to the **Sonora** area, where there are beautiful caverns to be seen. They're about eight miles west of Sonora and then seven miles south on Route 1989.

Continue east again on I-10 making your next stop **Kerrville**, in the heart of the Texas Hill Country. The name comes from James Kerr, a supporter of Texas independence who died in the Civil War. The town has a reputation as being a health center thanks to its low humidity and clean air. You'll see the name Schreiner everywhere. The young Charles Schreiner, who became a Texas Ranger at age 15, came to Kerrville in the 1850s and started raising sheep and goats. His wool and mohair ranching business became so big and successful that eventually the town became the mohair capital of the world. While in Kerrville, take time to see the *Cowboy Artists of America Museum* and the *Hill Country Museum*.

In nearby **Old Ingram** (leave Kerrville on Route 27 and continue northwest for seven miles; Old Ingram is located on the *Old Ingram Loop*), you'll find several art galleries and antiques shops.

Return through Kerrville on Route 27 to the historic town of **Comfort**. Founded by German pioneers in 1854, the name comes from their desire to name it "Gemuetlichkeit" which roughly means peace, serenity, and comfort. The simpler English word Comfort won out. Take some

Bluebonnets, the state flower of Texas

time to wander around downtown; it's a *National Historic District* filled with homes and businesses dating from the early settlers. Check out the *"Treue der Union"* (True to the Union) Monument on High Street, between Third and Fourth Streets. It was erected to honor residents of Comfort who during the Civil War did not approve of slavery and openly swore their loyalty to the Union and were subsequently killed by Confederate soldiers. It is the only monument to the Union located south of the Mason-Dixon Line.

Your next destination is **Boerne** (about 17 miles east of Comfort, off I-10). Also founded by German immigrants, the town is named for author Ludwig Boerne whose writings encouraged many Germans to come to the New World. About a mile from Main Street on Route 46, you'll find the *Agricultural Heritage Center*, with many farm and ranch tools used by the pioneers. Before heading back into San Antonio, consider visiting the *Cascade Caverns* (take exit 543 and follow signs). There are guided tours of the cavern which includes a 100-foot waterfall.

"Treue der Union"
Monument—
Comfort, Texas

Treue der Union

130

SPECIAL EVENTS

If you happen to be touring this part of Texas during any of these events, join in the festivities.
- In April, Fiesta takes place in San Antonio. This is a week-long festival with a water parade, art shows, food, and more.
- Come May, the Kerrville Folk Festival goes on for 11 days. It's the largest outdoor music festival in the state.
- For four days every August, the Texas Folklife Festival happens in San Antonio. It includes folk dancing, costumed craftspeople demonstrating crafts, and traditional cuisine.
- In September, the town of Del Rio celebrates its historic past with a festival called Deis y Seis de Septiembre. There's Mexican food, music, and all-around festivities.
- Another German Town in the Hill Country, Fredericksburg celebrates Oktoberfest every October with dancing, eating, and arts and crafts.

Awesome Arizona

Distance: 436 Miles Round-Trip, Phoenix
Time: Allow at least three days
Highlights: The Grand Canyon, shopping, museums and galleries, spectacular desert scenery, golf and tennis, hiking, horseback riding.

Incredibly colored canyons, tree-sized cactus, sunsets that elicit tears—Arizona's scenery stays with you forever. From **Phoenix**, it's an easy drive to the state's most beautiful sights.

Phoenix has come a long way since its cowtown days. Today, Arizona's capital is a sprawling metropolis offering a plethora of big-city pluses (museums, shops, restaurants, theaters), an astonishing range of sporting activities, and over 300 days of sunshine a year. If you're into fresh air and sporting, you'll fit right in with the local Phoenicians. Within the urban limits, there are over 50,000 swimming pools, 75 golf courses, 1000 tennis courts, and a man-made ocean for surfing. If that's not enough, you can go soaring, hang gliding, windsurfing, horseback riding, and hiking, too. Some of the city's top attractions include the *Heard Museum* which showcases art and artifacts of Southwest Native Americans; the *Arizona Biltmore Hotel*, a landmark structure designed by the famous American architect Frank Lloyd Wright; and the *Desert Botanical Garden*, where you can learn all about the extraordinary local plants and flowers.

The drive north from Phoenix to the *Grand Canyon* is peppered with attractions, never far from I-17. One of the first stops to consider making is *Arcosanti* (about 65 miles north). This is a prototype of a futuristic city employing what is called "arcology"—a synthesis of architecture and ecology.

The whole metropolis is inspired by a vision of the Italian architect Paolo Soleri. It's open daily for tours.

Further north is *Montezuma Castle National Monument*, a five-story, 20-room cliff-dwelling that was built by Native Americans more than 800 years ago. Though visitors cannot enter the castle itself, there is a self-guided trail offering excellent views of the structure.

Sedona is also on the way (take Route 179 to Alt 89 which runs parallel to I-17 to **Flagstaff**). As you approach it, the landscape all around becomes so magnificent, you'll want to pull over to take pictures. But hold back a bit, because the closer you get, the more spectacular it is. Everywhere you turn, terra-cotta rocks and cliffs tower above junipers, cypress, and piñon pines. So spectacular is the scenery that it has been the backdrop to more than 65 Hollywood Westerns. There are Jeep excursions through the red-rock landscape (hold on tight, they're not kidding when they talk about the 45 degree grade). Sedona is also considered the art-gallery capital of Arizona and has a Spanish-styled shopping complex called *Tlaquepaque* filled with intriguing boutiques.

Just north of Sedona, you'll find the steep-walled *Oak Creek Canyon*, studded with thousands of ponderosa pines. You can hike around, take a ride down the natural slide, snap

GOOD NIGHTS

For staying in the Grand Canyon area, make reservations far in advance at the El Tovar Hotel (602) 638-2401. This grand old hotel is perched on the south rim of the Grand Canyon. It was built in 1908 of native boulders and Oregon pine.

photos, or even try for a trout (it's necessary to buy a license in Sedona).

At Flagstaff, head north on U.S. 180 which will take you right to the Grand Canyon. Five million years ago, a stream that became the Colorado River began its meandering to the Gulf of California. Today, the north and south rims are nine miles apart, but the distance is so daunting that certain species of trees and animals appear on one side of the canyon but not on the other.

The *South Rim* is open all year around and features nature walks including rim hikes, excursions into the canyon, mule rides, and bus tours. For the very best Canyon views, consider taking a sightseeing flight in a helicopter or small plane. Or, for a completely different perspective, sign on for a summertime raft trip down the roaring Colorado.

From there, go east on Route 64, then head south on U.S. 89 to Flagstaff where you can pick up I-17 to return to Phoenix.

Valley of the Sun—Phoenix, Arizona

Balloon Festival, Valley of the Sun
Phoenix, Arizona

132

SOUTHWESTERN NATIONAL PARKS

■ *CARLSBAD CAVERNS NATIONAL PARK*

Carlsbad, New Mexico

One look around at the desert-like landscape that characterizes the foothills of the Guadalupe Mountains and one would never suspect that below lie dozens of cave systems with spectacular formations.

These limestone caverns were formed about 200 million years ago, during the Permian period, from an inland sea reef. The Carlsbad Cavern is the most famous of them; its Big Room is considered the largest underground room in the world (the ceiling is as high as a 60-story building).

Fresh-air activities: Year-round ranger-led cave walks, nature walks, and camping.

For more information: Carlsbad Caverns National Park, 3225 National Parks Highway, Carlsbad, NM 88220. (505) 785-2232.

■ *GRAND CANYON NATIONAL PARK*

Grand Canyon, Arizona

Everyone knows what the Grand Canyon looks like. America's most magnificent natural setting that has been filmed, photographed, written about, sung about...you name it. But no amount of research or knowledge can prepare you for the moment you actually lay eyes on this vast spectacle.

One of the seven natural wonders of the world, the Grand Canyon is 10 miles across at its widest point, up to a mile deep, 227 miles long, and a living record of 1.5 billion years of geologic history.

It's home to an astonishing variety of plants, over 220 species of birds, 67 species of mammals, 27 of reptiles, and 5 of amphibians.

Fresh-air activities: Camping, hiking, horseback riding, mule-back trips, boating, white-water rafting, nature walks, and bird watching.

For more information: Grand Canyon National Park, Box 129, Grand Canyon, AZ 86023. (602) 638-7888.

■ *PETRIFIED FOREST NATIONAL PARK*

Holbrook, Arizona

Here you'll find the world's largest showcase of petrified coniferous trees. Nearly 100,000 acres are covered with these hauntingly beautiful solid logs. Once trees, they fell in a swamp and were converted by mineralization to brilliantly colored rocks of jasper and agate.

Fresh-air activities: Year-round hiking, nature walks, and picnicking.

For more information: Petrified Forest National Park, Box 2217, Petrified Forest, AZ 86028. (602) 524-6228.

Lake Pleasant—Phoenix, Arizona.

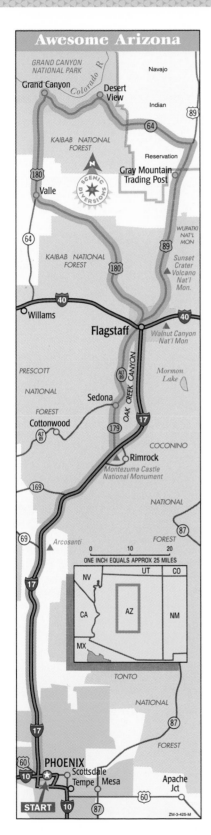

BIG BEND NATIONAL PARK

Maverick, Texas

On the U.S.- Mexican border, Big Bend is a wildly beautiful park that's home to thousands of western plants and animals (including mountain lions, cougar, fox, coyote, and pronghorn antelope). Much of it remains as raw and wild as it was when the first Europeans passed through back in the 1600s: the rocky pine-and-juniper-covered Chisos Mountain Range, deep multi-colored canyons with refreshing waterfalls, and the vast desert.

Fresh-air activities: Camping, boating, fishing, hiking, bird watching, horseback riding, picnicking, and pack trips year round.

For more information: Big Bend National Park, TX 79834. (915) 477-2251.

GUADALUPE MOUNTAINS NATIONAL PARK

Pine Springs, Texas

Texas' highest mountains, the Guadalupe Range rises out of the state's arid desert lands. The most prominent features are El Capitan, a 2,000-foot limestone cliff and Guadalupe Peak, the highest point in Texas at 8,749 feet. Also noteworthy are McKittrick Canyon, with its contrasting vegetation (lush maples next to yucca plants) and The Bowl, a high forest of Douglas fir and ponderosa pine.

There are pictographs in caves and rock shelters that indicate prehistoric Americans occupied many of the canyons as early as 12,000 years ago.

Keep your eyes open for mountain lions, bears, wild turkeys, and hawks.

Fresh-air activities: Camping and hiking year around.

For more information: Guadalupe Mountains National Park, HC 60, Box 400, Salt Flat, TX 79847-9400. (915 828-3251.

WILD ABOUT WILDLIFE

When visiting our national parks, keep the following in mind with regard to the animal kingdom:

helpful hints...

- Never sneak up on animals.
- Don't disturb nests and other habitats.
- Don't touch animals or try to remove them from their habitat for the sake of a photograph.
- Don't get between animal parents and their young.
- Never surround an animal or groups of animals.

133

TOURING TUCSON

Like Phoenix, Tucson has changed dramatically over the years. What used to be a rough Old West town, with tumbleweeds chasing shadows down the streets, is now a flourishing urban center. Stroll around the Arizona-Sonora Desert Museum, inspect the Kitt Peak National Observatory's astronomical instruments, and check out Old Tucson, the movie location where John Wayne used to battle outlaws. If you have time, consider saddling up for a ride in the Saguaro National Monument, a forest of cacti that can grow up to 50 feet tall.

California & Nevada

*W*ith a thousand miles of beaches, vast deserts, towering mountains, deeply cut valleys, and its fast-paced cities, California is one of the top tourist destinations in the country. Add to that the sensations of nearby Nevada—the gambling, the outdoor activities, the desert terrain—and you've got plenty of exploring to do. Here are five driving tours designed to take you through and to some of these two states' most magnificent areas.

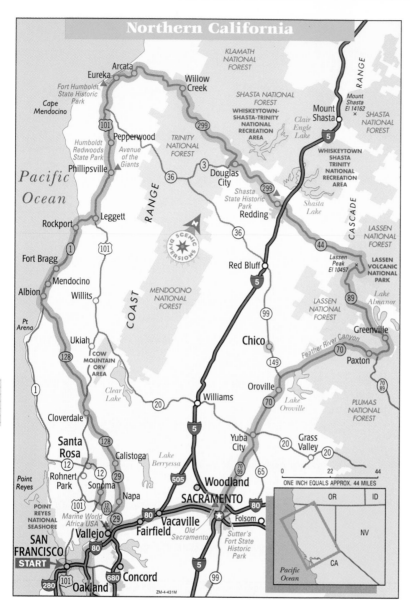

Northern California

Distance: 845 Miles Round-Trip, San Francisco
Time: Allow at least seven days
Highlights: San Francisco and Sacramento, wine country, outdoor sports including skiing in winter, Lassen Volcanic National Park, redwoods, coastal scenery, mountains, lakes.

You'll need at least a week to visit all the attractions and scenic areas north of **San Francisco**. Here you'll find the state's capital (**Sacramento**), *Redwood Country*, the *North Coast*, and *Sonoma County* and *Napa Valley*, the country's biggest wine-producing regions.

From San Francisco (see p. 141 for things to see and do in town), head north on I-80. In **Vallejo**, you'll find *Marine World Africa USA*, a wildlife theme park. There's also a very worthwhile *naval and historical museum*. Carry on to Sacramento, which, in addition to being the capital of the state, is considered the "Camellia Capital of the World", due to its abundance of the flower. See *Sutter's Fort State Historic Park*, *Old Sacramento Historic District*, the *State Capitol*, *Governor's Mansion*, and take your pick of museums (there's an art museum, a local history museum, a museum devoted to Ford automobiles, and a science center with hands-on exhibits and a planetarium).

Take Route 70 north. Just after the turn off for Route 149, it goes through *Feather River Canyon*, a densely scenic area. Turn left onto Route 89 shortly after you pass through **Paxton**. This takes you right through the *Lassen National Forest* to *Lassen Volcanic National Park*. Like Yellowstone, Lassen Volcanic National Park has thermal

TO B & B OR NOT TO B & B

Like everything, Bed & Breakfasts have their pros and cons.

Pros

a) They're reasonably priced.
b) You get to see how a local family lives and sets up home.
c) You can usually have a cup of tea in the middle of the afternoon without having to order room-service and pay for it.
d) A home-cooked breakfast is included in the price (usually a continental breakfast is served).

Cons

a) The bath is most likely down the hall and to be shared with fellow guests.
b) You may have to walk through somebody's living room to get to your room.
c) You won't have a personal telephone.
d) There are none of the services (such as a concierge and in-room meals) that you'd have at a hotel.

The choice is yours!

wonders such as mud pots, fumaroles, hot springs, and the like, but it's quite a bit smaller. *Lassen Peak*—the park's grande dame (10,457 feet) is one of the most recently active volcanoes in the lower 48 states (the last series of eruptions started in 1914 and continued for about seven years). The acreage surrounding it is home to forests, streams, and waterfalls.

Turn left onto Route 44 towards **Redding**, which is in the shadow of *Mount Shasta*, and bounded by the Coast Range on the west, the Cascades in the north, and the Sierra Nevada on the east.

About six miles west of Redding on Route 299 is the *Shasta State Historic Park*, which has the remains of a gold-rush town with several well-preserved buildings. About two miles further west is the *Whiskeytown-Shasta-Trinity National Recreation Area* where you can swim, fish, go boating, and picnic.

Continue west on Route 299 and before long, you'll be in the *Coast Range* . Carry on to the coast and turn left onto U.S. 101. In **Eureka**, see the *Fort Humboldt State Historic Park*, where Ulysses S. Grant was stationed in 1854; the *Clarke Memorial Museum* (regional history); and *Old Town*, with buildings dating back to Eureka's early days.

U.S. 101 takes you right through *Humboldt Redwoods State Park*, where giant redwoods grow. You'll pass through many groves including the spectacular *Avenue of the Giants*

Humboldt Redwoods, California

south of **Pepperwood** and north of **Phillipsville**.

At **Leggett**, turn right onto Route 1 which takes you down the coast. Stop to see **Fort Bragg**, which was a military post set up in 1857. Then move along to **Mendocino**, an artists' colony and popular resort community filled with New England architecture.

Just beyond **Albion**, turn left onto Route 128 which will take you right through the heart of wine country. Sonoma and Napa are California's most famous wine-growing valleys, and they make wonderful touring country. Start by stopping in the *Sonoma County Wineries Association's Visitors Center* (5000 Roberts Lake Road, Rohnert Park), where you can find out more about where to go via an interactive video terminal. The Napa Valley is less than half an hour away and is chockablock with wineries. Keep in mind that the Napa Valley is California's biggest attraction after Disneyland, so it can be very busy. In addition to touring the wineries, you can go hot-air ballooning, cycling, hiking, and picnicking. There are also several wonderful inns, restaurants, and shops.

From there, take Route 29 south to I-80 back to San Francisco.

RESORT REPORT

Minutes away from Lake Tahoe is **Squaw Valley**,**U.S.A.**, where the

Napa Valley, California

Wells Fargo building—Shasta State Park, California

Winter Olympic Games were held in 1960. It's home to the *Resort at Squaw Creek,* a wonderful winter destination with over 4,000 acres of world-class downhill skiing terrain, cross-country ski trails, a heated pool, spa, ice skating rink, and lots more. Come warm weather, there's golf, tennis, horseback riding, hiking, mountain biking, and swimming in a three-pool water garden. On top of that, there are all the attractions of nearby *Lake Tahoe.* The resort has 405 accommodations, all of which are tastefully decorated (many with original artwork) and all of which have forest or valley views. For more information, contact the Resort at Squaw Creek, 400 Squaw Creek Road, P.O. Box 3333, **Olympic Valley**, CA 96146; (916) 583-6300.

DID YOU KNOW

- Los Angeles was founded in 1781 as El Pueblo de Nuestra Senora la Regina de Los Angeles (The Town of Our Lady, Queen of the Angels).
- Lake Tahoe's water is so clear that a white dinner plate can be seen at a depth of almost 200 feet.
- One of the redwoods in *Big Tree State Park*, was so wide that a dance floor was built on its stump.
- At 2,425 feet from lip to basin, *Yosemite Falls* is the world's second tallest, after Angel Falls in Venezuela, and is 13 times higher than Niagara Falls.
- The annual frog-jumping contest held on the third weekend of May in **Angels Camp** was inspired by Mark Twain's short story, *The Celebrated Jumping Frog of Calaveras County.*

Gold Country and High Sierra

Distance: 902 Miles Round-Trip, Sacramento
Time: Allow between seven and ten days
Highlights: Sacramento, three national parks, casinos, raw natural beauty, Lake Tahoe, mountains, hiking, biking, swimming, fishing, mountaineering, downhill and cross-country skiing in winter.

The *Sierra Nevada* is the largest single mountain range in the country. It's a single block of earth, 430 miles long and 80 miles wide. For this diversion, we take you from **Sacramento** over this magnificent landscape across the border into Nevada. We visit the sparkly city of **Reno** and resorty Lake Tahoe and then the wildernesses of *Yosemite*, *Kings Canyon*, and *Sequoia National Parks*. From there, we take you back to Sacramento through *Gold Country.*

A gateway to the Gold Country as well as the state capital, Sacramento has some very interesting sights to see. Wander around *Old Sacramento*, a national historic landmark encompassing 28 acres and more than 100 restored

Sequoia National Park, California

and re-created buildings. And be sure to see the *California State Railroad Museum*, a highpoint of any visit to Old Sacramento. There are actually sights, sounds, and smells of the old railroads. Other attractions include the *State Capitol Building*, *Sutter's Fort*, the *California State Indian Museum*, the *Crocker Art Museum*, *Governor's Mansion*, the *Towe Ford Museum*, and the *California Citizen Soldier Museum*.

From Sacramento, head east through the Sierra Nevada Mountains on I-80. Plan to make your first stop *Donner Memorial State Park*, where there's a museum that commemorates a party of pioneers who tried to cross the mountains during the terrible winter of 1846-47. Many of them died from exposure and hunger; some went crazy and resorted to cannibalism. Continue east to **Truckee**, a 19th-century town that sits astride a mountain pass. Take a walk down its main street, Commercial Row. It's lined with false-front buildings.

Continue east on I-80, crossing the border into Nevada and before long, you'll be in Reno. A town that prides itself on its big-city amenities, but small-town friendliness, it was originally a trading post on the wagon train routes. It later developed into an important railhead for the nearby **Virginia City** mines. Today it's a gambling and entertainment center as well as gateway to extensive outdoor recreation in the Sierra Nevada Mountains. Highlights include the *Fleischmann Atmospherium-Planetarium*, the *Nevada Historical Society Museum*, and an extensive mineral collection preserved within the *School of Mines Museum* on

AN AUTHOR-ITY

Mark Twain once said of Lake Tahoe, "As it lays there with the shadows of the mountains brilliantly photographed upon its still surface I thought it must surely be the fairest picture the whole earth affords."

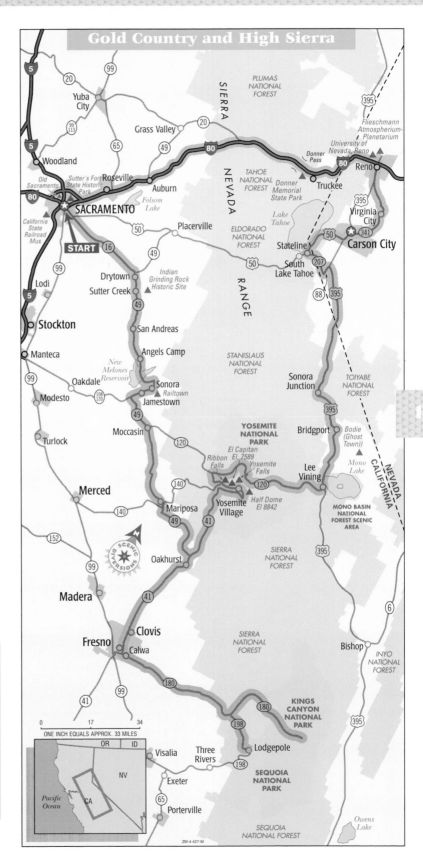

Gold Country and High Sierra

139

the *University of Nevada* campus.

From Reno, take U.S. 395 South to Route 341 to Virginia City, which was one of the richest cities in North America and is Nevada's most famous mining town. Perched on the side of *Mt. Davidson*, it's beautiful. Visitors can tour some of the old mansions, visit the opera house, poke around some art galleries, and take a ride on the *V & T Railroad*.

Continue south to **Carson City**, the state capital. It was named for the frontiersman Kit Carson. The most noteworthy building is the silver-domed Capitol constructed in the 1870's from native sandstone. Take time to tour the downtown historic and old home districts (guided tours are available).

From Carson City, it's a short drive west to *Lake Tahoe* (take U.S. 50), perched on the California-Nevada line. One of the most well-known year-round resorts, the area offers both gambling and outdoor activities, especially skiing (and other wintertime activities). With an average of 350 inches of snow each year and sunshine 75% of the time, it really lives up to skier's expectations.

On the southern end, you'll pass through **Stateline**, which used to be a famous stop on the Pony Express route and is now a major casino center.

Take Route 207 through Daggett Pass, turn left on Route 88 to U.S. 395 south which will eventually cross the border back into California. Turn right on Route 120 for Yosemite National Park, a monumentally beautiful park climbing across the Sierra Nevada from 2000 feet to 13,000 feet. You'll soon come to a visitors center where you can find out more about the park's attractions, hiking trails, and other activities. The natural wonders in the park are numerous. It's home to two of the world's highest waterfalls (*Upper Yosemite* and *Ribbon*); *El Capitan*, a gigantic mass of unbroken granite; and *Half Dome*, one of our country's

Half Dome—Yosemite National Park, California

most famous peaks. There is also a grove of giant sequoias, some magnificently scenic high country, and more than 750 miles of trails.

Take Route 120 across the park and then head south on Route 41. Follow this all the way to **Fresno** and then follow Route 180 to Kings Canyon National Park. Along with adjoining Sequoia National Park, Kings Canyon was set aside to preserve groves of giant sequoia trees. Sequoias are the planet's largest trees (in volume), with trunks averaging 35 feet in diameter, while redwoods are the world's tallest trees (sequoias grow to about 250 feet, redwoods tower up to 300 feet). Both are the last surviving species of a large genus of ancient times. Between the two parks (which are administered as one park), there are more than 1,300 square miles of rugged Sierra landscape. Though most of the main attractions in both can be reached by car, plan to do some exploring on foot to get the most out of your visit.

Retrace your steps to Fresno and then head north on Route 41, turning left onto Route 49 which is a consistently scenic route through Gold Country. Along the way, you'll pass

Fleischmann Atmospherium-Planetarium— Reno, Nevada

through many mining towns, some of which have been impeccably preserved or restored.

Just after **Drytown**, turn left onto Route 16 to return to Sacramento.

San Francisco and Monterey Bay

....

Distance: 261 Miles Round-Trip, San Francisco
Time: Allow at least two or three days
Highlights: San Francisco, coastal scenery, art colonies, fishing communities, beaches, water sports.

A series of hills crested with gingerbread mansions and glass-and-chrome towers, **San Francisco** is one of the world's most captivating cities, especially when the fog horns blow, the sea gulls soar overhead, and the cable cars trundle by. Combine a visit here with a coastal drive to the pair of coast-hugging hamlets (**Carmel-by-the-Sea** and **Monterey**) and you have a made-to-order perfect weekend trip.

You can take your time exploring San Francisco's patchwork of neighborhoods taking breaks in the dozens of bohemian coffee shops. Be sure to walk up to *Telegraph Hill* from which you can see the bay either bundled in fog or clear as a window with the *Golden Gate Bridge* hogging your attention. Window-shop on fashionable *Union Square*. Watch the sea lions that have colonized the docks off *Fisherman's Wharf*. Eat dim sum in *Chinatown* or deliriously good pasta in *North Beach*. The list goes on and on.

From San Francisco, take the coast road (Route 1) south, passing wave-smashed beaches all the way to **Santa Cruz**, a resort town on the north end of Monterey Bay. Here you'll find sensational swimming and surfing

beaches. There's also a boardwalk with a carousel dating back to 1911 and a 1924 rollercoaster, plus amusement arcades, eateries, and other ocean-side attractions. Other Santa Cruz attractions include the *Mission Santa Cruz* which is actually a replica of the original one that was destroyed in 1857, the *Casa Adobe* (Santa Cruz's oldest house), and the *Mystery Spot*, a very puzzling 150—foot circle where some of the laws of gravity are broken.

Follow Route 1 south along the bay to Monterey, which was the old Spanish and Mexican capital of Alta California. There's a self-guided walking tour map available at the Chamber of Commerce which takes you to all of the historic buildings in the *Monterey State Historic Park*. Be sure to spend some time on Fisherman's Wharf, where there are all sorts of shops, seafood cafes, paneled pubs, and boat trips to take (including whale-watching cruises). Take time too to see the *Monterey Bay Aquarium* on Cannery Row, the fish-canning factory author John Steinbeck made famous.

From nearby **Pacific Grove**, you can follow the legendary *Seventeen-Mile Drive* (toll required) which takes you through consistently knock-your-socks-off beautiful scenery (rugged headlands topped by golf greens, windswept cypresses, white-sand beaches pounded by the bravely foaming Pacific) to Carmel.

Carmel's charming eccentricities—a ban on neon, house numbers, and traffic lights—keeps it postcard-perfect. It's a felony to cut down a tree here, so *Ocean Avenue* resembles not so much a street as a park, lined with cypress, pines, and flower beds. Inns and restaurants are tucked away in Hansel-and-Gretel cottages and red-tiled adobes, and an astounding number of bakeries, antiques shops, and maritime galleries hide in the brick-lined alleys just off the main drag. There's a perfect little beach at the foot of the avenue, and the surrounding scenery is splendid, especially at wildly beautiful *Point Lobos State Reserve* (bring binoculars to spy on the sea lions and otters).

Head inland on Route 68 and then take U.S. 101 north back to San Francisco. If you're a John Steinbeck fan, consider

Hyde Street Trolley Car—San Francisco, California

141

HAVE CRAYONS, WILL TRAVEL

To help youngsters get the most out of family trips, encourage them to keep travel logs. Start them off with a large sketch book (and a roll of tape), so they can draw what they see and collect flowers, ticket stubs, and any other little souvenirs they find along the way. When they get older, encourage them to go out "shooting" with an instamatic camera so they have their own photos.

stopping in **Salinas**, where the author was born. The house is now a restaurant and gift shop in the town's nine-block historic district.

From there, continue north on U.S. 101 for 108 miles to San Francisco.

CALIFORNIA AND NEVADA NATIONAL PARKS

CHANNEL ISLANDS NATIONAL PARK

Santa Barbara, California
Five islands—Anacapa, Santa Cruz, Santa Rosa, San Miguel, and Santa

Barbara—comprise this serenely beautiful national park. Nicknamed "America's Galapagos," it's home to a wide variety of marine mammals and many unique plant species.

Fresh-air activities: Visitors can hike, swim, bird-watch, and camp year round.

For more information: Channel Islands National Park, 1901 Spinnaker Drive, Ventura, CA 93001. (805) 658-5700.

LASSEN VOLCANIC NATIONAL PARK

Susanville, California
With great lava summits, huge mountains created by lava streams, rugged craters and steaming sulphur vents, Lassen Volcanic National Park holds the same wonder for tourists as Yellowstone.

Lassen Peak (10,457 feet) erupted in 1914 beginning a 7-year cycle of sporadic volcanic outbursts, making it one of the most recently active volcanoes in the lower 48 states. The acreage surrounding the park is home to forests, streams, and waterfalls.

Fresh-air activities: Naturalist programs, fishing, camping, hiking, and boating from May to October; ski tours in winter.

For more information: Lassen Volcanic National Park, Mineral, CA 96063. (916) 595-4444

REDWOOD NATIONAL PARK

Orick, California
The world's tallest tree—367.4 feet high—stands in this northern California park along with hundreds of other towering redwoods. These trees—some of which have been growing a thousand years or more—once were widely spread across North America, but today they can only be found along this very moist stretch of coast.

The park also takes in 46 miles of Pacific coastline scalloped with pebble and sand beaches and sea-carved cliffs. It's prime bird watching territory with everything from

Point Lobos State Reserve, California

gulls and cormorants to great blue herons.

Fresh-air activities: Camping, hiking, bicycling (along Avenue of the Giants), and fishing year round. Field seminars on birds, photography, and park ecosystems are conducted summer weekends.

For more Information: Redwood National Park, Drawer N, 1111 Second Street, Crescent City, CA 95531. (707) 464-6101.

■ SEQUOIA AND KINGS NATIONAL PARKS

Three Rivers, California
Situated in the heart of the Sierra Nevada Mountains, Sequoia National Park—along with next-door Kings Canyon National Park—has two major claims to fame. First, it contains the highest peak in the lower 48 states (Mt. Whitney—14,494 feet). Second, it has 26 groves of mammoth sequoia trees. Sequoias are the planet's largest trees with trunks averaging 35 feet in diameter, while redwoods are the world's tallest trees (sequoias grow to about 250 feet, redwoods tower up to 300 feet).

The largest of the groves is the Giant Forest, centerpieced by the earth's largest living tree—the General Sherman. The tree stands 272 feet high, is 36 feet in diameter, and weighs 1,450 tons.

Fresh-air activities: From June to October, camping, fishing, hiking, and horseback riding; skiing in winter months.

For more information: Sequoia National Park, Three Rivers, CA 93271. (209) 565-3341.

■ YOSEMITE NATIONAL PARK

Yosemite Village, California
Yosemite has the Ice Age to thank for its good looks. Glaciers left the area strewn with spectacular granite peaks and plunging waterfalls.

Five of the seven continental life zones are represented in the plant and animal species that live in the park including more than 75 mammal species, hundreds of birds, and over a thousand species of flowering plants and trees.

Fresh-air activities: Naturalist programs, camping, hiking, biking, swimming, fishing, mountaineering, overnight muleback saddle trips between June and October; downhill and cross-country skiing in winter.

For more information: Yosemite National Park, Box 577, Yosemite Village, CA 95389 (209) 372-0200.

■ GREAT BASIN NATIONAL PARK

Baker, Nevada
Extending from the Wasatch Mountains in Utah to the Sierra Nevada in California, and from Idaho south to Arizona, the Great Basin showcases the contrasting worlds of the desert and the mountains. During a visit to the park (a very small portion of the basin itself), you can see everything from sagebrush and juniper to alpine meadows strewn with wildflowers, glacial lakes, and stands of bristlecone pines, the oldest living things on earth.

A BRIDGE WITH A VIEW

San Francisco's Golden Gate Bridge is not only one of the longest single-span suspension bridges in the world, but perhaps the most beautiful and the most famous. Linking San Francisco to Sausalito, it was designed by Joseph Strauss and built between 1933 and 1937 at a cost of $35 million. For one of the best views of the city itself, follow the handicapped-accessible walk up to the toll plaza level, where you'll also find landscaped gardens.

143

The Golden Gate Bridge—San Francisco, California

Spanish-Moorish court house—Santa Barbara, California

The park is also home to Lehman Cave which is one of the largest limestone caverns in the West.

Fresh-air activities: Naturalist-led tours and hiking year round.

For more information: Great Basin National Park, Baker, Nevada 89311. (702) 234-7331.

California's Central Coast

Distance: 244 Miles, Los Angeles to San Simeon
Time: Allow at least two days
Highlights: Los Angeles, coastal scenery, missions, mountains, wineries, Hearst Castle, outdoor activities.

For this drive, we combine a visit to **Los Angeles** with a drive up the coast which is one of the most spectacular drives in the state (and entire country).

Chances are, you already know what you want to see and do in the Los Angeles area. There's *Beverly Hills* and the movie studios, beaches, museums (the *Museum of Contemporary Art*, the *Los Angeles Museum of Art*), and a complete galaxy of family attractions (including *Disneyland* and *Knott's Berry Farm*).

Big Sur, California

From Los Angeles, head north on U.S. 101 to **Santa Barbara**, a California mission town. Here you'll find beautiful Mediterranean-style buildings festooned with fragrant blossoms. A "red-tile" walking tour takes you through the historic district to all the highlights, including the *Santa Barbara Mission*. For the best view in town, go up to the tower of the *Spanish-Moorish court house*. As you travel up the coast, you'll find several missions as you go along.

Continue up the coast passing non-stop beautiful scenery (the *Santa Ynez Mountains* loom up on your right, while the island-dotted *Santa Barbara Channel* shines like a huge sheet of mica on your left.

U.S. 101 takes you north by *Pismo Beach* (with 23 miles of white-sand beaches) and to **San Luis Obispo** which is centered around the historic *Mission San Luis Obispo de Tolosa*, founded in 1772 by Father Junipero Serra. There are over two dozen wineries in this area, many offering tours and tastings.

From there, it's a short drive north on Route 1 to the fishing village of **Morro Bay**. The number one attraction here is the massive volcanic spire that juts out almost 600 feet above sea level. At *Morro Bay State Park*, you can hike, go horseback riding, picnic, and camp. There's also a natural history museum.

Morro Bay is where *Big Sur*, an 80-mile stretch of coast begins. Considered a coastal drive of unparalleled beauty, it meanders its way up to just below **Monterey** plunging past parched canyons, sweeping meadows, and steep cliffs that fall sharply into the foam. Though we don't take you all the way there in this diversion, it's a drive not to miss (see page 141 for more information on the Monterey area).

Your last stop on this itinerary is **San Simeon**. Built by newspaper magnate William Randolph Hearst, the *Hearst Castle* is an opulently furnished mansion on top of a hill called La Cuesta Encantada. Nearly 30 years were spent building the Spanish-Moorish castle that's surrounded by Italianate gardens and stuffed with artwork from around the world.

Back in the 1930s, guests such as Charlie Chaplin, Clark Gable, and Cary Grant would visit the publisher who lived here at that time. Today, guests can tour the property and buildings.

From there, you can continue north up the coast or return to work your way back down to Los Angeles, taking in the attractions you might have missed on your way up.

SANTA MONICA: THE ARTS SCENE

If you love to gallery hop, you'll be in heaven at *Bergamot Station*, a fairly new attraction in **Santa Monica**. Located on the corner of Olympic and 26th Street, this former industrial site is now occupied by a collection of galleries. Many top L.A. galleries have relocated here including *Patricia Faure Gallery*, *Ernie Wolfe Gallery*, *Craig Krull Gallery*, *Peter Fetterman Gallery*, and *Shoshana Wayne Gallery*. There's also a café here and eventually there will be two theater stages, plus a restaurant owned by Chef Rockenwagner, one of the city's most highly regarded chefs. For information, call (310) 829-5854.

SANTA MONICA: INN-SIDE STORY

If you're looking for someplace wonderful to stay in the Los Angeles area, try *Shutters on the Beach*. Propped up on the sands of Santa Monica bay, Shutters (for those in the know) is right near the city's historic pier and within walking distance of all the beachfront activity, the shopping districts, and the city's restaurant and nightlife scene. On top of that, its just a quick drive into L.A. itself and 20 minutes from the airport. Throughout the hotel, there is original artwork including pieces by David Hockney, Roy Lichtenstein, and William Wegaman. All guest rooms are beautifully decorated and have views of the ocean.

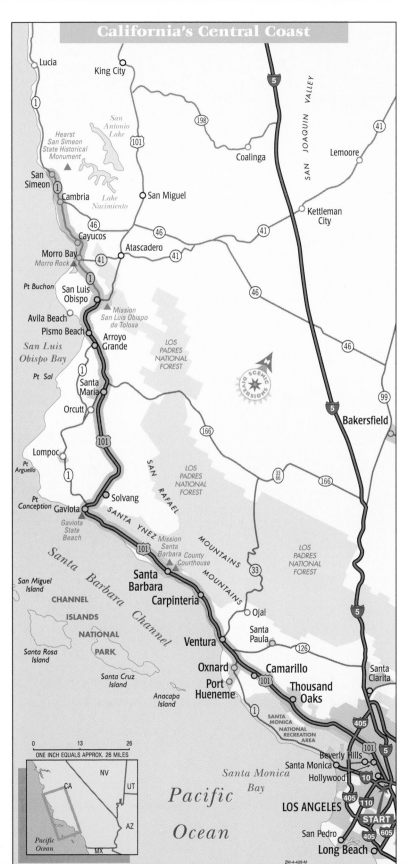

145

Each one has its own whirlpool tub in the bathroom. There are three restaurants, plus a health and fitness center. For information, contact Shutters on the Beach, One Pico Boulevard, Santa Monica, CA 90405; (310) 458-0030.

Southern California

Distance: 513 Miles Round-Trip, Los Angeles
Time: Allow at least three or four days
Highlights: Mountains, desert, missions, beaches, Disneyland, spas, tennis and golf, swimming, outdoor activities.

Sensational scenery punctuated with historic towns and a handful of cities—what more could you want on a driving tour? For this trip we take you east of **Los Angeles** through the *San Bernardino Mountains* to the resort towns of **Palm Springs** and **Palm Desert**. We then show you the way to the *Salton Sea* and cut across part of the *Colorado Desert*. From there, we wind our way up the coast, from **San Diego** back to L.A..

East of metropolitan Los Angeles, you'll find some amazing landscapes. Some of it can be seen almost immediately. Start by taking I-10 out of the city. Just northeast of **San Bernardino**, you can follow the "Rim of the World Drive" (Route 18) through the San Bernardino Mountains. Leaving **Crestline** you will wind past several lakes and lofty peaks looming up to over 11,000 feet. *Lake Arrowhead* is one of this alpine region's

most special places, popular with Hollywood name-names.

Follow the rim drive around to Route 38, which you can follow back to I-10 continuing to head southeast.

Take Route 111 to Palm Springs, a celebrity playground in the desert. Ever since 1930, Hollywood film stars have been retreating to this resort area to dip into the good spa life, the golf and tennis, and the year-round perfect climate. The most noteworthy attractions include the *Palm Springs Desert Museum*, the *Village Green Heritage Center* (devoted to local history), *McCallum Adobe* (the town's oldest building, now a museum filled with photos of Hollywood stars and other mementos from Palm Springs earlier days), *Cornelia White's House* (the 1893 home of a pioneer woman), *Ruddy's General Store* (a re-creation of a 1930s-era general store), and *Moorten's Botanical Garden* where you can see over 3000 varieties of desert plants.

The highlight for many people's visit to Palm Springs is a ride on the *Aerial Tramway* up Mt. San Jacinto. Be prepared for a bit of nail-biting. It's a 50 degree angle to 8,516 feet. It's worth it though. On a typical day, from the top, you can see the *Coachella Valley* from *Joshua Tree* to the Salton Sea.

A short distance south of Palm Springs is Palm Desert, another desert resort community. Take time to see *The Living Desert* here. It's a 1,200-acre nature park that recreates desert life (both the plants and wildlife).

Follow Route 111 to Route 86 and head south to **Salton City** and the Salton Sea. This inland saltwater lake was created when the Colorado River flooded through a broken canal gate. It's more than 35 miles long and up to 15 miles wide and is a sanctuary for sea birds (many of which can be seen at the national wildlife refuge at the southern end of the lake). It's also a popular recreational area with swimming, boating, water-skiing, and fishing.

Head west on Route 78 which will take you right through the *Octillo Badlands* and into the *Anza-Borrego*

Zoo—San Diego, California

Desert. Before long you will go from desert to mountains (the Volcan Mountains) which have been colonized by pine trees. The route is especially beautiful from **Ocotillo Wells** to **Julian**. Consider pausing for lunch or to poke around the artsy shops of Julian, a picturesque little gold rush town. From there, head south on Route 79 and pick up I-8 west for San Diego.

San Diego is the kind of city everybody wishes they could live in. It has a wonderful year-round air of festivity and an ideal climate. Sightseeing highlights include *Point Loma* with *Cabrillo National Monument*, *San Diego Bay*, *Seaport Village* (docked nearby is the 1864 Windjammer Star of India), restored *Old Town*, *Mission Bay Park*, *Sea World*, and *Balboa Park* with its wonderful gardens, museums, and world famous zoo. Sightseeing tours abound. Take a trolley tour of Old Town or to nearby **Tijuana**, Mexico. Or board a boat to experience the delights of the harbor.

Take I-5 north from downtown San Diego for about ten miles to the Ardath

San Diego, California

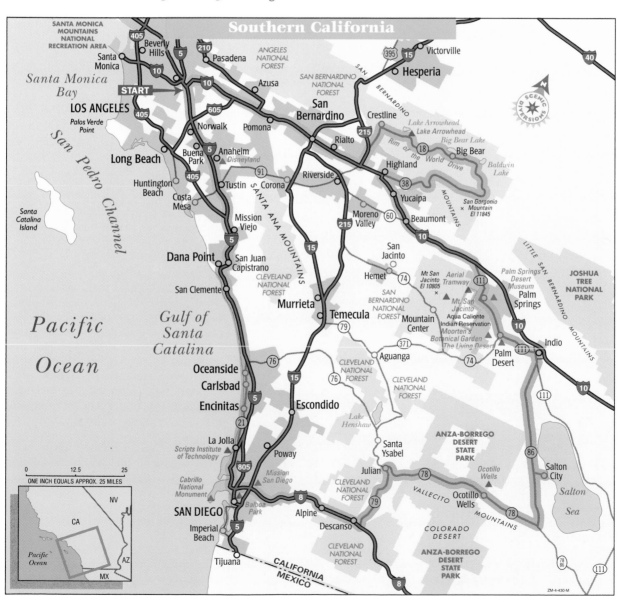

147

Road turnoff to **La Jolla** (pronounced 'La HOY-a'). A sophisticated seaside town, it's rife with museums, galleries, shops, and restaurants. Be sure to see *La Jolla Cove* (which is a popular spot for divers), *Whale Point*, and the caves in the cliffs below town, and don't miss the *Museum of Contemporary Art* or the marine aquarium at the *Scripps Institution of Oceanography*.

From La Jolla, take the coast road (Route 21) north through the beach communities. You'll pass lovely beaches and windswept bluffs. Consider stopping to see the 1,900-foot pier that protrudes into the Pacific at **Oceanside**, a very popular spot for surfers.

From Oceanside, take I-5 north, making a stop at **San Juan Capistrano**. The centerpiece of town is the *Mission San Juan Capistrano*, which is considered "The jewel of the missions." Built in 1777, it is a magical building.

Wrap up your trip with a visit to *Disneyland* in **Anaheim**. Though not quite as extensive as the Florida property, Disneyland is a mecca for amusement park aficionados. The highlight of its 76 acres is a ride called "Star Tour" in which visitors are ushered aboard StarSpeeders which blast off on a madcap flight to the Moon of Endor, using the same flight simulator technology used to train military and commercial pilots.

From there, it's an easy drive into Los Angeles.

CALIFORNIA CITY SCENES

California's three main cities have completely different personalities. There's San Francisco, the sophisti-cated northern city; Los Angeles which has long lured ambitious people in the film industry; and San Diego in the south, a resort-like city not far from the Mexican border. Here are some of the highlights:

■ San Francisco

A cosmopolitan blend of cultures, outstanding scenery, fine dining, and entertainment gives San Francisco a unique charm. Highlights include the *Golden Gate Bridge*, *Museum of Modern Art*, *M.H. DeYoung Museum*, *California Academy of Sciences*, *North Beach*, *Fisherman's Wharf*, the famed cable cars running from the wharf to downtown *Union Square*, *Golden Gate National Recreation Area*, *National Maritime Museum*, *Alcatraz*, *Chinatown*, the *Presidio*, *Telegraph Hill*, *Nob Hill*, *The Embarcadero*, *Old Mint*, *Palace of the Legion of Honor*, *Palace of Fine Arts*, and *Opera House*.

■ Los Angeles

This sprawling southern California basin actually encompasses many small cities. Los Angeles proper has the stunning *Music Center*, *Little Tokyo*, *Chinatown*, landmark *Union Station*, *El Pueblo de los Angeles State Historic Park*, *Griffith Park* (with observatory, old locomotive collection, and zoo), *Exposition Park*, *UCLA* and *USC*, *Southwest Museum*, TV studios, and *Sunset Strip*. **Santa Monica** and **Malibu** are attractive beach towns. Movie studio tours are offered in **Hollywood**, **Burbank**, and *Universal City*. **Beverly Hills** features some of the most expensive homes in the country.

■ San Diego

Highlights of this lovely coastal city include *Cabrillo National Monument*, restored *Old Town*, *Mission San Diego*, *Balboa Park* with its aerospace museum, relic buildings from the 1915 and 1935 California-Pacific Exposition, *Old Globe Theater*, *Spanish Village Arts and Crafts Center*, *Museum of Art*, *Natural History Museum*, and one of the world's leading zoos.

IT'S ALL DOWNHILL

Whoever said that life is a series of ups and downs, is wrong. In San Diego, California, you can take the Palomar Plunge, which lets you soar down 5,000 feet of *Mount Palomar* on a 21-speed Rockhopper mountain bike. Your journey begins with a van ride to the peak and it's crowning observatory. From there, you're safety outfitted with jackets, helmets, goggles, and cycling gloves and sent on your 16-mile way (with an experienced tour leader guiding the pack and a van holding up the rear). Tours cost $75 and include lunch and a commemorative photo, a certificate of achievement, and a T-shirt. For information, call Gravity-Activated Sports, (619) 742-2294.

Mission Bay Park, harbor excursions, *Sea World*, and the trolley to **Tijuana** are other sightseeing attractions.

OTHER URBAN AREAS

■ Palm Springs

This elegant resort community, home of the rich and famous, offers an aerial tramway, championship golf courses, tennis, bicycling, a desert museum, and desert canyons filled with palms.

■ Sacramento

The splendid state capitol here has been nicely refurbished. *Old Sacramento Historic District* includes an outstanding railroad museum and many early buildings. See also the *Crocker Art Museum*, *Sutter's Fort*, governor's mansion, and the science center. The *American River Parkway* has bike paths. The Sacramento River is popular for float trips.

■ San Bernardino

This city is the gateway to mountain resorts around *Big Bear* and *Arrowhead* lakes. Nearby Riverside has an *Indian Museum*, *Riverside International Raceway*, and the *Mission Inn*.

■ San Jose

Center for the electronics and computer industries also features *Winchester Mystery House*, small wineries, *Lick Observatory*, and *Great America* theme park in nearby **Santa Clara**.

A Day at the Beach

P H O T O   T I P S

helpful hints...

Since you're in Southern California, chances are pretty good you're going to go to the beach. If you want to take home some good lasting memories of your visit or visits, familiarize yourself with the following tips gathered from professional photographers.

• Use a waterproof camera. Rather than risk getting your treasured 35 mm camera wet or sandy, consider splurging on an inexpensive waterproof camera. These simple-to-use cameras can go right in the water with you.

• Know your equipment. Testing out a new flash, a new lens, or even a new kind of film should be done before going on your trip. Otherwise, you risk losing some shots you may never have the opportunity to take again.

• Stock up on film before leaving home. The cost of film at resorts and beach shops can be astronomically high.

• Pack lens cleaning paper and extra batteries. Finding out that your lens is dirty or your batteries have died, when you have two minutes of a fiery sunset left, is no fun.

• Keep equipment in the shade. Under no circumstances leave cameras, film, and other paraphernalia in the sun or a hot car.

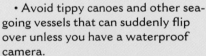

Film, especially, is easily destroyed by heat.

• Avoid tippy canoes and other seagoing vessels that can suddenly flip over unless you have a waterproof camera.

• Use a slow film if it's sunny. You don't need a faster film than ISO 25 or 64 until the sun goes down or if it's cloudy.

• Avoid shooting midday. Most professional photographers only shoot in the early morning and late afternoon when the light is very good. When the sun is high and bright, you risk having all sorts of reflections spoil the shots.

• Don't unload your camera in direct sunlight. Go to your car, a nearby building, or a shady tree—don't think your body shadow is enough to protect it.

• Ask permission to photograph people. Rather than snap away, take a minute to ask a person if they would mind being in your photograph.

• Label rolls of film. Too many photographers toss rolls of film into their bags only to find out later that they can't tell one beach from another. Take a minute to jot down the necessary information.

Pacific Northwest

*I*f it's beautiful scenery you're after, don't miss traveling through the Pacific Northwest. Between Washington and Oregon, there's a whole combination platter of terrains to see. All along the coast of both states, the mighty Pacific dramatically crashes in, waves breaking prismatically on rocky headlands. Move inland and fir-covered foothills and mountains—the Olympic Range in Washington, the Coast Range in Oregon—immediately take over. Further inland, the snow-capped Cascades—which were formed by centuries of volcanic activity—divide the Northwest from the Canadian border to south of Oregon. As a result, the west holds the moist Pacific air (the coastal hills are said to be one of the wettest spots on earth) and the east is largely dry, desert terrain.

Though natural beauty is what visitors most look forward to, the Pacific Northwest is also home to a handful of deeply interesting cities. The two biggest hubs, Portland and Seattle, are both progressive minded, architecturally interesting, internationally influenced, and...fairly easy to get to know. Of course, they have all the ingredients a big city should have: the museums, the restaurants, the shops, the nightlife.

There's more that makes it fun, however. For one thing, it's easy to drive. Not only are roads well-maintained and marked, but even the major ones—including interstates—slice right through the kind of scenery you see on the pages of Condé Nast Traveler.

Columbia River—Portland, Oregon

Looking Around Oregon

Distance: 854 Miles Round Trip, Portland
Time: Allow seven days
Highlights: Portland, Columbia River Gorge, coastal scenery, mountains, forests, national park, outdoor activities.

A state of unparalleled natural beauty, Oregon now has another huge attraction. Increasingly, its *Wilamette Valley* (which stretches 110 miles between **Portland** and **Eugene**) which is being colonized by electronics companies seeking cheaper land, no sales tax, and good public schools. Its good looks are not being compromised, however. You will find some of the most mesmerizingly beautiful scenery ever, from the wave-smashed shores of the coast to the deep inland forests.

Start by exploring Portland, which was named after Portland, Maine, in 1845 by Francis W. Pettygrove. Whether the name would be Portland or Boston was decided by Pettygrove and A.L. Lovejoy, two

early settlers, by the toss of a coin. The popular *Powell's Bookstores* offer a great self-guided walking map of downtown for free. It's available at hotels, restaurants, tourism offices, and of course, the bookstores themselves. Don't miss *Pioneer Courthouse Square* (notice all the red bricks have names of donors on them), Michael Graves' *Postmodern Portland Building* and its sculpture of Portlandia above the entrance, and if it's Saturday, the *Portland Saturday Market* under the Burnside Bridge on 1st Avenue in *Old Town*. Also take a drive up to the *West Hills* where you'll find the *International Rose Test Garden* and *Japanese Gardens* crowning a hilltop.

From Portland, take U.S. 30 west which roughly follows the Columbia River to the coast. You'll then turn left onto U.S. 101, to make your way down the coast.

Unlike some costal routes, Route 101 really hugs the shoreline, twisting and turning with the sea-carved points and inlets. You will see the Pacific foaming, waves lashing the coastline on one side, and thick green forests and mountains on the other. Every once in a while, you'll pass huge stone monoliths (such as Haystack Rock south of Cannon Beach) that rise dramatically from the ocean floor.

Along the way, there are a handful of towns to see such as **Cannon Beach** and **Newport** which are lively summer hubs with shops selling Native American and Alaskan crafts, marine-themed art galleries, and seafood eateries. In addition to these towns, consider stopping at the *Tillamook Cheese Factory*, where you can see how the cheese is processed before ordering a grilled cheese lunch; the *Sea Lions Cave*, where you ride an elevator down 208 feet to see a cave filled with these barking muscular creatures; the *Oregon Dunes National Recreation Area*, which offers 42 miles of high windswept dunes; and scenic viewpoints all along the way.

Turn inland at **Reedsport** on Route 38. Then turn right onto Route 138 at **Elkton** and follow that south to connect with I-5 which you can hop on and take a few miles to **Winston**. Here you'll find the *World Wildlife Safari*, where elephants, tigers, monkeys, and other animals from Africa, Asia, and South America roam a 600-acre park while visitors view from inside their cars. Don't miss the cheetah compound, which has the largest collection of these lightning-fast animals in North America.

Head back north on I-5 and then go east on Route 138. This cuts through the *Umpqua National Forest* and takes you right to *Crater Lake National Park*. Set in a dormant volcano, the focal point of this park is Crater Lake with over 21 square miles of water encompassed by cliffs towering more than 2,000 feet above the lakes surface. The *Rim Drive* (33.4 miles) is a scenic road running around the rim of the crater itself. It takes you around the caldera, to all the observation points and hiking trails. It opens in early July and closes after the first heavy snowfall.

From the park, head east on Route 138 and then follow U.S. 97 north. Much of this route (south of **Bend**) closely follows the route of a wagon road used by the pioneers. About 25 miles south of Bend, turn right to get to the *Newberry National Volcanic Monument* (it's about 14 miles east of U.S. 97). Ancient Mt. Newberry once soared up to 10,000 feet, but over many thousands of years, collapsed, forming a crater. There are two lakes there now—Paulina and East Lake—

and a wide range of volcanic features and deposits. Take time out to hike the trails through the crater and around the rim.

Continue north on U.S. 97 to the *Lava Lands Visitor Center* (just south of Bend). Here you can learn all about

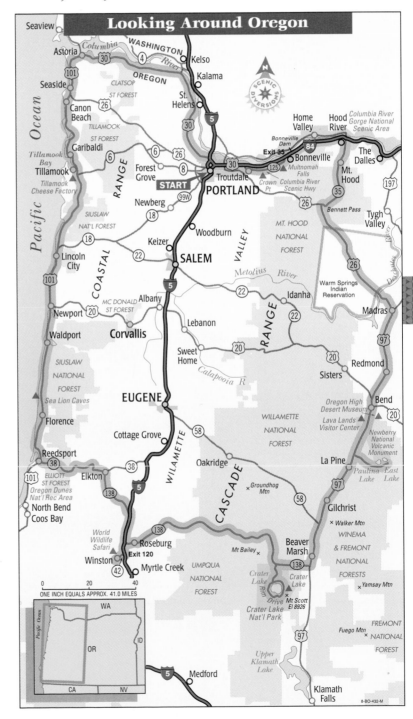

Saturday Market—Portland, Oregon

Yaquina Lighthouse—Newport, Oregon

TAKE A BITE OUT OF OREGON

An oregon apple that is. In the city of Hood River they take their fruit serious, with produce being responsible for over 26% of the towns annual income. Stop by the River Bend Country Store located at 22363 Tucker Road and try some local flavor in the form of homemade preserves, local and organic produce, gift baskets, and craft items.

the dramatic formation of the *Cascade Range*. The building is on the edge of a huge lava flow that emanated from *Lava Butte*, an extinct volcanic cone. You can drive to the top for a far-reaching view of the Cascades. Just up the road you'll find the *Oregon High Desert Museum* with nature trails, living wildlife displays, and all sorts of informative exhibits.

Continue north on U.S. 97 to **Madras**, where you'll turn left onto U.S. 26. This route cuts right through the *Mt. Hood National Forest*, dotted with lakes, springs, and peaks. Turn right onto Route 35 and follow it right up to the town of **Hood River**. As you approach the town, Mt. Hood, the highest elevation in Oregon at 11,239 feet, will be on your left.

Your last stretch of the trip is a drive alongside the *Columbia River*. From Hood River, take Route I-84 west. Take the time for a short detour at *Bonneville Dam*. The fish ladder at the *Bradford Island Visitor Center* and display ponds at the fish hatchery, are informative and entertaining. About five miles west of Bonneville Dam, you can pick up the *Columbia River Scenic Highway*, which was dedicated in 1916, culminating the efforts of several engineers and craftsmen who built the dry masonry walls and the bridges and tunnels designed to blend harmoniously into the contour of the land.

Along this route, you'll pass several waterfalls that are too tall to fit into one photograph and go through leafy woods and deeply cut gorges. Meanwhile, the mighty Columbia River runs alongside—shining like a huge mirror when the sun's out.

Be sure you allow time to pull off the road and follow hiking trails to waterfalls which have lovely names like *Bridal Veil Falls*, *Mist Falls*, *Horsetail Falls*, and *Oneonta Falls*. Most famous is *Multnomah Falls*, which splashes its way down 620 feet. You'll also find an occasional shop or gallery. There are a handful of restaurants as well, and an observatory called *Vista House* poised on the top of *Crown Point* from which you won't be able to take your eyes off

the view. This scenic highway ends in **Troutdale**, where you can get back on I-84 and return to Portland.

WILD ABOUT WILDLIFE

You don't have to be an Audubon type to appreciate the wildlife in the Pacific Northwest. Who wouldn't be thrilled to spot a bald eagle perched on top of a tree trunk? A red fox charging through a field? A pair of whiskered sea lions cavorting about in a harbor?

The vast areas of untouched wilderness make the Pacific Northwest a beautiful sanctuary for hundreds of species of birds and mammals. Fortunately, the Pacific Northwesterners are wild about their wildlife. With state nicknames such as *"Evergreen State"* and *"Beaver State,"* what do you expect? They're proud and protective. They're also meticulous about identifying and understanding the various types of wildlife. You'll find many small gallery-like museums with conscientiously assembled displays of the various wildlife and their surrounding environments.

If you own binoculars, by all means, take them along. You'll most likely use them as much as you use the maps in this book. Here's what to keep your eyes open for:

■ BY THE BEAUTIFUL SEA

Whales
Watching Whales. Along the coasts of both Washington and Oregon, you'll find charter boats that take you out into the deep to observe these magnificent creatures at close range, but you don't have to leave terra firma to see them. Several major headlands along Oregon's coast offer spectacular vantage points. On Washington's *San Juan Island*, there's a wonderful whale watch at *Lime Kiln Point*. If you're lucky, passing pods will put on shows complete with a little spyhopping, breaching, and lobtailing—the various flips and acrobatic moves they make. Keep your eyes open for killer whales (also called Orcas), minke whales, and dall porpoises.

In the spring and late fall, the longest migration of any mammal—the 12,000-

mile voyage of the Pacific gray whale—takes place a few miles off the coasts of Washington and Oregon. You can see them from the coast or climb aboard one of the charter boats.

A Whale of a Museum. If you want to find out more about these loveable mammals, stop by *The Whale Museum* in **Friday Harbor** on San Juan Island. Actually, don't just stop—allow yourselves plenty of time, a couple of hours. It's filled to the brim with whale exhibits. There's also a gift shop with whale magnets, whale paper weights, whale mobiles, whale postcards, whale books and posters, whale pins—well, you get the picture.

Seals and Sea Lions

If you spot something rubbery bobbing like a buoy in the water, look harder, it's probably a harbor seal. Harbor seals are the most commonly spotted marine mammal in the Northwest. They're full time residents of *Puget Sound* and the coasts of both Washington and Oregon. They're usually between four and six feet long and a mere 100 to 230 pounds. Sounds big, but not when you spot an elephant seal. Their adult males can grow up to sixteen feet in length and weigh over two tons. The latter is an infrequent, but notable visitor to Puget Sound.

Two species of sea lions are seen in the region. The Steller's which can weigh up to 2,000 pounds and the smaller, less common California sea lion.

How can you tell a sea lion from a seal? By their ears. California and Steller's sea lions have small rolled up ear flaps; harbor seals don't. Other differences are in their propelling techniques which only become apparent underwater.

For a close-up look at hundreds of these adorable creatures, be sure to visit the Sea Lion Caves, north of **Florence**, Oregon, on the coast. These caves are the year-round home for Steller's sea lions. You ride an elevator down 208 feet to a viewing gallery and watch these 200-pound bulls riding in waves,

snoozing with their young, claiming territories. It's a sight you'll never forget.

Marine Birds

From sea gulls that hang suspended in air like kites to great blue herons standing in shallow water like caryatids—the variety of birds along the Pacific Northwest coast is astonishing.

Some of the most common include loons, grebes, cormorants, and sea ducks such as scoters, harlequin ducks, buffleheads, and mergansers.

In Washington's San Juan Islands, you can see American bald eagles poised on top of trees all along the shore. Look for a white speck—the males have white heads that stand out. These islands also are home for other birds of prey such as osprey, turkey vultures, red-tailed hawks, golden eagles, and northern harriers.

More bald eagles can be seen in Oregon's Klamath County which host the largest wintering population of bald eagles in the contiguous U.S.

■ INTO THE WOODS AND BEYOND

Woodland Birds

You'll hear lots of woodpeckers in Pacific Northwest woodlands and dozens of little birds such as robins, thrushes, wrens, creepers, sparrows, warblers, and vireos.

The famous and rare spotted owl that has become a controversial issue between naturalists and loggers lives on Washington's Olympic Peninsula.

Wizard Island—Crater Lake National Park, Oregon

Puget Sound & The Olympic Peninsula

Distance: 605 Miles Round Trip, Seattle
Time: Allow at least four or five days.
Highligts: Historic buildings, coastal scenery, castle, national parks, rain forests, outdoor activities.

A visit to **Seattle** should unquestionably include a trip to its nearby *Olympic Peninsula* and neighboring cities of *Puget Sound*.

This is where pioneers called it quits after venturing across the continent. The area is not only scenic, but home to many historic buildings.

Allow yourself plenty of time to see Seattle, then venture out heading north of the city on I-5. If you're interested in aircraft, consider taking a tour of the *Boeing Company's* facility in **Everett**. By volume, it is the largest building in the world.

Continue north to **Mt. Vernon**, where you'll exit for Route 20. This takes you right out to *Whidbey Island*. There's a bridge connecting it to the mainland at this point. You can also reach the island by ferry from **Mukilteo** (just south of Everett). A wonderful vacation island, Whidbey is a mere fifty miles long and shouldn't take more than an hour to go from one end to another. It's a popular place for Seattle-lites to weekend. There's hiking, biking, and many other relaxing opportunities.

From **Keystone**, you can catch a ferry to **Port Townsend**, on *"The Peninsula,"* which is what Washington's westernmost piece of land is commonly called. You could easily fill several days discovering Port Townsend's Victorian past which has been beautifully preserved in many buildings. This small Victorian town, which crowds around the water's edge on the northeastern corner of the Olympic Peninsula, is one of four U.S. seaports that has preserved its Victorian heritage (Mendocino, California; Galveston, Texas; and Cape May, New Jersey are the others). Downtown—which takes less than ten minutes to walk from one end to the other—is full of splendidly preserved commercial buildings that were built in the 1800s. Uptown—which is literally "up" on the top of a bluff overlooking downtown—is home to impeccably restored Victorian mansions with cupolas, bay windows, gingerbread detail, and wraparound porches. A wide and shallow-step staircase connects the two; it was built to accommodate ladies' wide-hooped skirts.

From Port Townsend, follow Route 20 south and pick up U.S. 101 west. You'll pass through **Port Angeles** which is a commercial logging center and shortly afterwards, find yourselves surrounded by beautiful alpine scenery. You are right on the edge of *Olympic National Park*, which covers more than 900,000 acres of wilderness including 7,966-foot *Mount Olympus*. For the most far-reaching, spellbinding views, follow the road to *Hurricane Ridge* just before Port Angeles.

Once back on U.S. 101, the road twists and winds its way through foothills, forests, and alongside shiny blue lakes. Consider following Route 112 to **Neah Bay**, home of the *Makah Indian Reservation* or turning off just after **Fairholm** to see the *Sol Duc Hot Springs*.

Then continue back on U.S. 101 and look for signs for the road leading to the *Hoh Rain Forest*, which under no circumstances should be skipped. It takes about an hour to reach the end, where there are several trails to follow. The trails take you through halls of moss-draped trees, with firs shooting up as much as 300 feet, with every inch of the ground colonized by vegetation.

South of the Hoh Rain Forest, U.S. 101 runs alongside the sea, offering glimpses of the powerful surf and driftwood-studded beaches. Then it's back into the interior by *Lake Quinault*, a glacier-fed

Space Needle—Seattle, Washington

lake surrounded by more rain forests to explore. The *South Shore Road* winds around it.

Further south, in the lumber town of **Hoquiam**, stop at the *Victorian Hoquiam Castle*. This lavishly appointed 20-room mansion was built in 1897 by a lumber baron.

From there, drive east to **Olympia**, the state capital. Situated at the head of Puget Sound with Mt. Rainier and the Olympic Mountains as its skyline, Olympia is an attractive city punctuated with meticulously maintained parks. See the *Capitol Group Government Buildings*, the *Pabst Brewing Company*, and the *State Capital Museum*. Don't leave before sampling the Olympia oysters.

Take I-5 up to **Tacoma**, (third-largest city in Washington after Seattle and Spokane). It's home to many Victorian buildings as well as modern structures including the *Tacoma Dome*, the largest wood-domed structure in the world. There are many parks and more seafood eateries than you'll have time for. Take time to see *Point Defiance Park*, *St. Peter's Church*, the *Tacoma Art Museum*, and *Wright Park*, one of the finest arboretums in the Pacific Northwest . From there, it's a short drive to Seattle, via I-5.

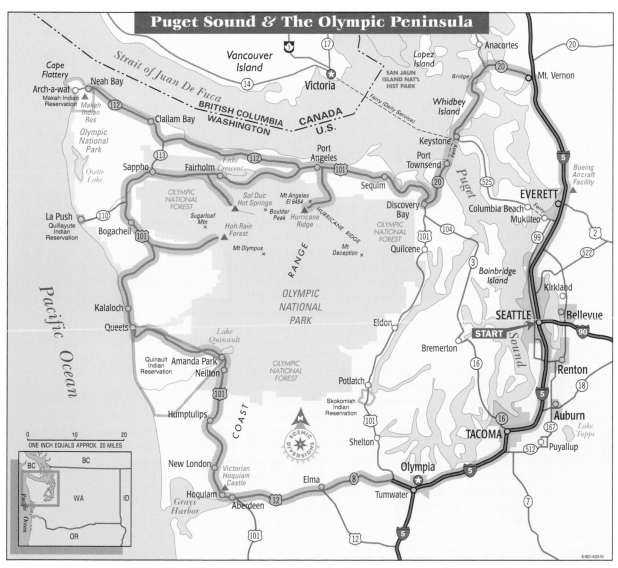

157

Mt. Rainier, Washington

NATIONAL PARKS

Until you've seen the forests and mountains of the Pacific Northwest in person, it's impossible to imagine just how beautiful they actually are. These two states are blessed with so much natural beauty that between the two of them, there are four national parks (three in Washington). All four are strikingly scenic wilderness preserves designed for your enjoyment. If you're serious hikers or mountain climbers, you will know what to bring. If you're just interested in following a handful of trails, do yourself a big favor and take rain gear as well as binoculars. You'll most likely have need for both wherever you wander.

■ CRATER LAKE NATIONAL PARK, OREGON

When a transplanted Kansan named William Gladstone Steel first laid eyes on *Crater Lake* in 1885, he was so moved that he decided to devote his life to its preservation. It is he we have to thank for keeping this marvel of nature out of the hands of homesteaders, lumber companies, and prospectors, and for encouraging Teddy Roosevelt to make it a national park back in 1902.

Crater Lake was formed about 6,840 years ago when then 12,000-foot-high Mt. Mazama erupted and blew its top off. It left a crater, 20 square miles in area, which eventually filled up with water from rain and snow, forming a lake 1,932 feet deep (the deepest in the U.S.).

Though this spectacle is clearly the centerpiece of the park, there are 183,189 acres of forests and meadows—teeming with wildlife—woven with hiking trails surrounding it. There is a scenic road running around the rim of the crater itself.

Getting There: From **Portland**, take I-5 to Eugene, then Route 58 east to U.S. 97 south to Route 138 then west to the park access road. From **Klamath Falls**, drive north on U.S. 97 to Route 62 for the southern entrance. From **Medford**, take Route 62. Route 62 runs through the park to the southern entrance.

Visitors Center: Located at *Rim Village* on the southwest shore. Maps and books available. Park exhibits. On summer evenings, rangers give campfire talks at *Mazama Campground* and at *Rim Center* at Rim Village. Open June through September, daily.

Activities: Hiking, biking, boat tours, campfire programs.

Camping: There are two campgrounds in the park: *Lost Creek* and *Mazama Campground*. In addition, there are other campgrounds in the surrounding national forests.

Hiking Trails: There are over 100 miles of trails throughout *Crater Lake National Park*. Among the most beautiful are *Discovery Point Trail* which is where the lake was originally discovered in 1853 by a miner who called it *Deep Blue Lake* (it was not made public for 31 years); *Garfield Peak Trail* with a view of Wizard Island which is actually a small volcanic cone; and *Watchman Lookout*, offering 360 degree views (on a clear day, you can see Mt. Shasta in California, 105 miles away).

For more information: Crater Lake National Park, Box 7, Crater Lake, Oregon 97604. (503) 594-2211.

■ MT. RAINIER NATIONAL PARK, OREGON

Seen from **Seattle** (which is 60 miles away), this sky-poking giant is impressive, but go up close, and you'll be bowled over by its massiveness and beauty. Native North Americans called it "Tahoma" (Mountain of God), today's

Train Sculpture—Tacoma, Washington

residents simply refer to it as "*The Mountain.*"

Washington's grande dame of volcanic peaks (now dormant some 2,000 years), *Mt. Rainier* towers up to 14,410 feet, a good two miles above some of the surrounding foothills of the Cascade Range.

Its expansive dome is covered with a patchwork of glaciers, including 26 that have been named and 50-odd smaller ones that remain anonymous.

Getting There: From Seattle, take I-5 south about 13 miles to exit 42B, then follow Route 161 south and pick up Route 7 to Route 706 which will take you directly to the Nisqually Entrance in the southwest corner of the park. There are four other approaches: via Carbon River in the northwestern part, Ohanapecosh in the southeast, Chinook Pass from the east, and White River, from the northwest.

Visitors Centers: There are four visitors centers in the park: at Longmire, Paradise, Sunrise, and Ohanapecosh.

Activities: Hiking, mountain climbing, fishing, naturalist programs. In winter, snowshoeing and cross-country skiing.

Camping: There are several major campgrounds in the park including *Cougar Rock*, *Ohanapecosh*, and *White River* as well as smaller, more primitive campgrounds and backcountry camping is permitted (a permit must be obtained).

Hiking Trails: Three-hundred miles of hiking trails thread throughout the park. One of the most popular is the *Wonderland Trail* which clings to the mountainsides, crosses alpine meadows, and fields of glacial snow.

For more information: Mount Rainier National Park, Tahoma Woods, Star Route, Ashford, WA 98304. (206) 569-2211.

WEATHER OR NOT

helpful hints...

Fortunately, rather—miraculously—Port Townsend, Washington is blessed with beautiful weather since it is in one of the Olympic Mountains rain shadows. It gets under 20 inches of rainfall a year. Indeed it is miraculous considering that between 12 and 15 feet of rain falls annually on the mountains themselves.

■ *NORTH CASCADES NATIONAL PARK, WASHINGTON*

Nicknamed the "American Alps," North Cascades National Park encompasses 504,780 acres of pristine wilderness. Here, you will see rugged mountain peaks covered with snow, snowfields and glaciers, cascading waterfalls and streams, and thick forests.

Tacoma Harbor—Tacoma, Washington

The park is divided into two intensely scenic units. The northern area—on the Canadian border—includes Mount Shuksan and the Pickett Range with glaciers, peaks, and high lakes; the southern area includes the "Eldorado high country" and the Stehekin river valley, a glacier-carved canyon.

In addition to the park, there's *Ross Lake National Recreational Area* (184-square-miles lying between the north and south portions) and 97-square-mile *Lake Chelan National Recreation Area* (adjoining the southern area), plus the *Mt. Baker-Snoqualmie*, *Wenatchee*, and *Okanogan* national forests all around.

Getting There: The North Cascades Highway—Route 20—is the major route to the park. From the west, you can pick it up north of Mt. Vernon from I-5; in the east, in Okanogan from U.S. 97. Route 20 takes you between the northern and southern portions of the park.

Visitors Centers: Information centers at Marblemount and Colonial Creek are only open in the summer months.

Activities: Backpacking, hiking, fishing, hunting, camping.

Camping: There are several campgrounds in the area: at North Cascades National Park, Lake Chelan National Recreation Area, and Ross Lake National Recreation Area. Permits must be obtained for backcountry camping.

Hiking Trails: Between the northern and southern portions of the park and the two neighboring recreational areas, there are about 360 miles of hiking and horseback riding trails.

For more information: North Cascades National Park, 800 State Street, Sedro Woolley, Washington 98284. (206) 856-5700.

159

Alaska & Hawaii

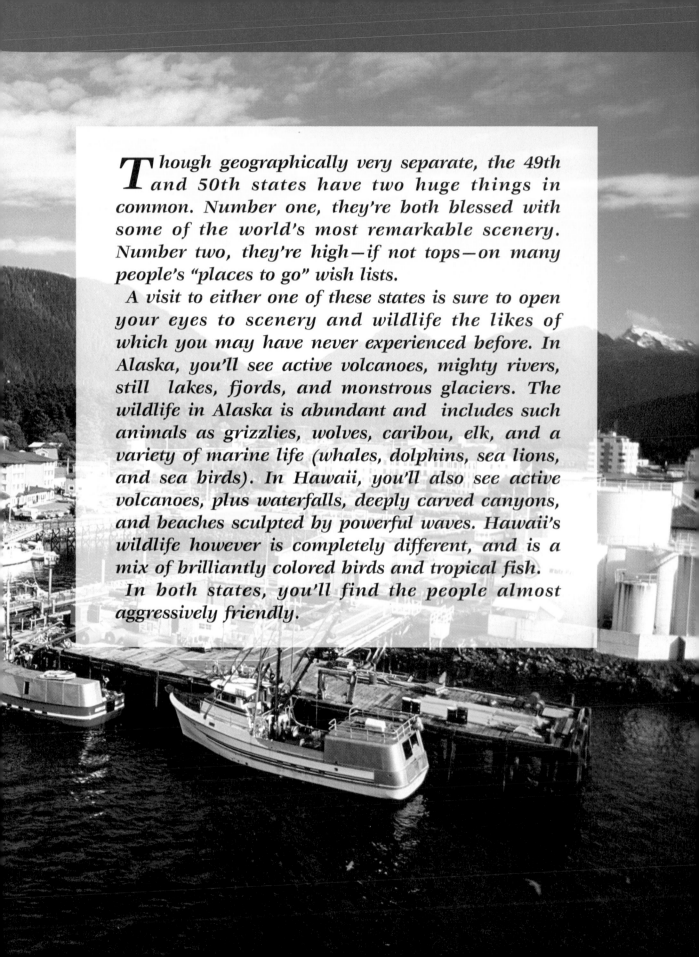

*T*hough geographically very separate, the 49th and 50th states have two huge things in common. Number one, they're both blessed with some of the world's most remarkable scenery. Number two, they're high—if not tops—on many people's "places to go" wish lists.

A visit to either one of these states is sure to open your eyes to scenery and wildlife the likes of which you may have never experienced before. In Alaska, you'll see active volcanoes, mighty rivers, still lakes, fjords, and monstrous glaciers. The wildlife in Alaska is abundant and includes such animals as grizzlies, wolves, caribou, elk, and a variety of marine life (whales, dolphins, sea lions, and sea birds). In Hawaii, you'll also see active volcanoes, plus waterfalls, deeply carved canyons, and beaches sculpted by powerful waves. Hawaii's wildlife however is completely different, and is a mix of brilliantly colored birds and tropical fish.

In both states, you'll find the people almost aggressively friendly.

George Parks Highway, Alaska

Astounding Alaska

Distance: 939 Miles Round Trip, Fairbanks
Time: Allow at least a week
Highlights: Mountains, rivers, glaciers, fjords, wildlife, pioneer and Indian artifacts, railroad history, two national parks, hiking, winter sports.

Long considered one of the most beautiful states, Alaska hardly needs an introduction. It's a state many individuals dream of visiting: a land of Arctic scenery; strong, but vulnerable animals; and a population of hardy people.

Alaska is home to not one or two, but eight of our country's national parks, all of which contain some of the world's most extraordinary scenery. Just to give you an idea: *Denali National Park and Preserve* is home to *Mount McKinley*, the highest peak in North America (20,320 feet). More than eight million acres of the *Gates of the Arctic National Park and Preserve* lie above the Arctic Circle. *Kobuk Valley National Park* has the extraordinary presence of the *Great Kobuk Sand Dunes*, a rare spectacle here. At 13,200,000 acres *Wrangell-St. Elias*

National Park and Preserve is the largest national park in the national park system. The park also has the greatest concentration of peaks over 14,500 feet in North America including *Mount St. Elias* which—at 18,008 feet—is second in height only to Mount McKinley.

For this diversion, we take you south from **Fairbanks**, the heart of Alaska's interior, to the port city of **Valdez** and *Prince William Sound*, via the *Richardson Highway*. This highway parallels the *Trans-Alaska Pipeline*, taking you through mountain passes and over roaring rivers. From Valdez, you will backtrack a bit and then head west on Route 1 which will take you over to the *George Parks Highway*. You'll then head north back to Fairbanks, skirting around Denali National Park.

During the summer, the temperature in this part of the world is typically in the eighties and there's up to twenty hours of light in a day.

Start in Fairbanks, Alaska's second-largest city. It has come a long way since it started life as a Gold Rush settlement. For a bit of background on the area's natives, the culture, and wildlife, stop by the *University of Alaska Museum*. You don't have to go far from the city to see wildlife. In fact, caribou have been known to wander through town. Just two miles away, *Creamer's Field* is a waterfowl refuge for ducks, geese, and cranes during the spring and fall migrations. Before heading south, consider going to see the bubbling mineral waters just north of Fairbanks, *Manley Hot Springs,* and to the east, *Chena Hot Springs*.

Your first stop as you head south of Fairbanks on Route 2 (which is the start of the Richardson Highway) is **North Pole**, where the United States Postal Service traditionally sends mail to be answered by Santa's elves. Just to the south is **Big Delta**. Stop in to see the museum in the *Big Delta State Historical Park*; among its displays are pioneer relics and Athabascan Native artifacts. **Delta Junction**, just down the road, is the northern terminus of the *Alaska Highway* (which is the only road linking Alaska with the lower 48 states).

Travel south to **Glennallen** the gateway to Wrangell-St. Elias National Park and Preserve. The ranger station for the park is located at **Copper Center** off the *Edgerton Highway*. The park is breath-taking: peaks and glaciers; glaciers and peaks. Most activities are wilderness-oriented, therefore travel and other facilities are limited. From here you can follow a 61-mile long, extremely rough, gravel road to the historic mining towns of **McCarthy** and **Kennicott**, a national historic landmark. These historic mining towns continue to attract visitors interested in learning more about Alaska's history—one rich with stories of the gold rush days and legendary strikes.

Valdez, the southern terminus of the *Trans-Alaska Pipeline* and situated on Prince William Sound (which is made up of fjords, glaciers, and islands) is next. You can take tours of the pipeline, a ferry trip to the fishing port of **Cordova**, a "flightseeing" tour, or cruise to the *Columbia Glacier* (4 miles wide and over 200 feet high at the face).

From there, retrace your steps on the *Richardson Highway* turning left onto Route 1 at Glennallen. This road takes you past glaciers, mountains, rivers—Alaska just as you pictured it.

If time permits, spend some time exploring **Anchorage**. Otherwise, head north onto Route 3 at **Palmer**, the George Parks Highway.

This route also has a parallel running mate—the *Alaska Railroad*. If you're interested in learning about the railroad, stop in at the *Transportation and Industry Museum of Alaska* in **Wasilla** (west of Palmer).

The George Parks Highway runs parallel to the eastern edge of Denali National Park and Preserve, home to the towering Mount McKinley. If you have time, take a guided tour into the park's wilderness to see bears, moose, wolves, Dall sheep, lynx, fox, snowshoe hares, and whatever other animals decide to show up.

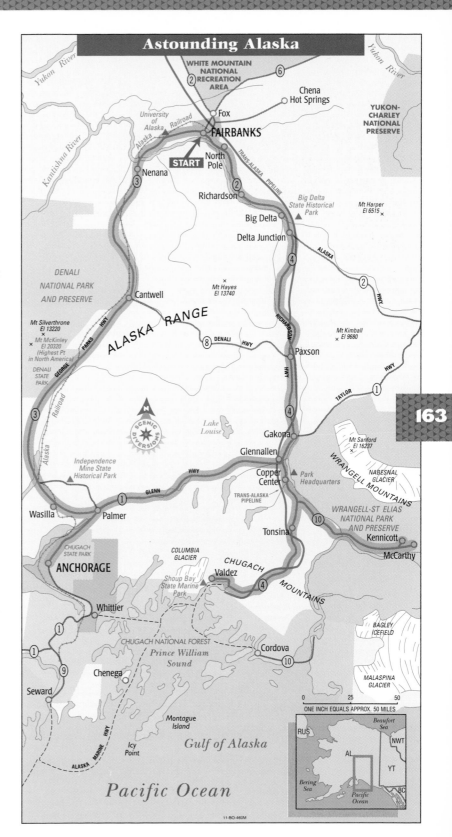

163

Rainbow Falls—Hilo, Hawaii

Hawaiian Journey

Distance: 238 Miles Round Trip, Hilo
Time: Allow five days
Highlights: Volcanoes, dramatic cliffs and canyons, sugarcane and coffee fields, dense green jungle, flowers, national park, grasslands, range animals, beaches, coral reefs, water sports.

The Big Island (a.k.a. Hawaii) is an island with a Dr. Jekyll and Mr. Hyde personality. With active volcanoes, it is both haunting and fearsome, while also offering the epitome of relaxed comfort in a number of cushy, waterfront hotels.

Hawaii is home to *Mauna Kea* and *Mauna Loa*, twin volcanic peaks. Mauna Kea, which soars to a whopping 13,796 feet, is the largest island-based mountain in the entire world. Mauna Loa looms up to 13,679 feet. A third volcano, *Kilauea*, is one of the world's most active craters.

You can easily spend a week here, dividing your time between exploring the intensely interesting geologic wonders and dipping in the sea. Most visitors stay on the west or what's known as the *Kona*—or farther north, the *Kohala—Coast*; the names are almost interchangeable.

For this route, we suggest starting in the lush and tropical town of **Hilo** (on the east coast) and circling around the island counterclockwise.

In Hilo, be sure to see at least one of the flower nurseries which grow orchids, one of Hawaii's biggest exports. In fact, Hawaii's orchid industry is the largest in the world. Also check out the plantation-era buildings downtown and the *Lyman Mission House and Museum* (276 Haili Street), a 19th-century missionary home. The two-ton *Naha Stone* (in front of the *Hilo Library* at 300 Waianuenue Avenue) is one of the island's most famous artifacts. According to legend, the man who could lift it would become king of all the islands. The young Kamehameha (who became Hawaii's first king) apparently did. Don't miss *Banyan Drive*, which is famed for its many banyan trees that were planted by visiting celebrities. Just off the drive is *Liliuokalani Gardens*, a 30-acre park with views of Hilo, *Mauna Kea*, and the *Hamakua Coast*. The *Suisan Fish Market* at the end of the drive comes alive in the early morning (from 7:30 a.m.) when fishermen return with the morning's catch.

From there, head north on Route 19, following the Hamakua Coast. A sensationally scenic drive, this route takes you atop high cliffs (known as pali) that plunge into the Pacific. Along the twisting, winding way, you'll pass waterfalls, valleys, and signs indicating where scenic viewpoints are. In the village of **Honomu** (15 miles north of Hilo), there are two incredible waterfalls—*Akaka Falls* (442 feet) and *Kahuna Falls* (400 feet).

When you reach Route 240, follow it to the end to *Waipio Valley*, home to some of Hawaii's most powerful kings including Kamehameha. There's a lookout tower, from which the views of the northeastern end of the island are mesmerizing.

Backtrack to Route 19 and turn right, heading west now to **Waimea** (Kamuela). Here you'll find *Parker Ranch*, which is one of the world's largest independently owned cattle ranches. There's a museum and tours. Waimea offers a dramatically different landscape than most of the island. Stretching off in every direction are cattle-dotted grasslands.

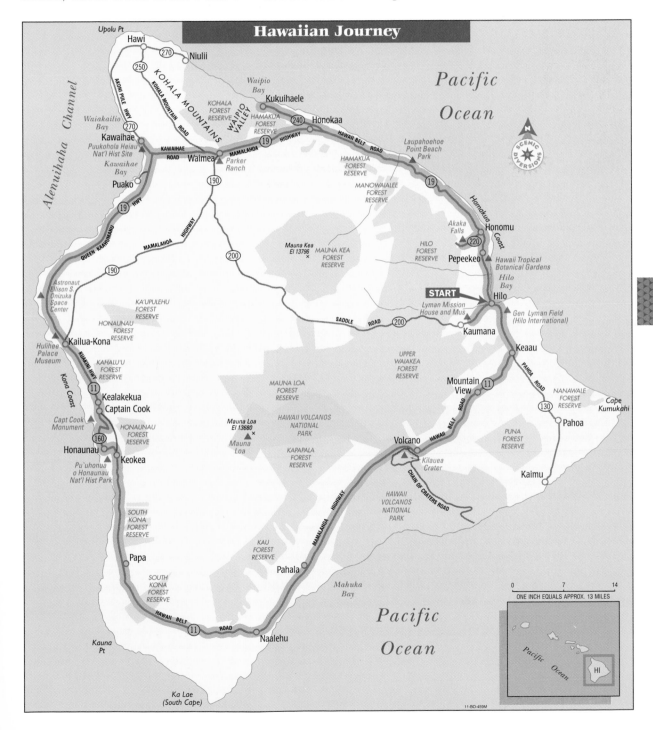

Continue on Route 19 west over to the coast, then take Route 270 north. Just off Route 270 at **Kawaihae**, there's a 15th-century temple and altar (the *Puukohola Heiau National Historic Site*) which was dedicated to the god of war by King Kamehameha I. Apparently, he invited his main rival to the dedication and had him killed.

Return to Route 19, follow it south and you'll pass some of Hawaii's most elegant resorts. At **Puako**, Route 19 becomes the *Queen Kaahumanu Highway*. **Kailua-Kona**, the *Kona Coast's* major town, is home to a string of beachfront condominiums, hotels, shops, restaurants, and bars. This area is where Hawaiian royalty settled back in the 19th century. Take time to see *Hulihee Palace* (5718 Alii Drive), a museum that was formerly a summer house owned by the Hawaiian royal family and the grounds of the *King Kamehameha Hotel* (near the *Kailua Pier*), where you'll find the restored headquarters of King Kamehameha the great, who died here in 1819.

Head south on Route 11 and you'll pass through coffee fields en route to **Kealakekua**. Kealakekua was where British explorer captain James Cook was killed in 1779 after a battle with the local Hawaiians. There's a monument marking the spot.

Continue south on Route 11 to **Keokea**, which connects to Route 160. Take this eight miles south to *Pu'uhonua o Honaunau*—the City of Refuge, an ancient holy ground. In the past, this was where anyone who had broken sacred laws could find sanctuary.

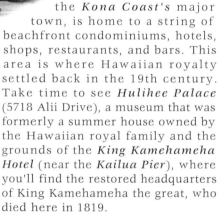

Captain Cook Monument
Kealakekua, Hawaii

Route 11 takes you around the south side of the island to *Hawaii Volcanoes National Park*. Here you can have an upfront look at an island still being born. There are two young volcanoes—Mauna Loa and Kilauea—which are still active. The latter has erupted 50 times since 1980. The park is otherworldly beautiful with a lunar-like landscape, firepits, fumaroles, and lava flows frozen in time. From there, it's just a 28-mile drive back to Hilo.

TRAVEL TIP

For travelers who like to shop, consider adding a roll of wide heavy-duty tape to your packing list. It's one of those things that you'll find a hundred reasons to use once on the road and wonder how you ever lived without it. It's especially good for reinforcing bags and boxes bulging with new purchases.

Black Beach, Hawaii

PACK (FLASH) LIGHT

When traveling to tropical island destinations, consider taking a small flashlight along. On many islands, brief power failures occur with some frequency. Also, guest rooms are often tucked away in densely covered jungle areas, down long unlit—or partially lit—pathways.

helpful hints...

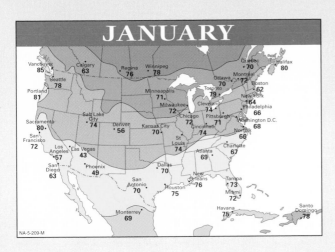

AVERAGE MONTHLY TEMPERATURE

MEAN MONTHLY RELATIVE HUMIDITY

is shown in bold numbers

Celsius	Fahrenheit		Celsius	Fahrenheit
Over 38°	Over 100°		-7° to 4°	20° to 40°
27° to 38°	80° to 100°		-18° to -7°	0° to 20°
16° to 27°	60° to 80°		-29° to -18°	-20° to 0°
4° to 16°	40° to 60°		Below -29°	Below -20°

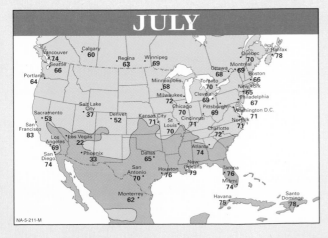

CITIES & TOWNS

Index

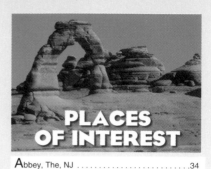

PLACES OF INTEREST

171

172

NATIONAL HOTEL/MOTEL CHAINS

Best Inns of America
(800) 237-8466

Best Western International
(800) 528-1234

Budget Host Inns
(800) BUD-HOST (283-4678)

Budgetel Inns
(800) 428-3438

Canadian Pacific Hotels
(800) 828-7447
(800) 268-9420 (In Canada)

Choice Hotels Int'l, Inc.
(800) 4-CHOICE (424-6423)

Clarion Hotels
(800) 252-7466

Colony Hotels and Resorts
(800) 777-1700

Comfort Inns
(800) 228-5150

Days Inn of America
(800) 325-2525

Dillon Inns
(800) 253-7503

Doubletree, Inc.
(800) 528-0444

Doubletree Guest Suites
(800) 424-2900

**Downtowner – Passport
International**
(800) 251-1962

Dunfey Hotels
(800) 843-6664

Drury Inns
(800) 325-8300

Econo Lodges of America
(800) 446-6900

Embassy Suites
(800) EMBASSY (362-2779)

Essex Inn
(800) 621-6909

Exel Inns of America
(800) 356-8013

Fairmont Hotels
(800) 527-4727

**Fiesta Americana Hotels
and Resorts**
(800) 223-2332

Forte Hotels
(800) 225-5843

Fairfield Inn by Marriott
(800) 228-2800

Four Seasons Hotel
(800) 332-3442
(800) 268-6282

Hampton Inns, Inc.
(800) HAMPTON (426-7866)

Harley Hotels
(800) 321-2323

Helmsley Hotels
(800) 221-4982

Hilton Hotels
(800) HILTONS (445-8667)

Holiday Inns, Inc.
(800) HOLIDAY (465-4329)

Hospitality International
(800) 251-1962

Howard Johnson Hotels
(800) 654-2000

Hyatt Hotel
(800) 233-1234

Inter-Continental Hotels
(800) 327-0200

**L-K Motels and Country
Hearth Inn**
(800) 282-5711

LRI Inc.
(800) 223-0888

La Quinta Motor Inns, Inc.
(800) 531-5900

Loews Hotels
(800) 235-6397

Marriott Hotels
(800) 228-9290

Motel 6
(800) 4-MOTEL (466-8536)

Nendel's Inns
(800) 547-0106

New Otani Hotels
(800) 421-8795

New York Inn of America
(800) 777-6933

Nikko Hotels International
(800) 645-5687

Omni Hotels
(800) THE-OMNI (843-6664)

Preferred Hotels
(800) 323-7500

**Princess Hotels
International**
(800) 223-1818

Quality Inns
(800) 228-5150

Radisson Hotels Int'l Inc.
(800) 333-3333

Ramada Inns
(800) 228-2828
(800) 854-7854

Red Carpet
(800) 251-1962

Red Lion Hotels and Inns
(800) 547-8010

Red Roof Inns
(800) 843-7663

Regent International Hotels
(800) 545-4000

Registry Hotel
(800) 247-9810

**Residence Inn by
Marriott, Inc.**
(800) 331-3131

Rodeway Inns
(800) 221-2222
(800) 228-2000

Sandpiper Resorts
(800) 237-0707

Scottish Inns
(800) 251-1962

**Sheraton Hotels and
Motor Inns**
(800) 325-3535

Shoney's Inns/Sholodge
(800) 222-2222
(800) 233-4667

Sleep Inn
(800) 252-7466

Sonesta Hotels
(800) 776-3782

Stouffer Hotels and Resorts
(800) HOTELS1 (468-3571)

Sundowner
(800) 648-5490

Super 8 Motels, Inc.
(800) 800-8000

Travelodge
(800) 578-7878

Village Resorts, Inc.
(800) 367-7052

Wellesley Inns
(800) 444-8888

**West Coast Hotels and
Motor Inns**
(800) 426-0670

Westin Hotels and Resorts
(800) 228-3000

**Wyndham Hotels and
Resorts**
(800) 996-3426

175

RENTAL CAR AGENCIES

Advantage Rent-A-Car
(800) 777-5500

Alamo Rent-A-Car
(800) 327-9633

Allstate Rent-A-Car
(800) 634-6186

Avis Rent-A-Car System
(800) 331-1212

Budget Rent-A-Car
(800) 527-0700

Dollar Rent-A-Car
(800) 412-6868

Enterprise Rent-A-Car
(800) 325-8007

Hertz Corporation
(800) 654-3131

National Car Rental
(800) CAR-RENT
    (227-7368)

Thrifty Rent-A-Car
(800) FOR-CARS
    (367-2277)

Value Rent-A-Car
(800) GO-VALUE
    (468-2583)

Staff for
SCENIC DIVERSIONS

John Stephens, *Managing Director;* **Cary Wilke,** *Production Director;*
Tim Carter, *Editorial Director.*

Editorial
Craig R Coughlan, *Associate Editor;* **Misty Riddles,** *Editorial Assistant.*

Design
Kristin Watson, *Design Coordinator;* **Timothy R. Herber, Marc W. Land,**
Design Assistants; **Carrley Mason, Andrea E. Thompson,** *Graphic Designers.*

Desktop Publishing
Cyd Arhelger, *Coordinator.*

Cartographic Production
Tom Deiley, *Manager;* **Rebecca Bergmann, Pat Flach, LaVonne Miller,** *Coordinators;*
Terry L. Anderson, Kate Barteau, Debra A. Cabaniss, Rudy L. Carson, Allison Caseres,
Brian C. Casey, Consuelo R. Montez, Jill A. Nix, Malcolm Scott Olsen, Hank Ramirez,
Dana Rose Smith, Lee S. Stewart, Rebecca M. Walker, Terri Wiedenfeld, Diana L. Wood,
Cartographic Technicians.

Digital Cartography
James Craft, *Manager;* **Glen A. Pawelski,** *Coordinator;* **Johnny Zavala,** *Digital Analyst;*
Charles Daggett, Chris Gray, Ellen L. Parman, *Digital Technicians.*

Map Research and Acquisition
Kate Smith, *Coordinator;* **Josephine Below,** *Acquisition Specialist;* **Iva Hobson,**
Jo Lynn Puehse, *Research Assistants.*

Map Content
Karen L. Novian, *Manager;* **Frances S. Hohmann, Evelyn Rolfe,** *Coordinators;*
Lisa R. Allerkamp, Sandy Babbitt, Nancy G. Below, Linda DeVazier, Wanda Fischer,
Dolores R. Gonzales, Rudy C. Gonzales, Sylvia Harmon, Ellen K. Hymer,
Carolyn Meier, Irma Rios, Carol Rust, David A. Warnell, *Compilers and Editors.*

Map Production Services
Stan Elliott, *Print Production Coordinator;* **Sherri R. Marcee,** *Reprographics Coordinator.*

Travel Information Services
Ross E. Morres, III, *Manager;* **Elizabeth Daggett,** *Coordinator;* **Lupe D. Castro,**
Cheryl Argona, *Travel Planners.*

REMEMBER

No Matter where you go in the United States, a Gousha
map can help you find your way.

ROADMAPS
Detailed highway maps of all 50 states and Canadian
provinces.

AREAMAPS
Large-scale regional maps covering the Continental
U.S. and Mexico.

METROMAPS
Major U.S. metropolitan areas, with insets of downtown
areas.

CITYMAPS
Fully indexed street maps of U.S. cities.

RECREATION MAPS
Road maps that highlight outdoor recreation activities.

For more information
E-Mail
HMGousha@aol.com
General Information: H. M. Gousha Main Office
(210) 995-3317; Fax (210) 995-3217
Subsidiary Rights
(210) 995-3317 x 252; Fax (210) 995-3217
Marketing/Order Administration
(800) 270-2242; Fax (210) 995-4492
National Sales Office
(708) 382-4290; Fax (708) 382-4288
Travel Information Services
(210) 995-3317; Fax (210) 995-3217

ILLUSTRATIONS CREDITS

ABBREVIATIONS: *Illustrations appear on pages listed at; r-right, t-top, b-bottom, or l-left of page. FC- Front Cover, BC- Back Cover,*
C&VB-Convention and Visitors Bureau, V&CB - Visitors and Convention Bureau.

Alabama Bureau of Tourism & Travel: 85, 86
(Dan Brothers).
Alaska Division of Tourism: 162.
Atlantic City C&VB: 33.
Bake, William A.: 6-7, 20-21, 60-61, 76-77,
100-101, 160-161, BC.
Basin and Range Photography: FC (Bob
Rosenquist).
Ben & Jerry's: 8.
Boston C&VB: 19.
Boulder C&VB: 113.
Brown County C&VB: 58.
Bucks County Tourism Commission, Inc.: 36b,
36t, 37.
Cape Cod Chamber of Commerce: 12.
Cape May County Dept. of Tourism: 34
(Victor D. Sylvester).
Charleston Area C&VB: 62,63.
Conner Prairie: 59b, 59t.
COREL Professional Photos CD-ROM: 26,
42b, 42t, 47, 63, 87b, 87t, 99, 102,
103, 104t, 106, 108, 110, 111, 112,
114t, 115, 119, 126b, 130b,137b,138b,
140t, 141, 142, 143, 144b, 153, 155,
156, 158t,160, 164, 165, 166, 168,
168, 169, 172, 174.
Corrie, Chris: 125, 126t.
Dade County & The Greater Miami C&VB:
72t, 74, 75.
Daytona Beach Area C&VB: 71.
Dechert, S. J.: 15.
Denver Metro C&VB: 114b, 117.
Des Moines C&VB: 92.

Gatlinburg C&VB: 82.
Gettysburg Travel Council: 44.
Gibbson, Scott: 134-135.
Helen C&VB: 68t.
Holland Area C&VB: 53.
Hot Springs Nat'l Park: 84b, 84t.
Idaho Department of Commerce: 104b (L.
Culovich).
Lake Lanier Islands Authority: 67, 68b.
Langford, Mark: BC
Lexington C&VB: 79.
Louisville & Jefferson County C&VB: 78.
Maine Office of Tourism: 11.
Mariano Advertising: 87b.
Merry Go Round Museum: 56b.
Mielke, Bruce: 52.
Miglaus, Janis: 152, 153.
Minnesota Office of Tourism: 50b, 50t.
Missouri Division of Tourism: 93, 94.
Napa Valley C&VB: 137t.
Nashville C&VB: 81 (Robin Hood).
Natchez C&VB: 89.
National Parks Service: 129t, 138t.
New Hampshire Office of Travel & Tourism
Dept.:17t.
New York State Dept. of Economic
Development: 22, 25, 28b, 29, 31, 32.
Norman Rockwell Museum: 17b.
North Carolina Division of Travel & Tourism:
65, 66t.
North Dakota Tourism Dept.: 90-91, 95t, 98.
Ohio Division of Travel & Tourism: 56t
(Charles Engle).

Oklahoma City C&VB: 122t, 124.
Olympic Regional Development Authority:
29.
Orlando/Orange County C&VB, Inc.: 69.
Pennsylvania Dutch C&VB: 38, 39.
Phoenix & Valley of the Sun C&VB: 131,
132b, 132t.
Photodisc, Inc.: 14b., 120-121.
Reno News Bureau: 140b.
Retama Park: 127.
San Antonio C&VB: 128t (Tim Thompson),
128b (Al Rendon).
San Diego Convention & Visitors Bureau: 147
(James Blank), 149b (Bill Robinson).
Santa Barbara Conference & Visitors Bureau:
144t (Tom Tuttle).
Savanna C&VB: 64.
Schuemann Architectural Photography: 55
(Bill Schuemann).
Schulz, Peter J.: 51.
South Dakota Tourism: 95b, 96.
Stone Mountain State Park: 66b.
Tacoma/Pierce County V&CB: 158b, 159.
Terril, Steve: 150-151.
Tony Stone Images: 48-49 (Mitch Kezar).
Tulsa Chamber of Commerce: 122b.
Vermont Dept. of Travel & Tourism: 10t (Jim
McElholm).
Virginia Division of Tourism: 46.
Wilmington Delaware C&VB: 40.
Ziglar, Stephen: 18.
Zoological Society of San Diego: 146.

Dollie and Darcy illustrations by Robert Slomkowski.

The 1933 Ford Victoria (Vicky) on the back cover is owned by Roger Kelley of San Antonio, TX.